OUT OF THE WOODSHED

Out of the Woodshed

A Portrait of Stella Gibbons

Reggie Oliver

BLOOMSBURY

First published in Great Britain in 1998
Bloomsbury Publishing Plc, 38 Soho Square, London W1V 5DF

Text copyright © 1998 by Reggie Oliver

The moral right of the author has been asserted

A CIP catalogue record for this book is available from the British Library

ISBN 0 7475 3995 2

10 9 8 7 6 5 4 3 2 1

Typeset by Palimpsest Book Production Limited,
Polmont, Stirlingshire
Printed in Great Britain by
Clays Ltd, St Ives plc

CONTENTS

For Laura,
Daniel and Anna, Benjamin and Ruth,
Sonia, and all subsequent descendants

While reading Mr J. I. M. Stewart's novel *An Acre of Grass* I came, with surprise, upon the following:

'Authentic satire, although it can possess high rationality, must spring from something deeply traumatic in the first place. Unless, as a child, an authentic horror pounced on you in the woodshed, don't think of it as your field.'

I copied this into the notebook in which I keep passages I want to remember, and wrote beneath: 'Well, thank you Mr Stewart, from the woodshed's original creator. She was practically born in the place. But fortunately the door happened to be ajar.'

Stella Gibbons, 1966

Introduction

Introduction

It is not often said that sanity is akin to genius, but it ought to be. Stella Gibbons's most famous work, *Cold Comfort Farm*, is an expression of a kind of sublime sanity. It represented, both personally and artistically, a repudiation of wilful irrationality; yet – and this is something only the sane can do – it also gently mocks what it approves. Stella believed in what she called the Higher Common Sense, even though its author, the Abbé Fausse-Maigre, is unquestionably a comic creation. Her later works explore its implications, and in her penultimate and unpublished novel *The Yellow Houses* she refers again by name to the Higher Common Sense. By then its meaning has changed slightly, but only because time, grief, experience and wisdom had deepened her understanding of it. It therefore seems a pity that Stella is remembered only for that inspired first novel, and that her other books, though popular in their day, have been virtually forgotten.

With every new generation of readers, of course, a generation of writers is lost. This is to be expected of a certain kind of popular writer: the Marie Corellis of one era give way to the Jeffrey Archers of another; each of them as bad as their predecessors, but bad in a way which we somehow find acceptable in our own time. But there remain a vast number of writers, some of great merit, who fall into neglect simply because fashion and a new set of writers of equal excellence supersedes them. Only a few outstanding ones survive.

Stella Gibbons falls into the intermediate category as a writer who is remembered and celebrated for one book. *Cold Comfort Farm* will be read and enjoyed for as long as the English language and the English sense of humour last. It has been filmed, dramatised, musicalised, translated, and has even survived being set as an A-level text. Phrases from it, notably 'Something Nasty in the Woodshed', even words ('sukebind' is now in the *Oxford English Dictionary*) have entered the national consciousness and are quoted by politicians and media personalities who neither know nor care about their origin. Even those who know the name Stella Gibbons may not be aware that she wrote twenty-three other novels (twenty-five if you include two as yet unpublished), much journalism, one children's book, three volumes of short stories and three volumes of poetry (four if you count her *Collected Poems*). Her other work, while not as immediately captivating as *Cold Comfort Farm*, has a great deal to recommend it and is just as much a reflection of her complex and intriguing personality.

'That book', she used to call *Cold Comfort Farm*, and she sometimes resented the fact that this was all she was remembered for. Stella herself would like to have been remembered as a poet. Her first published book was a volume of poetry which was highly praised at the time, and she continued to write verse to the end of her life.

Once she told me she had been reading a biography of Gérard de Nerval, the Romantic poet who promenaded a lobster on a ribbon through Paris and had a tragic love affair with the unfortunately named Jenny Colon. One particular anecdote in the book struck her. He had been walking through Paris – lobsterless on this occasion, I think – and had seen a starving girl begging at a street corner. This had made him, he said, want to go back to his room and write and write. Stella found this attitude deplorable – mainly, I suspect, because she recognised a similar desire in herself to shut out the world and concentrate on her own imaginative life. But there was a strong puritanical streak in her which always put certain duties above an obligation to her talent. Genius to her was a privilege and not an excuse. This view is not a very popular one (particularly among geniuses), and it is arguable that Stella's adherence to it may have adversely affected her work.

That is not to say that her approach to writing was unprofessional: far from it. Stella was a writer by trade, and could have been nothing else. Equally her daughter Laura never remembers a time when she felt neglected in favour of her mother's work. From her early twenties Stella had supported herself, and, on occasion, her brothers Gerald and Lewis, by writing. For some years after she was married she was the chief breadwinner in the family; but she would never have described herself as a feminist, and was suspicious of the term. Her opinions were both deeply conservative and ahead of her time, notably on ecological and animal rights issues. I remember how she constantly oscillated between the *Times*, the *Telegraph* and the *Guardian*, irritated in turn by the set pattern of opinions expressed in each. In short, like all interesting people she was a mass of contradictions.

It is those contradictions in her life and work that I have attempted to explore in this biography. My hope in so doing is that readers' understanding and enjoyment of *Cold Comfort Farm* may be enhanced, but more especially that they may be tempted to discover her other novels and her remarkable poetry. I would also like to convey some sense of the very unusual and lovable person she was. To many people who knew her in the last years of her life the overwhelming impression she gave was one of serenity and gentleness, but her serenity was hard won and her gentleness was tempered in private by a pleasing acerbity. She never lost the astringent quality which informs and inspires 'that book'.

I feel also bound to dispel a myth about her life and work which has found its way into a number of articles about her, and even into the otherwise excellent entry in the *Dictionary of National Biography*. This is that *Cold Comfort Farm* was the product of a wild and adventurous youth, and that thereafter she 'dwindled into a wife' and her genius was tamed and neutered as a result. The reality is more complex. The more I have read her work, the more I have come to feel that it is all of a piece – including the poetry – and that the novels written after *Cold Comfort Farm* constitute the working out and, to some extent, the more mature expression of themes and ideas present in that early masterpiece.

I felt it necessary to offer some sort of critical appraisal of her work, despite my having no particular gift for, or experience in, the art of criticism. Biographies of artists which do not offer some assessment of their work, or which are content simply to quote from reviews, always seem to me to be telling only half the story, and often the less interesting half. If judgements in this book appear over-generous, it is not out of partisanship or some deliberate policy of promoting Stella's work; it is simply because I find so much of her writing personally sympathetic. The poet Rilke wrote: 'Works of art are of an infinite solitariness, and nothing is less likely to bring us near to them than criticism. Only love can apprehend and hold them, and can be just towards them.'

Stella had a rather grudging admiration for Rilke, mainly because she read him as a result of someone telling her that she *ought* to read Rilke. As it happens, being forced to read a book that she did not want to read was one of the factors which led to the writing of *Cold Comfort Farm*.

I am indebted to the many people who assisted me in my researches with unstinted generosity. First of all I must thank my cousin Laura Richardson, Stella's daughter, for approving the idea of the book in the first place, and for all her subsequent help, especially with photographs and many personal reminiscences. I would like to thank her sons Benjamin and Daniel for giving me access to correspondence and diaries, and for allowing me to quote from Stella's work. I would also like to thank Ben's wife Ruth for her translations from German. If I have mentioned Laura, Daniel and Benjamin less than their importance in Stella's life deserves, it is for two reasons: firstly, out of respect for their privacy; secondly, because they may feel they want to tell their own story in their own time. I do not, however, feel that this restraint on my part has in any way distorted the portrait of Stella as a whole.

My mother, Stella's sister-in-law, Renée, has been an almost inexhaustible source of stories, and has kindly allowed me to make use of Stella's many letters to her, as well as her own diaries. My father too has been of invaluable assistance. To them go my profound love and gratitude.

I am also greatly indebted, in no particular order, to the following: Patricia Angadi; Elizabeth Jenkins, Mrs Morgan and Mrs Pennels at the North London Collegiate School; Howard B. Gottlieb and Margaret R. Goostray of the Mugar Memorial Library, Boston, Massachusetts; G. T. Withers, Ronald and Mrs Raymond-Cox; Stephen Powys Marks; Joan Stevens; Jane and Christopher Rye; the remarkable Ida Affleck Graves; Bevis Hillier; Mrs Valerie Southcott; Mr Richard Adams; Dr Barbara Reynolds; Barry Humphries; John and Diane Rose; my brother Charles and his wife Sarah; Caroline Oliver; Hilary and Pauline Graham; Karen

Introduction

O'Brien Sanderson; Joan Aiken; Blanche Cardale; Beth McDonald; Maggie Oxland; the Institut Français for information about the *Prix Fémina-Vie Heureuse*; Jim and Roger Marshall; Mike and Alice Sharland; Richard M. Kolbet, Special Collections Librarian at the University of Iowa; Mr William Young, Archivist, and the vergers and staff of the church of St Martin in the Fields; Maxine Powell at Manchester University; and Miss Tauba Heilpern for allowing me to make use of her thesis on the sources of *Cold Comfort Farm* which has many illuminating and interesting things to say on the subject, some of which I have borrowed (or stolen) and put into this book.

I am greatly indebted to Mr Michael Pick for allowing me to see letters written by Stella both to him and to his father, for telling me the story of the German version of *Nightingale Wood*, and for his perceptive and helpful comments on Stella's novels. Suzanne Goodwin, who was such a good friend to my aunt, has also been kind enough to talk to me and let me see Stella's letters to her.

I am very grateful to Dr Frederic Hunter MA for supplying me with information about Stella's journalism course at University College London from his thesis, *Grub Street and Academia: The relationship between journalism and education, 1880–1940, with special reference to the London University Diploma for journalism, 1919–1939.*

Many of my researches have been made much less arduous by my membership of the London Library, an institution Stella herself loved and belonged to for many years.

Finally, I would like to thank my wife Joanna, 'without whom', genuinely, this book would never have been written. It was she who urged me to write it. The idea of a biography had not seriously crossed my mind because I was content with Stella's books and my memories of her. But, once embarked on the work of researching Stella's life, I found the task richly rewarding. Unfortunately Joanna never met Stella, but this made her dispassionate appraisal of the book and her many suggestions for improvements all the more valuable. Joanna also accompanied me on many research expeditions, some of them fruitless, many of them both fruitful and enjoyable, and all the more enjoyable for her company. For that, as for so many other things, I am deeply in her debt.

CHAPTER 1

'Growing boys!
Growing devils!'

None of us entirely escapes from our family background, but the extent to which we do is often the measure of our maturity. Escape is more desirable, of course, from some families than from others. Where the Gibbons clan was concerned, the breaking of familial bonds was a necessary condition of happiness.

Charles Preston Gibbons, a civil engineer by profession, had six children: in chronological order Louise, Telford, Arthur, Gus, Fred, and Ruth who died young. To his offspring he bequeathed many of the characteristics we associate with the Starkadders of Cold Comfort Farm: sanctimonious arrogance, self-pity, rampant sexuality (in the males), violent swings of mood and a passion for self-dramatisation. He also passed on, to his granddaughter Stella at least, some more valuable traits, notably a lively interest in all the arts and a profound love of nature. Stella once told me that the Gibbons idea of heaven was to walk through a garden full of deep red roses and the music of Wagner. Male members of the Gibbons family attended concerts of his music *en masse*, and tears would flow. Richard Wagner was, in consequence, never a favourite composer of Stella's.

In July 1866, when still only seventeen, Charles Preston Gibbons married the twenty-seven-year-old Alice Elizabeth Knight, who had been widowed two years previously. Her maiden name is recorded both as Gibbons and Gibbins (on her birth certificate it is the latter) and she was actually a cousin of his. Both the bride's and groom's families came from the Deptford and Greenwich area of London on the south bank of the Thames. On the marriage certificate Charles Preston entered his age as twenty-one. The story behind these bare facts set down in the registers is unknown, but doubtless full of drama. Charles Preston's father, William Preston Gibbons, was a dyer, not an exalted trade, and the family was Irish in origin.

Alice Elizabeth seems to have been a gentle soul, known, in the early years of their marriage, by the pet name of Butterfly. Charles Preston's first male child, who was to be Stella's father, was born in 1869 and christened Charles James Preston Telford, but he was always called Telford, after the great Scottish civil engineer, the 'Colossus of Roads'. From the first the Gibbons household was turbulent. Charles Preston Gibbons was a violent man with a perverse craving for peace: he would fire blank cartridges at his study ceiling to quell the noise of his four young sons in the nursery above.

In 1878, leaving his family behind, Gibbons took ship for South Africa where his titanic energies found an outlet, and, among other exploits, he built the first bridge over the Orange River. On one of his return visits to England, he asked to see the family accounts. Among the bills that Alice produced were some for his sons' clothing. Gibbons immediately flew into a temper. Why should his sons need more clothing? Had he not seen to the purchase of clothing for them barely a year ago? 'But they're growing boys!' his wife remonstrated. 'Growing boys! Growing devils!' Gibbons replied.

This story entered family legend, and was passed on to me by his second son Arthur's second wife, Kitty. She also told me that on one occasion, rather later, Charles Preston marched up and down his dining room blowing a whistle and waving a green flag. Once he had attracted sufficient attention, he declared to his assembled family that he was practising to be a railway guard, because his children were spending so much of his money that this was the profession he would soon be forced to adopt. I doubt whether even the slightest suggestion of a joke was intended because I have studied Charles Preston's diaries. They contain not a glimmer of humour.

When the children reached adolescence, the troubles in the household were intensified. Gibbons, barely twenty years older than his sons, was attracted to their girlfriends, mistresses and even wives, as were these women, occasionally, to him. Stella's daughter Laura writes:

These rivalries between the brothers *and their father* underlay the constant falling-out between the various members of the Gibbons family. Every few weeks it was: 'That name is not mentioned in this house,' with an accompanying shudder and pursed lips, as one or other member of the family indulged in some escapade of which the others disapproved. Consequently sides were taken. (My mother thought a list should have been pinned up in the hall, and changed periodically, so that you knew what names you could mention, and what names you couldn't!) This sexual swapping, or however you like to describe it, was not done out of any belief in free love: on the contrary, it was accompanied by much guilt, remorse and indignation.

The paradox was that, despite these endless quarrels, members of the Gibbons family remained obsessively interested in each other's doings and constantly in touch. The banishments never lasted for long because the Gibbonses fed each other's appetite for drama.

The surviving diaries of Charles Preston Gibbons – Grandfather Gibbons – cover the years 1899 to 1911, and are revealing documents. They would be even more revealing if they were not written in almost illegible handwriting and if his daughter Louise had not cut passages out of some of the early volumes. The character that emerges from their pages is a bizarre combination of Heathcliff and Pecksniff, or of Amos and Seth Starkadder. A photograph of Grandfather Gibbons dating from the 1920s shows him seated on a deckchair outside Louise's home in Finchley, north London. The features, vital and a touch malign, are those of an elderly satyr.

Grandfather Gibbons was in some ways a typical Victorian, in others decidedly not. His poetic preferences, after Shakespeare, were for Tennyson, Browning and Coventry Patmore, but he also read Ibsen, Wells and Shaw. Shaw, like Gibbons a Wagnerite, was a hero of his. In his diaries Gibbons records attending a talk by Shaw ('a grand Pioneer fearless lecture'); and on one occasion he enjoyed two minutes' conversation with the great man.

His religious views were unorthodox: he despised conventional religion, though he did attend services at something called the 'Ethical Church'. It was, of course, difficult for anyone so remorselessly preoccupied with himself to have any sort of religion. From time to time a severely limited apprehension of deity surfaces. On holiday in Eastbourne he encountered two groups of people (a family and a pair of lovers) and was indignant because they were not looking, as he would have wished, at 'God's splendid Landscape', but reading books instead. Against the date of his birthday he would often write the words 'whom God preserve'.

Signs of discord can be found in the very opening pages of his diary. The entry for 24 December 1899 contains this cryptic passage: 'Alice rowing [?] me at every opportunity because I don't enjoy her company. Poor thing she *would not* put oil into her lamp, and so the door is shut.' The reference to oil and lamps is baffling. Some kind of sexual allusion may be intended, but it seems more likely to be a biblical metaphor for poor housekeeping – a fault of Alice's which enraged him on numerous occasions. Alice is a Foolish Virgin who did not keep her lamp full.

The diaries often praise women other than his wife, in particular a Mrs Lydia Ceiley, who was thirty-nine when first mentioned. She was the wife of George R. Ceiley, a music teacher and organist of St James's, Piccadilly. An amateur actress of note, Mrs Ceiley was much given to recitations, her *tour de force* being one called 'The Venetian Revenge'. This extract from Gibbons's diaries, dated 26 December 1899, is typical of many:

> With a mind and spirit ever giving, and a face which daily becomes more and more the picture of her soul. And she honours me with something akin to reverence such as an ideally dutiful daughter would bestow on a patriarch. Little wonder that I reverence her so. It seems that she had been sent to show me how good a woman can be. . . . What a 'light from heaven' to come round about me on the way. What a harp wherefrom to draw celestial music. What a Comrade in the van against the powers of ill . . . .

Not surprisingly, his enthusiasm for Coventry Patmore is in evidence when he is with her. He often reads aloud, 'much to her delight', from Patmore's 'The Angel in the House', a poem which epitomises the worshipful side of male Victorian attitudes to women. In Gibbons's copy of the poem many of the more elevated passages have been heavily underlined in pencil. On one occasion, while enjoying yet another bout of mental anguish over his relations with Mrs Ceiley, he cries out: 'How could I sleep? Would Coventry Patmore have slept?' Generally speaking, in the presence of Mrs Ceiley, 'a sylph with a vestal soul' as he describes her, Pecksniff predominates; and when he is with his wife, Heathcliff takes over.

Though passages are often cut out of the diaries where 'Mrs C' is mentioned, it is clear that the relationship remained platonic, sometimes painfully so. In August 1900, he wrote:

> At home with a frugal meal – Ibsen, Shaw – then a strange letter to Mrs Ceiley. A supper of boiled skate which was almost unendurably pungent with Ammonia. Better still after this, in fact never physically better and mentally cleaner in my life. But how the more keenly I feel the burden of my restraints. A pig wallows in his sty. But ugh! the marriage bed time – I who know what it is to reverence a woman as I do Jehovah of the stars. . . . Often when I come to write my diary I am in such perturbation by the *Alice Hells* that my memory is two-thirds [?] gone.

'Alice Hells' is a phrase that occurs frequently and seems to refer to the rage and disgust which his wife's mild incompetence excites in him. On 7 September 1900 he wrote:

> Am I – I – to hunt for the Gas papers [business papers of his concerned with the Hoddesdon Gas Tank] misplaced by Alice Elizabeth. Good God. And the steamers on the river are Yelling and Helling [his house was near the mouth of the Thames at Gravesend]. I have no home. My home is not home. It is not an office. My office is only half an office. True the club is all right. And so is the street. Except that I can't afford to call a cab but must wait for a bus and sit beside the human rank and file.

Relations with all his children, with the exception of Louise, are at best uneasy during this period. The first reference to Stella's future mother and father occurs on 20 June 1900. 'Telford and Miss Williams are still staying here [Gravesend] (since the end of last week). I doubt whether I shall ever again feel at ease in the presence of either Alice or any of her children. There is not between us enough in common to rewrite the hostilities of the past.'

Telford was thirty-one, and it was not surprising that he and his father did not get on: two of a kind rarely agree. Temperamentally they were almost identical, even to their passion for Wagner. When Stella, aged ten, asked him if he would, or *could*, ever be happy, Telford replied: 'Never! Never though seated at the right hand of God!' The combination of brooding melancholy and melodramatic arrogance makes this a quintessentially Gibbons remark.

In the *Medical Directory* for 1901 Telford had given the house in Gravesend as his address. In 1897 he had qualified as a physician and surgeon at the London Hospital. After three years at a practice in Derby, he returned to marry and to look for a practice in London. Telford claimed to have fallen in love with Maude Williams, his bride-to-be, after hearing her sing in a choir. Presumably this was not a church choir because Telford was a staunch atheist. Maude – always called Maudie – was nine years his junior, pretty, dark and slim. Her background was, in a less violent way, as unconventional as his.

Maudie's father, Gerald Williams, was a stockbroker of a good family which claimed an ancestral link with Myles Standish, one of America's founding fathers. The writer Patricia Angadi, a second cousin of Stella and Gerald's great-niece, told me that Gerald was mentioned seldom, and then guardedly, in their family – some sort of disgrace attached to him. There were vague intimations that he had lost much of his money in a stock market crash and that he had married unsuitably. One legend had it that his wife was a barmaid called Florrie. Their marriage certificate, however, reveals that Gerald Williams (whose occupation is given as 'Gentleman') married Florence Marion Simon, daughter of Henry Arthur Simon, 'Barrister at Law', and no occupation is ascribed to her. The Bar was regarded as one of the four gentlemanly professions, but the name Simon suggests Jewish origins, so perhaps it was this that the Williams family found objectionable. The barmaid legend could well have originated in a typical Victorian pun on Florrie's father's profession, which later turned into a bitter kind of joke.

Gerald had two children by Florrie, Maudie (Maude Phoebe Standish Williams) in 1877 and Ruby in 1879. But Florrie took to drink and abandoned her daughters when they were eight and six respectively. Ruby once recalled to her great-niece Laura standing on a railway station watching her mother go off, and wetting herself with grief and anxiety.

Not long after his abandonment Gerald met another single parent, Ethel Lester, a short, dominant woman who had been on the stage. She had staring blue eyes, and a daughter called Nina. Gerald, Ethel and their respective offspring set up house together in South London. The two never married, perhaps because the errant Florrie could not be traced and therefore divorced, and Gerald used to refer to Ethel as 'my little house-keeper'. This unorthodox arrangement, rather than his unfortunate marriage, was probably the reason why Gerald was ostracised by the rest of the Williams family.

On 29 September 1900 Grandfather Gibbons went to his office in the Balls Pond Road as usual at 8.45 a.m. He bought a book by Oliver Wendell Holmes 'to make peace with Miss Wheatly'. In fact on that day he saw both his beloved Mrs Ceiley ('in highly efficient working costume. When is she not efficient?') and Nellie Wheatly, with whom his relations were perhaps rather less chaste. Having recorded these encounters in his diary he drew a little arrow, pointing to the space after the date, to insert the words 'Wired joy to Telford & Co.' It was the wedding day of Stella's future parents. Telford and Maudie married at Bromley registry office in Kent: both gave as their address the house in Beckenham where Gerald Williams was living with Ethel Lester.

For some time, Grandfather Gibbons was too bothered by the horrors of his own marriage to trouble about anyone else's. On 3 December he was writing: 'Through it all I terribly miss the only two elements possible for life – solitude and a comrade. To be [illegible] onto a being without an act or thought in common is terrible indeed and makes me hourly curse the law which binds me to a woman who will grovel, and the fate which keeps me from the accumulation of such wealth as would enable me to override or evade that law.' On the 23rd, he wrote: 'Alice's mouth is full of vileness again. And the day is black. But a little gleam of sun in the middle makes me hope. Yet an hour later and Hell is uppermost. That cursed Alice is at the bottom of it all.'

Telford and Maude Gibbons bought a house in North London:

21 Malden Crescent, Kentish Town, which was to be Telford's surgery and their home until they both died in 1926. Today Malden Crescent no longer consists of terraced houses, but is lined on both sides with grim council blocks from the sixties and seventies. However, the general atmosphere remains what it was at the turn of the century. The population is working- or lower middle-class, with a smattering of the artistic and eccentric around Camden Lock. There is something raffish and unconventional about the place. Its more successful inhabitants often migrate further up the hill to Hampstead, as Stella was to do.

On 28 December 1900, Grandfather Gibbons finally paid a call on the newly married couple. 'Camden Town & Malden Crescent and called on Telford for the first time. He & Maude were very cordial. We had tea and they were genuinely disappointed at my not staying to dinner.' By March 1901 the reconciliation was so complete that he was even sending his beloved Mrs Ceiley to consult his son: 'Telford was very gracious.'

By January 1901, Grandfather Gibbons had decided that his wife should move out of his home in Gravesend and take lodgings elsewhere. As he put it, for once succinctly and unsanctimoniously: 'Life is a struggle when couples are not pairs.' But by April the situation had not changed and he was ranting once more:

> Again an Alice Hell has driven my memory away and I write almost full of curses. I say almost, for there will always be a chamber in my heart into which curses cannot enter . . . then 2 letters to Mrs Ceiley, because I could not post the first I may not post the 2nd. I must give up writing to people to whom I can not, dare not, say what I would. It is a torture, a non life, a stifling – I wonder I survive it. I am a social martyr. I dare not speak except as prescribed by my 'peers'. It is a social tyranny. It is very terrible for society or any other power to tear people apart.

The first sign of troubles in Telford and Maudie's marriage occurred as early as 27 April 1901. The entry in Grandfather Gibbons's diary also demonstrated that, while cordial relations had been restored, his feelings for his son would never be warm. As with many great egoists, Grandfather Gibbons's attitudes were nearly always extreme. He could show devotion (Mrs Ceiley), loathing (his wife) or cold indifference (his children), but he was almost a stranger to the middle range of emotions which includes affection, tenderness and fatherly concern. He wrote: 'Alice had been at Telford's to consult him about her throat. Maude & Telford (so Alice said next day) had been discussing suicide "because the money is not coming in fast enough". Well, I understood that it was coming in well. Early days for the abandonment of hope – I think. Feeling terribly troubled about poor Mrs Ceiley.'

In May 1901 Grandfather Gibbons packed Alice off to live in Woking and took a room in Fortis Green, North London, with Mr and Mrs Ceiley and their two sons. As might be expected, reality began to tarnish his idealised picture of Mrs Ceiley the moment he was living under the same roof. She is still a martyr, but is guilty of 'unreasonable utterances', 'violent outbursts' and 'a belief that all the world is against her' – rather like Gibbons himself, in fact. He castigated her for indulging her teenage sons Hubert and Len whom he considered selfish, demanding and noisy. He particularly objected to their habit of eating oranges at all times of the day. The over-indulgence of children – something of which he was never guilty – became an obsession with him and many dull and anguish-ridden pages were devoted to the subject: 'I once more wish myself in a world, nay almost a universe, where children are not.' Despite all of this he managed to derive satisfaction from the equanimity with which he bore his sufferings: 'A proper description of my life just now would be that I am far too often and far too extremely put by circumstances – very strange circumstances – under conditions of great and intensely unpleasant mental strains; & I greatly wonder how I come out of them as clear-headed and high minded as I do.'

The diary for 1902 no longer exists, so there is no record of Grandfather Gibbons's reaction to the birth of his first grandchild, Stella Dorothea, on 5 January. Two more children were to be born to Telford and Maudie, but Stella considered herself luckier than her brothers because she had been born when the marriage was still young. In her autobiographical novel *Enbury Heath* she wrote of herself: 'She grew up in the wreck of hope and the slow, strange living-death of love, but because she was conceived in love, she was the happiest of the three, and she never forgot it.'

Grandfather Gibbons's diaries resume in 1903, by which time relatively cordial relations between himself and Alice had been resumed, although they continued to live apart. On 5 March he wrote: 'At 6 to Telford's where Alice had come up from Woking. An enjoyable fish supper, but Stella was too full of life to allow any to adults.' Other entries make it clear that Telford and his brothers sided on the whole with their mother. Grandfather Gibbons's meetings with his wife usually took place at the house of either Telford or Telford's sister Louise. On 17 March he went again: 'To Telford's to see Alice, but it was very uncomfortable. The baby is the Establishment.' On 18 December 1903 he recorded that Stella was ill, and on the 21st he wrote: 'To Telford's and found great distress about Stella's danger. I was too perturbed to stay.' By 30 January 1904 she had recovered: '. . . on to Telford's, where Stella was very soon banging on the 80 guinea Bechstein, and I feeling very uncomfortable thereat.' A few days later he was writing: 'When I remember Telford allowing his 2 year old to bang his 70 [sic] guinea Bechstein, and what the two lads [Len and Hubert Ceiley] do all week – I had to turn in to bed again for my heart got bad and my blood seemed to half curdle.'

The reason why Telford was allowing his two-year-old to bang the piano was that he was very anxious to give her every opportunity to be musical. Music was a passion with him and one of his few harmless consolations. He was disappointed when he discovered that, though fond of music, Stella had no particular gift for it.

Of Grandfather Gibbons's other children, with the exception of his daughter Louise, he wrote less. Gus was an accountant, and there is very little about him except a vague grumble that he could not handle money – a disadvantage if one is an accountant. Family memory recalls little about him except that he possessed a parrot which had a habit of perching on the shoulders of strangers and, in its excitement, vomiting down the back of their necks. Arthur, after a short and no doubt acrimonious spell in his father's engineering firm, became an actor and theatrical manager with a tangled private life. By the time Grandfather Gibbons's diaries began,

Arthur already had an estranged wife and a mistress to whom his father was becoming increasingly attached. To compound the confusion, both of these ladies were called Maud – the name seems to have had a fatal attraction for the Gibbons family. An unusually terse entry from Grandfather Gibbons's diary on 30 July 1904 read: 'Took Arthur to lunch and to task.' The one child who was virtually never mentioned was Fred. Very sensibly, he had emigrated to America and married there. Before 1908 there was but a single entry concerning Fred. On 12 April 1904 his father wrote: 'This morning a letter from Alice with portraits of Fred and his wife.'

Grandfather Gibbons's daughter Louise was, on his own admission, 'the most loved child of all', though even she 'has not a twentieth part of the graciousness of Nell [Wheatly, his aforementioned girlfriend]'. Perhaps, like Stella, she, being the eldest, was the one to be conceived in love before 'Alice-Hells' rumpled the marriage bed. Louise became a nurse, and in October 1901 she married a Dr Percy Pywell. By contrast with the passing reference to Telford's marriage, Louise's wedding was fulsomely described in the diaries. Louise was tall and slim with her share of the Gibbons temperament, while Percy was short, plump, jolly and extrovert. Though childless, they often held children's parties at which, much to Louise's disapproval, Percy would put cream cakes and jam tarts on top of his bald head and let the cream and jam trickle down his face. By this simple act he gave great pleasure to his young guests.

References to the infant Stella occur infrequently in Grandfather Gibbons's diary. He was mostly taken up with his tortured relations with Mrs Ceiley, Nell Wheatly and Maud Lydgate (Arthur's discarded mistress). In 1906 Alice's servant Ellen gave birth out of wedlock and took poison, but this incident merited only a casual mention.

Stella's brothers Gerald Preston Telford and Lewis O'Reilly were born in 1905 and 1909 respectively. In February 1908 Grandfather Gibbons paid a visit: 'I went to Telford's. Maudie had prepared a nice cup of tea & Stella was polished up to perfection. Gerald also was "on view" asleep in bed, and a fine show they made. Maudie herself looked well, and Telford, although not in good health & *not* polished up, still made, with Arthur who happened to be there too, a group of whom one may be excused for being proud.' In April 1908 he gave Alice two portraits of Stella 'in pretty gilt frames' with which she was delighted. 'Just after 5 o'clock tea, when Percy had gone up [to see Alice], and the evening sun was brightening the drawing room, Stella and her mother bounded up the garden. They were a charming pair. . . . Maudie sang two songs written and composed by herself – and very pretty they are. Telford was on holiday in Clacton.'

Then on 2 May 1908 Alice contracted erysipelas, a bacterial skin infection. Her rapid decline is described in painstaking and moving detail, though the tenderness of his account might have been more touching if Grandfather Gibbons had shown himself more tolerant of Alice's failings when she was in good health. On 20 May she died, and he wrote: 'God had decided to call her whom he had blessed with a soul of angelic kindness. . . . Gus and I slept in the dining room so as to be near Alice in body. How we were kept from mad raving, and tearing open the coffin, and beseeching God to spare us our dear one – I scarce can tell.' After the funeral he heard a street musician playing the cornet on Moorgate Station and asked his son Arthur what the tune was called. It was: 'Alice, Where Art Thou?'

He raised an obelisk to her in Brockley Cemetery in South London and visited it obsessively, laden with floral tributes. On 15 July Louise had a letter from 'poor Fred'. On 19 August Grandfather Gibbons wrote: 'I have not yet had Fred's letter shown to me.' On 1 September he 'began writing to Fred'. On the 20th he 'at last resumed my letter to Fred. But did not advance it very far.' It was not until well into October that Grandfather Gibbons completed his letter to Fred.

It is as if the pain of Gibbons's marriage to Alice had been wiped out by the pain of bereavement. There are no mentions of 'Alice-Hells' – nor any expressions of remorse or even regret. Telford's later conduct towards his own wife Maudie would mirror his father's to an extraordinary degree.

The pattern of family relationships and the deterioration of Telford and Maudie's marriage are charted by the occasional entry. On 12 October 1908 Grandfather Gibbons went to tea with Telford: 'Stella perfect.' On 9 November Telford was 'in grave fear of cancer of the throat. Found him and Maudie in a terrible state of mind.' But the fears proved groundless. On 12 November 1910 'Maudie is not happy. . . . Arthur is out of it with Louise – and for that matter Telford is also, & Maudie too in a measure because she more or less sits dutifully under the Telford regime, or the Telford prohibition[?].'

A pleasanter note intrudes on the 26th: 'From here to Telford's, and very pleased with all his 3 children. Stella [aged eight] astonished me, and Telford too by her reading. Gave her Brutus to the Crowd, and she took it splendidly, tho' she had never seen a line of Shakespeare before.' Then on 8 April 1911 came this entry: 'To Louise's by 7.15 and found a telegram despatched at 1.43 and asking "Can Mr Gibbons come over soon?"'. . . . Off I went. Maudie told me of some most unaccountable[?] behaviour of Telford's which grieved me greatly, and later Telford made much complaint to me of Maudie's manner and management. It was painful in the extreme.' Two days later he wrote: 'Maudie said I must have worked magic with Telford – for he began to be kind even when I went out for the sundries[?] on Saturday night, and had been most kind ever since.'

These entries give some indication of the misery of Telford and Maudie's marriage, a misery which can be laid largely at Telford's door. Maudie, like Alice, was a gentle soul and not the best person to manage the household of a doctor in one of the poorer districts of London. The worst really that can be said of her is that she failed to stand up to her brutal and domineering husband. According to Stella, the pain of it all was exacerbated by the fact that there was a sense in which they remained 'in love' for the rest of their lives, and therefore could not separate.

Relief was found in visits to Maudie's father, Gerald Williams, in Sydenham. There was a large garden for Stella to play in and her Aunt Ruby would pet her, while her grandfather, who had a vein of fantastic humour, would tell her marvellous stories. Stella recalled the Sydenham ménage in her short story 'Edwardian Afternoon', published in *Beside the Pearly Water*, in 1954. In it the nine-year-old Sophia (a name Stella also used for herself in the autobiographical novel *Enbury Heath*) notices with an innocent but observant eye the slight but subtle tensions that existed even in this comparatively well-regulated household. Stella's maternal grandfather seems to have been a cheerful, waggish type; Ethel, his 'little house-keeper', slightly forbidding and rather prim. Her daughter Nina, who followed her mother on to the stage, was the pretty and preferred one. Gerald's daughter, Stella's Aunt Ruby, was physically tiny. (Her great-niece Laura measured her once and found her to be only four feet eight inches in height.) She was not as gifted or attractive as Nina, and consequently her status was not as high in the household. Notwithstanding, Sydenham must have appeared to Stella a haven of happiness by comparison with her parents' dark house in Kentish Town.

Stella also knew happiness in the holidays which Maudie took with her children, unaccompanied by Telford. They generally went to Clacton which, along with other East Coast resorts, remained a favourite place of refuge to Stella in time of trouble. A number of her novels were set in Essex and its smug, restful coastal towns. In an article in *St Martin's Review* in July 1940 she recalled:

> When we were children we used to stay at an East Coast town in a small lodging house kept by a family. . . . The handsome bearded father had a club foot; the mother was stout and pale and talkative; kind, but with that malicious twist to her unceasing flow of gossip which gives salt to the speech of Essex people. I used to be put to bed early in what seemed to me a large room, papered in silvery white with twists of blue ribbon, and on the walls hung texts adorned with birds and wreaths of flowers in smooth, rich colours.
>
> My mother always left me a night light in case I should be frightened of the dark. I remember so clearly how I would lie in the big clean bed with its honeycomb quilt, noticing the fresh smell of the cotton sheets and watching the shadows on the white ceiling. Time seemed to go on for ever and ever, in a lovely dream of content and peace. All day I had enjoyed the feeling of the hot sand under my bare feet, and the smell of the sea, and the look of the dark seaweed against the rocks, the little ships sailing far out, the White Coons [a troupe of minstrels] on the jetty, the rose pink shells and trembling yellow foam; and as I lay there I dreamily knew that tomorrow would be as lovely as today had been.
>
> When I remember peace, I remember those long summer twilights in the bedroom that looked out towards the sea, when I was six years old.

Moments of happiness were also to be found nearer home. All her life Stella loved Hampstead Heath, and during walks there with her governess she made her first childhood friends. One of these, Anthony Rye, later a distinguished poet and the biographer of Gilbert White of Selborne, became a lifelong friend.

Rye recalled to his daughter Jane an early encounter with Stella on the Heath. They and some other children, accompanied by their governesses, were playing Ring-a-ring-o'-roses. After 'All fall down!' Rye saw fit to add the words '. . . on our bums!' The word 'bum' had recently entered his vocabulary, it sounded good and he felt that it deserved an airing. Unfortunately this piece of vulgarity was not well received by either the governesses or the other children and he was ostracised; but Stella came over to comfort him in his disgrace. It was early evidence, he said, of her strongly protective instinct, as well as a natural scorn for prevailing orthodoxies.

Another lifelong friend acquired from playing on the Heath was Ina Dornan, whose family, like Stella's, was Irish in origin. She was two years younger than Stella, and later came to be idealised and immortalised as Mrs Smiling in *Cold Comfort Farm*.

The shadow cast by Stella's father, Telford Gibbons, was long and grim, but he had his good points. He was, in the words of *Enbury Heath*, 'a bad man, but a good doctor'. In the same book Stella offered her considered verdict on her father, here called Hartly Garden:

> He was a most unhappy man, whose very great energies needed more outlet than his work as a doctor in a slum could give them; yet the timorousness and lack of self-confidence which he had inherited from his mother prevented him from turning his powers into satisfying channels.
>
> He was ambitious, but his ambition sprang from vanity, and when it was not fed by achievement, it turned sour and increased his misery. He did not possess the concentration and aptitude for hard, persistent study which would have burnished his gifts and brought him social and professional success. On every side he was thwarted, and he threshed insanely against the nets woven by his own most unfortunate character.
>
> Yet his gifts were great. In the practical execution of his work

he excelled. He worked like a demon, building a large practice of patients who loved him as much as they feared him, in the heart of a miserably poor and crowded district; and during the twenty years of his work there he saved many hundreds of lives by the exercise of his brilliant gifts of diagnosis and surgery. He let in light, sunshine and a kind of fierce laughter into the wretched rooms where his patients lived.

They called him the Fresh Air Doctor, because fresh air was what he most often prescribed. He realised the curative powers of light and sun some time before they became part of the stock-in-trade of clinics and general practitioners in very poor districts and he insisted, with oaths, on his patients sleeping with their windows open.

Sophia [Stella] used sometimes to ride on his rounds with him when she was a child, and she could remember in later years how, when his small cheap car appeared at the top of the street, windows would fly up all along its squalid length. 'Open the winder quick! 'Ere comes Dr Garden!'

The story goes that he once saved the life of a boy with a chronic asthma attack by strapping him on to the back of his motor bike and riding at breakneck speed to the top of Primrose Hill. A doctor tells me that a temporary cure might have been effected, not through the forcing of air into the boy's lungs, but from the adrenaline which a dangerous ride with a volatile medical practitioner would have pumped into his system.

When Telford's patients were too poor to pay, he would give his services free or take payment in kind. Hundreds of grateful Camden and Kentish Town residents attended his funeral in 1926. From accompanying her father on his rounds Stella acquired an intimate and sympathetic understanding of working- and lower middle-class urban life. Her authentic portrayal of it in early novels such as *Miss Linsey and Pa* is a distinctive and unusual feature of her work.

Charity for Dr Gibbons, however, ended at home. Depressive, mean with money (to his family) and a drunkard, he had a succession of affairs with the housemaids and governesses he employed. He tyrannised over the household and struck fear into its inhabitants. Stella's friend Ida Graves used to visit the house in Malden Crescent, which was also the surgery, in the early 1920s. She recalled: 'Stella's mother often had no light on. I said, "Why are you sitting in the dark?" and she'd say laughingly, "I like the dark, Ida."' Maudie was trying to manage on the meagre housekeeping that Telford gave her. Stella's daughter Laura recalls that her mother 'would have recurring nightmares about having to leave Highgate and be sent back to the dark house, the surgery, where she had grown up'.

In *Enbury Heath* Stella evokes the atmosphere of the surgery after his death:

> It was a tall, dark, narrow house with creaking stairs and a base-ment in which lived rats, which Sophia used to feed in defiance to her father's orders, and blackbeetles of which she had an almost mystical horror, as though they were symbols of everything evil in the world. . . . The Surgery was an unhappy house. So many miserable and violently ugly events had happened in it that they had soaked the walls and staircases in an atmosphere of oppression and terror. . . . There were two banisters missing from the hall staircase near the bottom; Dr Garden had torn these out in a fit of fury one night. On a cupboard door in the basement dining room there was a long, glancing scar; that was made when he had thrown a knife at their mother; and another scar, star-shaped, in the cloudy glass window between the dining room and the kitchen, marked where he had hurled a plate at the housemaid – the same girl who now sat in the kitchen, red-eyed and silent because he was dead.

As Stella makes clear in this novel, Telford was both oppressive and violent. He had indeed once thrown a knife at Maudie, and on one occasion he upturned the breakfast table, depositing the food intended for himself and five others on to his wife's lap. Whisky was his principal poison, though in later years he would dose himself with laudanum and veronal from his dispensary.

Until she was about twelve Stella was her father's favourite child. He was extremely proud of her obvious intelligence and taught her how to row, and even, later on, to box. He would frequently take her to the Zoo in nearby Regent's Park where Stella acquired a lifelong love of animals, particularly wild ones. But, as she approached puberty, Telford's attitude towards his daughter changed. Her figure was always sturdy, sometimes plump, and he began to call her 'fat' and 'the old bargee'.

This cruelty may have been motivated by a strong element of self-hatred. Stella had inherited the mental vitality and originality of the Gibbons family, but also many of its physical traits. Photographs reveal a striking facial resemblance between her and her father – the broad face, thin lips, firm chin and strong, regular features. In castigating Stella for looking like an old bargee, a figure he resembled much more closely than she did, Telford was, perhaps unconsciously, punishing himself.

In a letter to her friend the writer Suzanne Goodwin in 1975 Stella wrote: 'I had absolutely not one grain of self-confidence "in that way" [i.e. about her attractiveness to the opposite sex]; my father knocked it all out by continual jeering at my looks . . . and I was *not* plain. I think he feared I should attract men.'

Stella loved physical beauty, but she knew that there was a more precious beauty which came from within; and inner beauty was something her father would not have recognised, let alone acknowledged in his own daughter. The complex emotions Stella felt about her appearance are expressed in her best-known poem, 'Lullaby for a Baby Toad'. In it the mother toad comforts her child, which has just caught a glimpse of its reflection in a pool, with the old legend that it carries a jewel in its head:

> For if, my toadling,
> Your face were fair
> As the precious jewel
> That glimmers there,
> Man, the jealous,
> Man, the cruel,
> Would look at you
> And suspect the jewel.

At first Stella bitterly resented the fact that she resembled her father. She would have liked to look like her gentle, humorous mother. Both she and Lewis felt a certain envy for their brother Gerald, not so much because he happened to be the good-looking one as because he was the one who took after their mother in appearance. Less fortunately, Gerald inherited Maudie's weakness and lack of stamina.

Much later, long after he was dead, Stella felt that her likeness to her father gave her a measure of understanding for him. Old colleagues of his who instantly recognised her as Telford's daughter would tell her what a brilliant young medical student he had been. Through them she caught a glimpse of the remarkable man he might have been but for his demons, and she began to feel pity. While he was alive, however, her predominant feelings towards him were fear and distrust.

A key incident occurred when Stella was about eleven. One day Telford, in a fit of melancholic remorse, was threatening to commit suicide and Maudie in desperation had begged Stella, still his favourite child, to persuade him not to. As the ranting went on Stella noticed that Telford had a slight smile on his face and was deriving a secret pleasure from the scene, much as an actor might do from tearing a passion to tatters. She was appalled. To suffer from a fit of despair was one thing; but actually to enjoy causing a scene which brought misery to all around one was quite another. Moreover, it seemed to her that if one can be detached enough to revel in the outpourings of one's own emotional violence one can also control it.

This was the view which was to animate Flora Poste in *Cold Comfort Farm*. In Stella's comic fantasy the Starkadders were changed as a result into saner, more fulfilled human beings. No such transformation occurred in the real lives of the Gibbons family.

Soon after the incident of her father's apparent suicide bid Stella began to realise that it was a trait of the Gibbons family as a whole not simply to be prone to melodramatic scenes, but to take pleasure in them. She detected an element of pretence in their passion, and it was this early recognition which made her the enemy and scourge of pretentiousness throughout her life. Stella is a good example of the truth that it is not convention *per se* against which the young revolt, but whatever in their surroundings oppresses them. If what oppresses them is wildness, disorder, eccentricity, they are just as likely to rebel against that as against staidness and good form.

Stella eventually became inured to the family rows, except when they involved her mother whom she loved very much. In an interview with Jill Neville published in the *Independent*

Magazine on 26 August 1985 she remembered feeling 'absolutely detached but disliking it, thinking, Oh Lord, they're at it again.' Stella's immediate method of escape from this unhappiness was through her imagination. She recalled that even before she could read she was telling stories to her brothers Gerald and Lewis.

In an interview given to *Leader* magazine and published on 28 April 1945 she remembered:

> My brothers used sometimes to come to me and say tell us a 'Ticky' story. [Ticky was a character who later became the hero of a novel of the same name.] In the childhood version Ticky was an undersized obstinate creature, always making trouble. I never could exactly say what he was.
>
> More often my brothers and I got talking about all the 'Ticky' people as if they were real, and a story would develop out of that. Sometimes a story would continue for hours (or it seemed like hours) until we were weak and helpless with laughter. My mother, from whose family my story-telling comes, used to listen and laugh with us.

Once Stella was telling one of these stories to her mother and brothers in her attic bedroom and all of them were rolling about on the bed with laughter. Telford heard the sound. He came upstairs softly, hoping to surprise them, but their sensitive ears caught his tread. The laughter died. Telford came into the room and asked what the joke had been. Maudie explained that it was just some story of Stella's. Telford said: 'Stella never tells me stories,' then turned and left the room without another word.

When Stella could read, which she learned to do late and rather reluctantly, another world was opened up to her. 'We had an old bookcase,' she wrote in *Writers' Directory* in 1947 'carved from black oak and decorated with figures of Adam and Eve and bunches of apples, and herein I discovered Lord Beaconsfield's gorgeous Jewish romance *Alroy*, and Thomas Moore's Oriental poem *Lalla Rookh*. The glowing Eastern landscapes and brilliant figures charmed me, I am sure, because they were so different from the squalid, dull streets in which I walked every day.'

Her copy of *Lalla Rookh* was an elaborately bound Victorian edition with illustrations drawn by Tenniel and engraved by the prolific Dalziel brothers. Many of the engravings have been coloured by a childish hand (presumably Stella's). *Lalla Rookh* is a fair example of Romantic Western Orientalism, with a prose narrative connecting four tales in verse, a sort of Arabian Nights in miniature. The verse, if not very distinguished, is fluid and graceful, like nearly all Moore's work, and it is easy to see why it once had a tremendous vogue. A young girl would have found it eminently readable – especially with generous rations of Tenniel to help her along – though its themes of passionate love and violent death might not have been deemed suitable for her in a more rigidly controlled household. Dickens as a boy found a similar refuge in the Arabian Nights, which Peter Ackroyd describes as 'arguably the most important of all literary influences' upon him.

It was Stella's first brush with the Romantic, an intimation of the boundless nature of the imagination, a thrilling sense of the vastness and otherness of the world beyond her own. This sense was to inform and provide the theme of much of Stella's best poetry, and remained with her to the end. One of the quotations on the title page of her penultimate novel, *The Yellow Houses*, is from Paracelsus: 'Resolute imagination is the beginning of all magical operations.' Her last (and unpublished) novel *An Alpha* concludes with a journey to a strange Oriental city in the desert.

Alroy, by the nineteenth-century statesman Disraeli, who became Lord Beaconsfield, was another highly coloured Oriental tale, about a Jewish prince. It is full of magic and passion and ends with the hero's beheading. Stella was enough of a Gibbons to enjoy its exotic melodrama.

She also acquired from this bookcase a lifelong taste for the popular late Victorian works of Rhoda Broughton, Miss Braddon, Mrs Hungerford, Ouida and other female novelists of their generation. The writer Elizabeth Jenkins found her collection of their works 'enviable'. Stella often reread them, and would occasionally search the shelves of the London Library for further examples of their output. Ouida (whose real name was Louise Ramé, changed by her to the more romantic de la Ramée – the *nom de plume* being her own childish version of Louise) was a particular favourite and later inspired her fantasy novel *Ticky* (1943).

She described the effect of these books on her in her semi-autobiographical novel *My American* (1939): 'They were sturdy

OUT OF THE WOODSHED

late Victorian editions that wore well enough to shame the card-board backs of to-day; and their thick paper, good type, touch of gilding on the cover and charming end-papers thrown in out of sheer grace, made any reader sensitive to books feel that here was a friend; a good story well dressed.'

Another writer she discovered was the Alabama novelist Augusta J. Evans Wilson (1839–1909), author of *St Elmo* with, as she wrote in Chapter 4 of *My American*, 'its wicked Southern hero and Edna its lovely, learned heroine and the rich house bowered in Magnolia flowers'. Augusta Wilson seems to have exercised a peculiar fascination for Stella throughout her life. Two late articles of hers in *Punch* poke gentle fun at this author's lush, passionate fiction. It was perhaps from her that Stella first experienced the subtle pleasure derived from wallowing in over-ripe prose while at the same time laughing at it. There is love as well as mockery in the starred purple passages of *Cold Comfort Farm*. Wilson was the author of *Macaria, or Altars of Sacrifice*, which appears among the books in Flora's bedroom at Cold Comfort Farm. *Macaria, or Altars of Sacrifice* is such a typically Victorian title that I had always imagined it to be an invention until I found a battered copy of it among Stella's books. 'She liked Victorian novels,' Stella says of Flora Poste. 'They were the only kind of novel you could read while eating an apple.'

These writers have been largely forgotten. Rhoda Broughton and Mrs Hungerford are now little more than names, while Miss Braddon is remembered, if at all, for the melodramatic stage version of her novel *Lady Audley's Secret*. The name of Ouida is sometimes unfairly coupled with that of Marie Corelli, a vastly inferior writer; though it is surprising to find that, at the beginning of her career, Ouida was thought to be another *nom de plume* of Mary Ann Evans, better known as George Eliot. But these women were all esteemed and successful in their day. Moreover, they represented a tradition of serious, professional women writers who supported not only themselves but sometimes large families and feckless husbands by their labours. This was an inspiration to Stella, who was nothing if not a professional writer.

She also enjoyed, as she admitted in an interview with Libby Purves in 1981, 'a great deal of rubbish'. She read *The Girl's Friend*, 'a paper for kitchen maids', and penny novelettes called

Angel Novels which she found in the attic of her maternal grand-father's house. It was her father, however, who introduced her to the works of Rider Haggard, one of her first major literary passions.

As well as enjoying the fantasies of others, she was also creating her own. In her attic room she constructed an Egyptian temple out of cardboard which she populated with cut-out figures. There were times, she told me, when her waking thoughts were entirely dominated by this temple and its imaginary inhabitants. The first story she wrote, at the age of nine, was entitled 'Rida, a Tale of the Temple'. 'I wrote them [her stories] on sheets of wrapping paper stolen from my father's surgery,' she told the *Hornsea Journal* in 1975. 'There was a dispensary, for in those days doctors usually had their prescriptions made up on the premises.' She told Libby Purves that 'Rida' 'was very romantic and rather sad'.

Stella attributes her story-telling abilities mainly to her mother's side of the family, but Grandfather Gibbons also must have possessed the gift in a different way. In an article in *St Martin's Review* in April 1941 Stella recalled:

> When we were children, and he an old man, he used often to tell us about his adventures in the Africa of the 'eighties. One favourite story was of how he used to lie awake at night in his hut near the bridge [over the Orange River], the only white man among the African labourers, and hear, far off across the veldt in the silence of the night, the Zulu *impis* (regiments) on the march. They marched, he said, to a chant, and this was how it went –
> Ah-ahahahahah-*ah!*
> and on the final *ah!* the whole *impi* paused and stamped on the hard earth, bringing down the handles of their *assegais* (broad-bladed spears) on the ground as they did so. My brothers and I never used to tire of this story, and introduced the Zulu chant into our games, based on our beloved Rider Haggard stories.

Until I came across this vignette I had often wondered why, with the possible exception of *Lawrence of Arabia*, Stella's favourite film, during the time I knew her best, was *Zulu*. She saw it many times and often talked of it, particularly that moment towards the end when the Zulu *impis* salute the defenders of Rorke's Drift as fellow warriors by chanting and stamping from the brow of the hill. It was almost a visual re-enactment of her grandfather's tale.

Up to the age of thirteen Stella was educated at home by governesses. In *Enbury Heath* she wrote: 'They had a habit of departing in a hurry at the end of about four months, either in tears and very insulted about something and glad to be going, or else in tears and darkly hinting at an undying devotion to somebody and begging to be allowed to stay.'

The governesses were employed not simply so that Telford could pursue them when they were not educating his children, but because he positively did not want his offspring to be given any kind of religious instruction. This would have been almost inevitable had they been sent to a school. He was, Stella wrote in *St Martin's Review* in April 1957, 'an atheist: not the head-shaking and doubtful kind, well-tempered by agnosticism, but an active rebel against God in Whom he did not believe'.

Writing on her religious development in the third person, she continued:

> [Stella's] mother taught the child to say her prayers (Our Father, followed by a long list of relations and friends whom God was asked to bless); the mother's reason, she told the child, for doing so was based on fear of God: she was afraid to disbelieve in Him. The other grown-up members of [Stella's] family were equally confused in their religious life: it may be said without strong injustice that they, with the exception of one aunt [Louise?], paid lip-service to religion without any attempt to live it or believe it.
>
> In this dismal pagan atmosphere, where all the adults were unhappy and some of them violent, [Stella] grew into childhood, perfectly content with the picture that she made of the world all about her; and one evening, when she was aged about eight and standing at the window of her attic bedroom looking at the broad black chimneys of a factory outlined against the yellow light of sunset, she experienced a sudden, strong wish to be good. The feeling touched her: then it went away: and she did nothing about it, and she did not feel it again, unless the intense shame which she suffered the first time that she told 'a deliberate lie' was another form of the same impulse.

When [Stella], who is a woman strongly susceptible to what Keats called 'the principle of beauty in all things', was about eleven years old, she fell in love with someone, and took to attending the nearest church where this person was a singer and swinger of thuribles, in order to look at them. Saint X's was one of the churches built in London before the First World War under the influence of the Anglo-Catholic Movement, and it was very High indeed: [Stella] soon learned to say that 'at Saint X's we believe in everything except Transubstantiation and the infallibility of the Pope', but during the two years or so which she faithfully 'attended' and fasted and sang and genuflected there, she cannot recall having one genuine religious feeling, although she had plenty of feelings of other kinds.

It was somehow symptomatic of the topsy-turvy nature of Stella's early life that adolescent rebellion should take the form of going to church. The young man's name was Eric Ryder and the church was St Martin's, Gospel Oak, an eccentric Neo-Gothic structure designed by Edward Buckton Lamb. Ryder was the first of three men with whom Stella fell deeply in love.

Then, when Stella was thirteen, her father 'on a whim', as she called it, decided to change her mode of education. This whim was connected with the attempted suicide at the house in Malden Crescent of one of the unfortunate governesses. Apart from the alteration of names, the description of this event in *Enbury Heath* was, Stella told me, accurate in every particular, even to the book she was reading at the time.

Miss Vereker tried to kill herself one quiet sunny afternoon because Dr Garden had become bored by their intrigue.

He was out on his rounds, the little boys [Gerald and Lewis] had gone for a walk on the Heath with their mother, and Sophia [Stella], who was at this time thirteen years old, was sitting on the landing which led up to the attics, reading Thomas Moore's *Lalla Rookh*. Miss Vereker crept sobbing out of her bedroom and down to the dispensary, where she took enough veronal, she hoped, to kill herself.

Sophia, who had observed the sobbing and creeping with much disgust from her perch on the stairs, found her an hour

later on the sitting room floor, unconscious. It was Sophia who
fetched the cook and the parlourmaid and suggested that they
should carry Miss Vereker upstairs to her bedroom.

Sophia and the two servants knew exactly what had happened
and none of them felt sorry for Miss Vereker. The servants
thought that my lady had been asking for trouble and had got
it, and Sophia thought that Miss Vereker, of whom she had
been rather fond at first, was a silly tiresome nuisance and that
it would be rather a good thing if she died. But she never forgot
the picture that the two servants made, slowly climbing the stairs
with the big, unconscious girl swinging between them.

'Miss Vereker' did not die, but there were no more governesses
and Stella was sent to school for the first time in her life. The
establishment chosen was the nearest available and happened to
be a very good one – the North London Collegiate School, then
situated in the Camden Road, and so within walking distance of
Malden Crescent. Telford also sent his younger son, Lewis, to the
junior school there.

It was 1915, the second year of the First World War. The
conflict does not seem to have had a great effect on Stella, partly
because none of her close relatives was actively involved, partly
no doubt because she was too much preoccupied with domestic
conflict to worry about battles abroad. Only one anecdote directly
connected with the war survives. In an interview published in the
Independent Magazine on 26 August 1985 she told the writer Jill
Neville: 'During the First World War my father had us evacuated
to get us away from largely imagined Zeppelin raids. There was
quite a large library in that house and I read a book by Balzac,
Cousine Bette. It was full of bad people. I was so shocked that
people could behave like that that I had to go out and sit in a
cornfield and think about it.' Understandably, Jill Neville was
surprised: but what about the goings on at home, she asked?
'That was noisy but it was not exactly evil,' Stella replied. If it
was evil, it was the evil to which she was accustomed and not the
cold-hearted malignancy of Balzac's characters.

The North London Collegiate School is, as Stella remarked in
an article in 1938, 'one of the most interesting girls' schools in

England', and also one of the oldest. It was founded in 1850 by Frances Mary Buss, a great pioneering educationalist and the first headmistress in England. Far from being unsusceptible to cupid's darts – as the rhyme went – she seems to have been a passionate, motherly soul who nevertheless insisted on and obtained very high academic standards from her charges. When Stella went there the headmistress was Dr Sophie Bryant, Miss Buss's immediate successor. Sophie Bryant was the first woman Doctor of Science in Britain, the author of some ten books and a contributor of articles to the philosophical journal *Mind*, as well as being an ardent suffragist and campaigner for Irish Home Rule. Under this admirable woman academic standards were raised even higher than they had been under Miss Buss, but life could be difficult for those whose gifts were not of a strictly intellectual kind.

'At our school,' Stella wrote in an article for *Punch* in January 1957, 'you were expected to be a scholastic success or a missionary, and if you did not do that no-one on the staff cared what you became or how brilliantly you did it.' In *Enbury Heath* she referred to it as 'a cheap but excellent day school where she was extremely miserable, because a spoilt, arrogant, lazy and precocious child naturally cannot be popular with, or even accepted by, ordinary and properly brought up little girls'.

This is perhaps an exaggeration – Stella had a habit of being too harsh on herself – but certainly she found it difficult to adjust, her education hitherto having been haphazard and undisciplined. (She herself said that she had not so much been badly brought up as not brought up at all.) All at once she was confronted, for the first time in her life, with a highly regulated society. The Rules were a feature of the North London Collegiate, a relic of the Buss era. In an article called 'A School Moves House', published in *Good Housekeeping* in February 1938, Stella wrote that 'there were so many that the high-spirited, the dreamer and the wilful rather easily broke them. . . . If you broke a rule you signed in the Appearing Book . . . and when you had ten signatures, you had an imposition to do. This usually consisted of ten lines of poetry to learn. When you had a good memory – or perhaps even liked the poetry – you were given twenty lines to learn, as the present writer has good reason to remember.'

In 1933 she was interviewed for the school magazine, 'the first in a series of interviews with distinguished Old North Londoners'. She told the interviewers: 'There used to be signatures for talking on the stairs. . . . I was always rather a talkative person. . . . We weren't allowed to speak while we were waiting for a mistress – but of course we did!' In another interview she recalled how she would write stories for her fellow pupils, and how they would queue up to get the next instalment. They were mostly school stories and the heroine was generally a girl called Paddy, a nickname she gave to herself (in honour perhaps of her Irish Gibbons ancestry) and which later became an embarrassment to her. But the popularity which her story-telling abilities generated was tempered by her quick and sarcastic tongue, which came to be feared by those less intellectually nimble.

The poet Stevie Smith was an exact contemporary, who came to the London Collegiate in 1917. Stella did not know Stevie well. To Stella she seemed an aloof person, cleverer than most, with her own very intimate circle of friends which included her academically brilliant sister Molly. She remembered her dark eyes and the fact that, unlike her, she did Latin. Recalling her to me in later life, Stella seemed to feel that Stevie Smith had always looked down on her, and she remembered a slightly patronising review by Stevie of one of her novels. Though not prone to the vice of envy, Stella did admit to a twinge of it when Stevie won the Queen's Gold Medal for poetry. 'I suppose I shouldn't feel too bad,' she said to me once. 'I mean, she did write one or two really memorable poems. And, after all, on the whole I've had a much happier life than hers, so I shouldn't complain.'

Stevie Smith's attitude to the North London Collegiate was remarkably similar to Stella's. She found its endless rules oppress-ive and later wrote that her aloofness was a kind of defence against the intrusiveness of petty regulations – though, when Dr Bryant was succeeded as headmistress in 1918 by Miss Drummond, the regime became a little more relaxed. Stevie also found the school's exclusive preoccupation with academic excellence irksome. Like Stella she was able to pass muster in subjects of which she knew little by means of her gifts of expression, mathematics in consequence being the only stumbling block.

Though she never became a prefect, or even a monitor, Stella made two good friends, Stella Crow and Brenda Bennett, and took part in certain school activities. The school magazine, rather a desiccated item at that time, contains no record of her engaging in any sport – she hated organised games – but she became Vice President of the Senior Dramatic Club and featured strongly in the records of the Debating Society.

On 25 February 1920 she was reported as reading a paper on 'The Influence of Environment', evidence that this interest, which was to preoccupy her throughout her life, had taken root early. The paper apparently emphasised 'the fact that present inherited tendencies were due to past environment and that future heredity would be modified by present environment'. For a Gibbons the subject would have more than academic interest. At the end of the meeting 'Stella Gibbons proposed that more members should be forced to come to debates'. In March reward for her keenness came when she was made Hon. Secretary, and from that time she recorded the debates in a terse and often highly censorious style.

It is curious to find her so enthusiastic about debates, as she had a hatred in later life of arguments of any kind. Perhaps the formal environment of a debating club gave arguments an objectivity and decorum that she longed for at home – and the society certainly catered to her profound interest in ideas, particularly metaphysical and aesthetic ones.

Though not a particularly keen Old North Londoner, Stella maintained a certain tentative connection with the school. For a number of years in the sixties and seventies she rented a house called The Bryn, near Trevone in Cornwall, which belonged to Miss Drummond, the headmistress who had succeeded Dr Bryant, and Miss Odell, a fellow teacher. I stayed with Stella at The Bryn several times, and the names of Miss Drummond and Miss Odell belong to the mythology of my childhood. Stella made them the subject of a number of irreverent stories and verses with which she regaled her guests.

Her January 1957 article in *Punch* 'Oh, What's She Doing These Days?' is a mocking but affectionate study of the *North London Collegiate's Old Girls' Bulletin*, and the curiously terse and ambiguous prose which is still the rule in such publications:

Why should I like to read that Marjorie Allbutt (1917–1919)

will become a grand- mother for the fourth time this September.
Congratulations Marjorie!

The Marjorie I remember had a long brown plait tied at the
end with a stiff black ribbon and no grandchildren, and when
I used to see her every day she did but add one more faintly
distasteful drop to the generally tepid brew of the term. Why
do I get a small but definite kick out of imagining Celia Roberts
(1913–1918) *still living in Andover with her mother?* I don't
want to visit her; I should be dismayed indeed if she visited me:
nothing could be farther from my intention than writing to her
or her mother; I simply enjoy the small, neat picture that she
makes, moving around within the frame in her navy serge gym
tunic and white blouse. Perhaps I like the tableau because she
can't get out of it and make herself a nuisance.

She never herself contributed one of these vignettes to the *Bulletin*,
because she felt, wrongly perhaps, that it would not approve of her
peculiar success. In the same article she wrote:

Only one of us, a big fat laughing girl some years older
than me, became a comedienne; she was broadly, inescapably,
slapstickishly *funny* in a way that not even Miss Evans, the
sarcastic one, could have dismissed with her slight smile as
'very amusing', and she also made a great deal of broad and
inescapable money for herself.

The Bulletin always spoke of her with a note of slightly weary
reserve. 'Phyllis Court (1909–1914) *is appearing in another new*
musical comedy at His Majesty's Theatre. This is the third
leading part Phyllis has taken in a London musical play.'

(Couldn't keep off it, you see. Very regrettable. If it had been
Shakespeare now . . . that would have been quite different.)

If Stella never contributed to the *Bulletin*, neither did Stevie
Smith. What a bitter-sweet experience it would have been for
Stella to read: 'Florence Margaret Smith (1917–1919) *still lives*
with her aunt in Palmer's Green and has published a volume of
verse, "Not Waving but Drowning".'

During this period other members of the Gibbons family were

also in difficulties. In March 1920 Stella's uncle, Arthur Gibbons, together with a certain Sir Arthur Carlton, decided to mount a stage version of *Tarzan of the Apes*. Human actors played the apes, but other animal roles were taken by actual beasts of the jungle. Complete with its menagerie, the show was to begin with a two-week run at Brixton in South London, then tour, then come into the West End. The part of Tarzan was played by Ronald Adair and that of Jane by Ivy Carlton (Sir Arthur's daughter), who was to become Arthur Gibbons's third wife.

The tour was beset by trouble from the beginning: strikes, transport problems and a drunken elephant trainer. An actor in the original production, Roland Hope (known affectionately as 'the dice-player's motto'), recalled years later to Stella's sister-in-law that the elephant trainer would go on pub crawls with his elephant after the show. When his trainer became incapable, the elephant would loyally stand over him until he was able to get up off the ground and make his way home.

The play foundered in December 1920 before it ever reached the West End. It was a commercial disaster, and whenever reference was made to it in Arthur's presence thereafter he would murmur: 'The elephant alone cost six hundred.'

It was typical of Arthur Gibbons that he should decide that the reason for the tour's failure was that it had been mocked in a revue sketch called 'Warzan and his Apes', which had featured in a variety bill at the Victoria Palace Theatre in London. He sued the author, Dick Mortimer, and the resulting trial before Mr Justice Avory was a comic fiasco reminiscent of one of Beachcomber's fantasies. Lawton, Mortimer's counsel, was determined to turn the whole thing into a joke, and was abetted by the judge. When Arthur's counsel asked the actor who played the she-ape whether he had read the original story, Lawton interposed, 'How could he read the manuscript if he is an ape?' There was much laughter in court, and, not surprisingly, Arthur Gibbons lost – chiefly because Mortimer's sketch had been playing the halls already for about six years. It sometimes pays to have a sense of humour.

But Arthur was not always so unsuccessful. From 1924 until the early thirties he ran the Royalty Theatre, and made a good deal of money out of a once famous play by H. F. Maltby called *The Rotters*. He promoted and built the Duchess Theatre, but later lost all his money by gambling on the Stock Exchange. In 1935 the actor David Forbes Russell, visiting Gibbons as he lay dying, found a large, important-looking stranger sitting by the death-bed. Gibbons performed the introductions: 'David, the Bum! The Bum, David!' It was the bailiff.

Stella's opinion of her Uncle Arthur was low, but he must have had a certain style.

CHAPTER 2

'All the solitary things'

In September 1921 Stella embarked on a two-year Diploma in Journalism at London University. The course had been established in 1919 for the benefit of men returning from the First World War, but many women enrolled too, among them (in Stella's time) Christina Hole and Elizabeth Bowen, and later Leila Berg and Penelope Mortimer. There were lectures and examinations in English literature, economics, history, political science, natural sciences and modern languages. The acquisition of skills in typewriting and shorthand was encouraged, but had to be learned outside the university. In its early years the course was far from satisfactory and the National Union of Journalists protested that they had not been represented on the committee which set it up. But in 1922 Valentine Knapp, a distinguished working journalist, became chairman of the Journalism Committee at London University, and under his influence the course became more practical in its approach.

For Stella, the diploma was a necessity. There was little money to spare in the Gibbons household: much of it was drunk away or otherwise wasted. Stella knew she would have to earn her living soon, and that the only way she could conceive of doing so was by her pen. She had consulted her headmistress, Miss Drummond, who had not only recommended the course but also used her influence to secure her pupil a place on it. The end result, as Stella always stressed, was a diploma, not a degree: she was very conscious of having had a rather incomplete education.

For all that, University College offered her more joy and liberation than she had hitherto known in her life. When Stella met her old English teacher from the North London Collegiate by chance on the Underground, she told her that she was 'having a whale of a time'. The teacher smiled sadly and observed that that was not what one went to college for.

Her chief friend at this time was Ida Graves. I had heard her mention Stella in an interview on *Woman's Hour* in 1996. Letters sent to Ida via the BBC failed to reach her. Then, while going through what remained of Stella's correspondence, I came across an envelope with a single initial 'W' scrawled on it. It contained a death certificate and a letter from Ida dated 30 May 1977. From the information in this letter I eventually managed to contact Ida. The death certificate was that of a man called Walter Beck, a crucial figure in Stella's life.

Ida Graves was born in March 1902 and was, like Stella, a doctor's daughter. She too became a writer and in 1929, the year before the publication of Stella's first poetry collection, *The Mountain Beast*, the Hogarth Press had brought out Ida's first volume of verse. When I met Ida in 1997 Oxford University Press had only three years previously published a new collection of her verse, and she was still – at the age of ninety-five – producing work of distinctive quality and great technical verve. Though she was bedridden Ida's mental faculties were undimmed, and her capacity for conversation would have done credit to someone half her age. Only the previous year she had married again, to a jazz musician twenty-five years her junior. Her memories of Stella, whom she knew by her old school nickname of Paddy, were vivid but tinged with regret.

She was not doing the same journalism course as Stella, but attending the same lectures and tutorials on English literature, at which they sat next to each other. Ida in particular had many admirers who were, in the manner of the time, forever proposing marriage. Stella and she would mock the suitors' earnestness together.

In many ways their temperaments were different. Stella's wit was sharper and she had a dark, brooding side, the product of Gibbons genes and a Gibbons childhood. Ida was wilder and more bohemian, with an obvious zest for life which made her immensely attractive to men. Both, however, had a love of literature as well as a pronounced talent for it. Both were revelling in a new-found freedom.

'We would take any old bus from any old starting point,' Ida recalled, 'each taking sandwiches, and when the bus got to the end of its route we would get out and go for a walk in the country. We would start to go for a walk, but we would be so enthused and so hilarious, that we would have to stop and sit in a hedge, and chat and talk nonsense. Many of the jokes we shared – I don't know whether they started with me or her – found their way into *Cold Comfort Farm*.'

For example, Flora Poste's description of her schooldays and her attitude to games in the first chapter derives, according to Ida, from her. This seems probable, as Flora's education – 'expensive, athletic and prolonged' – bears no similarity to Stella's, which had been urban and academically intense.

They took pleasure in the lusher passages of popular romantic novels of the day. Stella decided that particularly fine examples should be marked in some way, perhaps by a star. This idea, in a more developed form, found its way into *Cold Comfort Farm*. Ida remembers that she and Stella amused themselves with impromptu parodies of contemporary writers, particularly poets: 'I was pretty good,' said Ida, 'but Stella was marvellous. We'd just pick a subject at random as we went along and do it in the style of de la Mare, or Housman, or whoever.'

Stella's own description of these walks in *Enbury Heath* has a different emphasis and marks the contrast in their characters:

> She liked best of all to blunder about London or to go for a whole Sunday into the country by herself or roaming along a hillside. She did not think about anything; she wandered along, falling over things and scratching her legs on brambles, vaguely looking forward to the sandwiches she carried in a little old square camera case made of leather, and chewing a piece of grass. If she was accompanied by a friend, she usually took a talkative one, to whom she could politely say 'Yes,' 'Indeed,' 'I should think not,' 'Oh,' and 'Did he, how odd,' without hearing more than three twelfths of what was being related. All the friends said she was so sympathetic, and Sophia would grin and feel a little ashamed.

Ida was nothing if not talkative.

Stella took Ida home and introduced her to her mother. Ida recalled the dark house in Malden Crescent and Maudie: 'Slim and rather badly treated. . . . she was very browbeaten. I liked her mother, and she liked me.' She did not remember meeting Telford, though she had a distinct recollection of the pall of fear which he cast over the household in general and Stella in particular.

Ida told me that her walks with Stella were riotous and full of jokes, but that 'Stella was quite different with other people – quite silent and boring, not funny at all . . . There was a side to her which was like Flora: very prim, orderly and well behaved. We made a joke of it. I used to say: "Oh, Paddy, if I get a wet sneeze and need a handkerchief, I never have one, but you always do!" I was more spontaneous.' She said she had once introduced a male cousin of hers to Stella, recommending her to him as most amusing and extremely good company. The cousin had taken Stella out to dinner and been disappointed, complaining that she was dull and taciturn.

I think the truth may have been that Stella was not so much dull as intimidating. Though not a feminist she detested condescension in men, and was unprepared to pander to their vanity with bright, inconsequential chatter. Like Flora she preferred to 'dine quietly with intelligent men . . . because then she could show-off a lot and talk about herself'. She told me once that she was at a dance with a young man in the twenties, and she had been talking away, 'perhaps rather brilliantly, I suppose, and this man just looked at me and said: "Miss Gibbons, promise me you'll never try to think." I'm afraid I laughed in his face.' It was an anecdote she worked into her 1949 novel *The Matchmaker*.

Ida introduced Stella to her circle of friends, among whom was Jean Gawthorne, whose sister Enid married Stella's brother Lewis in 1935. Other friends of Ida's were to have an influence on Stella's life in a different way.

In an interview for the *North London Collegiate Magazine* Stella says that her first literary work to be published was in the *University College Magazine*. The December 1921 issue contains a parody of 'the latest School of Decoratively-Melancholy Intro-spectives' entitled 'The Marshes of My Soul':

> Brackish . . . brackish,
> The Pools of weariness, flung in a glimmering chain
> Reach the horizon.
> And my thoughts, like purple parrots

Brood
In the sick light, trees
Blowing above those shallow pools
In whorls and whorls
Noiselessly
Printing a monotonous pattern upon the heavy air
Like watery curves upon the silken robe of a dying mandarin. . . .

It is fairly crude undergraduate stuff, though it does show her ability, later developed in *Cold Comfort Farm*, to flavour parody with a hint of genuine poetry. The last line, with its deliberate rhythmical bumpiness, would not look out of place in an early poem by Edith Sitwell – say one of the more loquacious stanzas of 'The Sleeping Beauty'. As a parody, it is a rather generalised attack on modernism and *vers libre*, which was just beginning to become fashionable.

But it does show that Stella had identified her enemy early. Her own poetry, though often profound, was never wilfully impenetrable and always well crafted. She distrusted *vers libre*, as some painters distrust abstract art because it looks undisciplined and too easy to achieve. She opposed not modernism itself – her favourite poet among her contemporaries was W. H. Auden – but its self-indulgent excesses. She did not care for pens that dwelt on guilt and misery unless they had to.

Another poem, 'Gypsy People', from March 1922 is more successful. It too is a parody, but of a more specific kind, guying the pseudo-rusticity of Georgian verse. With its fantasy of Mars and Venus as itinerant tinkers it is tempting to take it as a genuine attempt at pastoral neo-classicism, until some deliberate absurdity ('the great Olympian saucepans') makes us realise that the author is mocking. Later Stella was to be taken up by J. C. Squire, the standard-bearer of the Georgian movement.

A prose piece by her in the same issue of the College magazine, entitled 'The Doer, A Story in the Russian Manner', is interesting chiefly for its adumbration of themes and styles which were to find their ripe expression in *Cold Comfort Farm*. It begins:

The boughs of the almond tree, averted from the wind, trembled
with exquisite perversity. Hill thought they were like a frightened

virgin, but Stamer realised that they, like everything else, were meaningless. Leila looked at them and narrowed her eyelids. She was, as usual, quite inscrutable.

These people were sitting in a room looking out into an untidy garden, where the tall feathery grass waved round the thistles, just touching them or avoiding them. Gray was there too, talking about Psycho-Analysis. Not that he thought Psycho-Analysis mattered. Nothing mattered, except perhaps perception. . . .

Later in the story a matter-of-fact chicken farmer, Jones (the 'doer' of the title), comes to bear one of the characters away to live a less etiolated existence.

In this decidedly jejune tale some abiding preoccupations in Stella's work exist in embryo. There is the mockery of psycho-analysis and pretentious prose. In the setting up of Jones as the unromantic foil to the precious group of intellectuals described in the opening paragraph, the clash of two cultures, lies the germ not only of *Cold Comfort Farm* but of many of her other stories. We can even catch in Hill, for whom the trembling almond boughs 'were like a frightened virgin', a tiny glimpse of Mr Mybug, for whom every hill was a breast and every bud a phallus.

In August 1923 Stella completed her journalism course and obtained her diploma. Then, for the rest of the year, she was out of work. She explained her difficult situation at home to Valentine Knapp, chairman of the university Journalism Committee, through whose good offices in 1924 she secured a job with the British United Press, a news service similar to Reuter's. It was routine work for the most part, but it taught her to write concisely and it paid her £3 a week.

The agency took in cables from all parts of the world which they received from other, larger agencies as they passed through London on their way to the United States. BUP bought the London and provincial rights to these cables, decoded them, rewrote them and sold them to London or provincial papers for a retaining fee or lineage rates.

Stella's job was to decode some of the simpler cables and put them into readable journalese. It was, she reflected later, a good training for writers, provided they were not aspiring to the highest slopes of Parnassus. She also wrote up the 'mailers'.

These were news stories which were sent by mail rather than by cable on flimsy sheets of paper. As they were often written by foreigners and intended for the American market, the language was distinctly odd: 'Boris Bennoskwyz, hundred-year-old pesen from quent Old world hill village of Pitesci in Moldavia tells startlingly of nacked dances in mountains. Paysants says Boris is returning to the old-world gods blaming for harvest. Men and young girls orgying together. . . .' This example, or parody of one, comes from *Enbury Heath*.

In some ways Stella was not an ideal employee: her shorthand was only eighty words per minute and her typing was not neat. She could be vague and dreamy, but her writing was bright and confident. She knew how to convey a meaning simply and directly. Occasionally, when the agency was short of copy, she would write a 500-word article about some aspect of London life, its social events or its fashionably dressed women. Though not a particularly vain woman – and having no great illusions about her appearance – she remained throughout her life deeply interested in clothes.

This was the beginning of a truly independent existence, though, out of loyalty to her mother, she was still living at home. During the slack periods at BUP she was able to write her own fictional stories and, above all, poetry; and, for the first time in her life, she was able to take a holiday on her own. In the first year of her employment she went to Boulogne, and in 1925 to Switzerland. She told her daughter Laura that she would take long walks into the mountains, alone apart from a guide who could not speak English. Here, in a very particular way, she was able to experience what she called 'all the solitary things' for which she had such a passion. Her feelings for Swiss Alpine scenery are expressed in 'The Legend of the Mountain Beast', the title poem of her first collection of verse. Another poem, 'The Fabled Ones', which is subscribed 'Zinal 1925', is one of only two poems in the collection to be dated or located. Zinal is remote, nestling among some of the highest peaks in the Swiss Alps.

Her passion for 'the solitary things' may also account for Stella's very particular gift for drawing credible and sympathetic male characters in her novels. The love of solitude for its own sake is more common among men than women, and she understood the male hatred of interference, however helpful, in any solitary activity. Moreover, Stella was less disposed to share confidences than most women and liked to resolve problems by herself. Of the close and lifelong friendships that she made, several were with men.

In 1922 Stella's friend Ida was pursuing a different course, in which poetry played a significant role. One of her teachers at London University was A. L. Rowse, who was to become an eminent Shakespearean scholar. With the insouciance and naiveté of youth she had sent him a poem of hers instead of the essay he had requested. Rowse, who had poetic aspirations himself, was perhaps understandably annoyed and, at a seminar, berated Ida savagely in front of her fellow students. This excited their sympathy, for Rowse, who was in fact a year younger than Ida, was not a popular figure. Everyone gathered round her to commiserate when the seminar was over, and one of the students, a Jewish girl, invited Ida to a party that weekend at Angmering below the Sussex Downs. Ida arrived wearing shorts, daring for 1922, and attracted the attention of a young Jewish accountant named Herbert Marks. Within the year they were married. It was, she said, her way of escaping from a difficult home life: Ida was estranged from her mother, and had been billeted on an unsympathetic aunt.

Herbert Marks was well off and worked for a firm of accountants who managed the financial affairs of the United Jewish Synagogue throughout Europe. He was a brilliant linguist with a distinguished war record, but he had, according to Ida, a 'lugubrious nature' and 'sex with him was abominable'. Nevertheless they set up home in Golders Green and had two children in quick succession.

Marks was passionate about the arts in a rather earnest way, and was very anxious to mingle with creative people. His house became a meeting place for the young avant-garde, and Stella went there too. In her 1981 interview she told Libby Purves: 'I got in with a rather intellectual set, very trendy – though the word hadn't been invented in those days – in Golders Green. The men used occasionally to try to kiss me and also to talk to me about sex, like Mr Mybug does. . . . Lawrence was just beginning to be a cult with these people.' Mr Mybug of *Cold Comfort Farm* was an amalgam of these tiresome men, but if there can be said to be a model-in-chief for Mybug it was, as Stella later acknowledged, Herbert Marks. Ida willingly confirmed this. Like Mybug, Marks was Jewish, with 'fuzzled hair' (as Stella wrote in *Conference at Cold Comfort Farm*) and preoccupied with sex. Despite, or perhaps because of, his alleged sexual inadequacy, he began to look outside his marriage for gratification. As Ida remarked to me, it is a familiar pattern: Don Juanism and an obsession with sex are often a sign of failings in that department. D. H. Lawrence himself was a notable example.

There was a smattering of genuine talent among this *galère* of Lawrentian poseurs. One of the artists who had attracted the attention of Herbert Marks was the handsome and talented sculptor Eric Schilsky, with whom Ida fell passionately in love and he with her. He also became a lifelong friend of Stella's, though they were never romantically involved.

These new acquaintances fitted in well with the world of Stella's other great friend at this time, Ina Dornan, who had known her since they had played together on Hampstead Heath as children. She was in many ways curiously like Ida, vital and lively with artistic leanings and, though not conventionally beautiful, immensely attractive to men. She was the model for Mrs Smiling in *Cold Comfort Farm* and Celia in *Enbury Heath*, both affectionate and romanticised portraits. Like Mrs Smiling, Ina attracted numerous male admirers, often oddly named: the Bikki and Swooth of *Cold Comfort Farm* were, in fact, Buddy and Swerth in real life. She had a peculiar fascination for American writers: Paul Engle, author of *American Song*, a once highly acclaimed volume of poetry, was a lover; as was Leonard Ehrlich, author of *God's Angry Man*, a title which sounds a generation ahead of its time. Ina's relationships with these men were often simultaneous and invariably confused. An extract from Stella's sister-in-law Renée's diary for 1933 gives some idea of the amorous ferment in which she existed.

Mr Ehrlich who has come over from America . . . is Ina's latest young man. When they went down for the day to Ina's cottage at Hockley he made violent love to her, but Stella says this is because it always rains at Hockley and there is nothing else to do. To complicate matters still further, Buddy is still in England wanting Ina to marry him, and the other night Allan opened the door to find Swerth outside, very pale and exclaiming hoarsely that he couldn't get in touch with Ina. He has been in Danzig for quite a long time and we all thought he had gone out of Ina's life. So what with Ina well away with Mr Ehrlich and Buddy and Swerth both in London we may look forward I think to a pleasant winter and plenty to do in the long evenings. Mr Ehrlich is in love with an American woman poet called Geneviève Taggart [actually Taggard] who pushed her first husband off a liner and has now married again. But marriage, says Mr Ehrlich, means nothing in Geneviève's life.

The Women's Press anthology *The World Split Open* includes some of Taggard's work. It states that she was a 'committed feminist' and that she 'died of hypertension'. On her alleged way with husbands it is silent.

It was at about this time – in 1924, to be precise – that Walter Beck came into Stella's life. One of the reasons, she told Libby Purves, that she found the Golders Green Mybugs so tiresome was that she had fallen in love with Beck and was in no mood for miscellaneous flirtations. Her nature was, as she told her daughter Laura, 'boringly faithful'.

Walter Beck, sometimes called Jim, was a year older than Stella and worked for his family's cosmetics firm, of which he later became director. A naturalised German, he lived with his mother and sister in a house in Redington Road, not far from Hampstead Heath. He was good-looking and rich, and he and Stella first met on the Heath. Beyond that, the facts available are scanty. Stella was engaged to Beck, and told her sister-in-law Renée that she committed herself sexually to the relationship and would go away with him to hotels at weekends. They would sign the register as a married couple under false names and she would have to put on a wedding ring, an act she found peculiarly humiliating. Because Stella was deeply in love she tried to pretend that she found it all daring and exciting, but such a light-hearted attitude was alien to her.

'She was transformed by love. . . . The armour of irony, common sense, and honour . . . was cast aside, and she wore instead nothing but love's blinding bandages over her eyes': the course of the affair can be tentatively traced through fiction in Stella's novel *Bassett* (1934) in which, as she openly acknowledged, three characters called Shelling are portraits of Beck, his sister and his mother. Walter also appears, slightly disguised, as Juan Morales, a rich, shallow, spoilt young Argentine (who also lives with his mother and sister), in *Enbury Heath*, but it is in the former novel that the Becks' peculiar milieu is most carefully observed:

> In England, people often look slightly ashamed if they have lashings of money. If they do not look ashamed, they must be cads. But the Shellings were not English – they were German, and they were glad they had lots of money, and did not at all mind being thought cads. Nor was Baines House [where they lived] one of those shabbily comfortable houses. It was centrally heated, speckless, furnished by Tottenham Court Road at its best, and run like a first-class hotel.

Mrs Beck had a well-corseted Edwardian figure and a tower of fine brown hair. Her attitude towards her children was one of exasperated indulgence, but there was something loveless about the atmosphere of their house. Ida Graves remembered one day on an impulse giving Mrs Beck a hug, at which she burst into tears because she was so unused to such spontaneous gestures of affection.

It might appear that Beck and Stella had nothing in common, but he was not uncultivated. He read widely and had a passion for 'music and silence', according to Stella. She used to go to concerts with him and his mother and there acquired a lifelong love for nineteenth-century German and Austrian Romantic composers, in particular Schumann, Schubert and Brahms.

Stella's understanding of her incompatibility with Walter Beck can be summarised in a snatch of dialogue from *Bassett*. 'George' is George Shelling, the Beck figure:

> 'I,' said George rather sadly, 'live by the intellect. . . . And what do *you* live by?' he asked her smiling.
> 'I don't know,' she replied after the usual little pause for right

reflection. 'I'm still trying to find out. I think – like Keats, you know – "I am certain of nothing but the holiness of the heart's affections."'

'Oh ... affections,' said George ... 'I change mine every week.'

The quotation from Keats's letter to Benjamin Bailey was a favourite of Stella's, and a fuller version of it quite accurately conveys the essence of her philosophy: 'I am certain of nothing but the holiness of the heart's affections and the truth of imagination – what the imagination seizes as beauty must be truth – whether it existed before or not.' George's response may well have summed up Beck's approach to life, at least in Stella's eyes.

For her birthday in 1926 Walter gave Stella a copy of *Later Poems* by W. B. Yeats. It is inscribed: 'To dear Paddy from Lord Jim' with the date. Under it he has written the quotation: 'Be not too wildly amorous of the far.'

By that year Stella's work and the development of her social, artistic and emotional life meant that she had less time to support her mother. Lewis was still at school and Gerald, Maude Gibbon's favourite child, was pursuing a theatrical career of sorts in various touring and repertory companies, aided and abetted by Uncle Arthur. Maudie must have felt increasingly isolated. Ida Graves told me:

I have telepathic moments. I had gone to the swimming baths in Kentish Town one day and was just undressing when I had a violent feeling that Stella's mother was wanting me. I could almost hear her saying: 'It's urgent. Ida! Ida!' It was so insistent that I got dressed and went to see her. She was very ill with the most appalling headache. She said, 'Yes, I was calling you.' Stella by this time was working for her news agency and so couldn't get away. I gave Stella's mother aspirin and cups of tea, and some food, but I had to go back to my two children, and in the evening she died.

The date was 31 May 1926 and the cause of death was cerebral thrombosis. Maudie Gibbons was forty-eight years old.

Stella always felt that she could have done more for her mother during her last years. In later life Stella went to great lengths to support and comfort her elderly women friends, partly, she told me, to expiate these feelings of guilt.

Ida went to Maudie's funeral. She told me: 'Eric [Schilsky] came with me, and d'you know, it was awful but I suppose it was funny in a way. All during the clergyman's recital of the funeral service, Stella's father kept saying: "Oh, she was a bitch! She never cooked properly! What I had to put up with!" And every time the clergyman started up again, so did Stella's father. He must have been drunk.'

Once her mother had died, Stella had no reason to remain in the gloomy Malden Crescent surgery. She moved out and found a room in Willow Road near the Heath. It is a curious fact that, despite her unhappy childhood, none of Stella's subsequent homes was more than a few miles away from the one in which she had been brought up.

After Maudie had gone Telford's manner changed. As Stella put it in *Enbury Heath*:

> Perhaps her death wounded his spirit in some secret place which had been untouched by his other women, or perhaps he felt that his youth had died with her. Whatever it was, he changed. Though he did not stop drinking, he became gentle and quiet, and when heart failure killed him one evening in three minutes, in the interval between seeing two patients, all his relatives and women felt that he had been cheated out of a last, and a genuine, repentance.

Stella felt differently. 'She decided that six months of pensive grief did not atone for more than twenty years of bullying and unfaithfulness and cruelty.'

'Telford died, exactly as described by Stella in her novel, on 15 October 1926. Gerald was away on tour and missed the funeral, but was summoned back to a meeting at the surgery with the uncles and aunts and the family solicitor. Apparently Telford had died intestate, so his estate – what little of it there was – would be divided equally between Stella, Lewis and Gerald. The solicitor had just explained the consequences of Telford's neglect when something happened which Stella described in *Enbury Heath*.

Francis [Lewis] had stood up. He was very white and shaking. He said in a loud, drawling melodramatic tone which only Sophia [Stella] knew was meant to be quietly impressive:

'Just a moment. I've got something rather interesting here.'

And he held out a small folded paper.

It was Telford's will which had been entrusted to Lewis by his father. Lewis had produced it at his eleventh hour for no other reason than that he shared the Gibbons appetite for drama and wanted to scandalise his uncles and aunts.

The will made Gerald the sole heir. After the debts had been paid off and the surgery and practice sold, this amounted to a little over £2000. What possessed Telford to make this will and entrust his worldly goods to the one person least likely to make good use of them can only be guessed at. Gerald – weak, vain, charming and feckless – squandered the money in less than a year. Lewis, whose ambition was to follow his father's profession and become a doctor, was forced to leave school early and take a job. Stella was to make a home for both of them and, from time to time, extricate them from debt.

Lewis's quixotic gesture in producing the will, far from irritating Stella, endeared him even more to her – he was always her favourite brother. Lacking Gerald's good looks and easy charm, he was forced to work harder. After some unhappy experiences in love, he married well and held down a steady job.

Gerald was to be a source of anxiety to Stella for the rest of his life. His portrayal as Harry in *Enbury Heath* is unmistakable, shockingly so. It is possible that, when Stella wrote the book in 1935, she was hoping that Gerald would read and learn from it. It was, after all, dedicated to him and Lewis. Probably Gerald never read the book; certainly he never learned from it. Stella's judgement on him was both compassionate and severe:

Harry [Gerald] seemed to have been affected least by their horrible home life; this was because his manner was gay and charming, and he seemed to have a happy temperament, but actually the years of fear and insecurity had wounded him more deeply than they had wounded his brother and sister. He was a gentler person, who lacked the fighting instinct of Sophia and Francis [Stella and Lewis]; and the angry sounds and terrifying

46

anticipation of blows and unknown horrors which haunted his childhood had given him a true soul-wound; a painful sense of inferiority hidden deep under his gay, easy manner.

He thirsted for gaiety, crowds, noise and admiration to lull his own sense of insecurity. The idea of responsibilities terrified him; he wanted to escape from them, and to forget the ugly noises, shames and endless fears of his childhood.

Stella, Gerald and Lewis went to live in the Vale of Health, a cluster of old houses lying below the highest point of Hampstead Heath, in a valley beside a pond. Its name, Stella wrote in *The Woods in Winter*, 'dates from the time of the Great Plague, when (presumably rich) people came up from London into the purer air of Hampstead to escape the pestilence'. She rented Vale Cottage from Ina Dornan's mother. It adjoined Mrs Dornan's own house, which was believed to have once been lived in by Leigh Hunt. The connection, however tenuous, with Keats was an added attraction, and Stella kept in her sitting room there a plaster copy of Keats's death mask. D. H. Lawrence had also lived in the Vale, but this was of less interest to Stella.

Vale Cottage was not an excessively romantic or picturesque building in itself. It was (and still is) small, stucco-fronted and clad at the side in brown weatherboarding. Though it may have dated from the time of Keats and Leigh Hunt, it had probably been occupied by a mere groom or gardener. But it was only a step away from the Heath, in charming, evocative surroundings, and Stella loved the place.

During the months ahead Stella found that most of the domestic duties, especially the cooking, fell to her. Nevertheless she was always impatient to leave work and be at the cottage. The task of making a home was one she found fulfilling. Though she could write poetry in idle moments at BUP and later the *Evening Standard*, she could not make cushion covers there or paint bathroom shelves.

She remembered the period at Vale Cottage as a very happy one to begin with, though it was not long before her brothers began to drink heavily, bring girls back and take Stella's domestic efforts for granted. This was in spite of the fact that Stella was the highest and steadiest earner of the three, and the greatest contributor to the household budget. Some of her resentment at their unthinking masculine attitudes – 'chaps must be catered for, chaps must have a good time and live their own lives' – is expressed in *Enbury Heath*.

There were parties at which Ina and Stella's more literary and artistic friends mingled with Gerald's theatrical cronies. The atmosphere was lively but penurious, except during the brief period when Gerald's inheritance was being squandered. Stella would have liked more peace, time for 'all the solitary things', but she indulged her brothers' taste for hectic gaiety because she felt that they deserved it after their hellish childhood. There was a streak of self-abasement in Stella's character which was often accompanied by a certain priggishness. She would sacrifice herself for others and then resent the fact that these unasked-for sacrifices were not always acknowledged or reciprocated. Despite being aware of this tendency (as she shows from her self-portrayal as Sophia in *Enbury Heath*), she never quite rid herself of it. The burden that she occasionally placed on herself and others as a result was, however, mitigated by an ever-present self-mockery.

Besides the more mundane tasks of cleaning and tidying up after her brothers, she also had to deal with occasional crises in Lewis's emotional life. Gerald's amours were too fleeting and casual (on his side) to cause much trouble to himself or Stella; but Lewis, who was nearer in temperament to his sister, fell in love less frequently and more deeply. It was left to Stella to extricate him from the complex web of financial and emotional difficulties which were their invariable consequence. This dependency continued until Lewis's marriage in 1935.

In 1934 Renée wrote in her diary what Stella had told her of Lewis: 'Apparently he lived for about a year on two pounds a week with a dreadful neurotic girl who used to hit him and make awful scenes. He loved her very much and had a horrid time and literally starved.'

In *Enbury Heath* Sophia visits the parents of one of her younger brother's girlfriends to sort out a difficulty that has arisen. The father is a fireman and the family live in quarters above the fire station. It is a vivid and bizarre description, and, as Stella later told Renée, an exact account of what had actually happened. Lewis had used the word 'bloody' in a letter to his girlfriend and her mother had read the offending word. Stella visited the fire station to heal the rift caused by this breach of lower middle-class propriety. After the long and agonising ritual of tea and small talk, the mother simply took up the letter and dropped it into the fire with the words: 'We'll say no more about it.' (But of course nothing *had* been said about it.) The gesture struck Stella as being both absurd and impressive.

The ménage at the cottage lasted for four years, often uneasily. Stella tried too hard to protect and manage her brothers, but they felt the need to make an even wilder break from their past. While Gerald was riding the luxury of his inheritance, enjoying his brief moment of gaiety, Lewis was anxious to ride with him. Though Lewis did leave for a while to live with the girl who hit him, he came back, and in 1930 when Stella took rooms in nearby Fitzjohn's Avenue, Lewis came to live with her again.

It was in 1930, too, that Stella first made an impact on the literary world with her collection of poetry *The Mountain Beast*, published by Longmans. It anthologised the work she had been writing since the early 1920s, much of which had already been published in periodicals such as the *New Adelphi*, the *Saturday Review*, *Queen*, *Country Life* and the *London Mercury*.

'When I was a girl of about thirteen I discovered other people's poetry,' Stella wrote in an article in *St Martin's Review* in December 1940. 'I say other people's because *I* had been writing poetry since I was eleven, and my own was the only poetry I was interested in. But my father loved Shelley's poetry [Shelley, like Telford, was a resolute atheist], and he had a thick volume of the *Poetical Works*, with an orange-coloured flyleaf, that he found me reading one day and gave to me.' In her adolescence poetry became a passion. Her earliest models were the Romantics, in particular Keats. She was, as she said, 'strongly susceptible to what Keats called "the principle of beauty in all things".' This passion for beauty in all its forms was a Gibbons trait, but to it she added a love of order and harmony which was reinforced by her experience of disorder and disharmony in her early life. The tension between passion and tranquillity, each expressed in the other, is what gives her verse its peculiar intensity and vision.

She had no conventional religious belief at this time, but her love of the principle of beauty in all things was like an article of faith. In these early years she sometimes described herself as 'a committed pantheist', and there is a vein of pantheism in her poetry. The elements of nature such as Earth and Air, as well as beasts and trees, are imbued with a particular spirit, strange and beautiful but not always gentle. Though at times Stella seems to veer towards the more generalised nature mysticism found in Wordsworth, her outlook, on the whole, is more pagan, though she uses classical pagan imagery sparingly.

Her approach is exemplified in one of the first of her poems to be published. This was 'The Giraffes', which appeared in September 1927 in *Criterion*, then edited by T. S. Eliot. Inspired by having read that there were once giraffes in China, the poem is a vision of these creatures living their secret lives 'In Chi's stone vale of age-carved green.' It concludes:

> I hid the thought that suddenly
> Troubled my mind's tranquillity,
> 'What if those golden beasts should find
> The secret out before mankind?
> And if their draught of movement's wine
> Teach them before these books of mine?
> If they are nearer to the True
> Than Wisdom?' pierced doubt's arrow through.

In 1981 she told Libby Purves: 'It's really a poem about natural things being nearer to reality than books and ideas. . . . I don't know that I believe it now.' By that time her beliefs were cast in a more conventional and Christian mould, but she still retained strong feelings about the primal innocence and beauty of nature. Once, at a time of great emotional stress, she told me she had drawn solace from having read in the papers of a tribe of apes recently discovered in the jungle who had lived in a valley hitherto quite unknown to, and hence unmolested by, man.

'The Giraffes' was noticed and admired by Virginia Woolf and Elizabeth Bowen. Woolf wrote to Stella asking her to submit some poems to the Hogarth Press, and the same year noted in her diary that Dorothy Wellesley, who financed and edited the Hogarth Living Poets series, was proposing to include Stella among them. Nothing came of it, but as late as 1929 Woolf was still talking about 'The Giraffes' at a dinner in Newnham College, Cambridge. (Dorothy Wellesley, later Duchess of Wellington, was a poet and a lesbian. I have no idea how well Stella knew her, but one of the main characters in her novel *Miss Linsey and Pa* (1936) is a sophisticated lesbian writer called Dorothy who lives in Bloomsbury.)

Though very differently expressed, Stella's views as found in 'The Giraffes', 'The Fabled Ones' and many other poems were not far from those of D. H. Lawrence. This is curious since, though she greatly admired Lawrence's poetry, she found many of his ideas repellent and wittily caricatured them in *Cold Comfort Farm*. In this instance, however, expression was all. Stella at the time was moving in circles – introduced to her by Ida – in which Lawrence's ideas were being used by men to justify their harassment of women. Both Stella and Lawrence owed much of their thinking to the Romantic movement, and in particular Keats's desire 'for a life of sensations rather than of thoughts', or, as she more mystically put it in her poem 'Dreams': 'To *be* delight where once we knew delight!' To Stella, poetry at its best approached that state of ecstasy.

The Mountain Beast was dedicated to her mother. The poem which gives the collection its title, 'The Legend of the Mountain Beast', has a characteristic theme: the existence of a pure world beyond the reach of human corruption. Under the title are the words 'A man is walking in his garden on a moonlit night in June'. In pleasant, comfortable surroundings, he remembers his innocence which is associated with an Alpine landscape:

> Silence, soft as a flower,
> Rocks, white as a rose,
> And peaks that soared into the blue
> Beneath a cloak of snows . . .

He hears of a legendary valley where:

> . . . the light of the First Day
> Lingered in innocence –
> In last, long radiance
> Upon the worn world's rim . . .

Access to this valley could only come from following the Mountain Beast, a grey, half-human creature with deep sorrow in his face. The man fails to follow the creature and returns to his

OUT OF THE WOODSHED

prosperous life, with the regret that he had missed the opportunity to find his lost innocence. A mysterious poem of extraordinary power and beauty which selective quotation cannot convey, it reflected, among other things, the fact that Stella's holidays in the Alps offered an ecstatic and intense release from her home life and the banalities of decoding cables for the British United Press. 'The Fabled Ones', a slighter poem of considerable charm, is also set in an Alpine landscape, where the fabled ones of the title, 'a herd of snowy unicorns', live. Unicorns are a legendary symbol of purity; and they embody the liberation from human impurity that she felt in these surroundings.

In many of her best poems Stella reveals her awareness that the voice of her imagination, which summoned her away from mortal sorrow into a realm of non-human purity, was a siren call. The world of pain and suffering must be faced. This is from 'The Whisper':

> A demon whisper sighed,
> 'Here is your heart's love.'
>
> 'Leaves greener than the sea,' it sighed
> 'Dancing within a sea-blue sky,
> Music blown forth from shells,
> And clouds in harmony.'
>
> 'Turn then your heart from Man,' it said
> 'Follow a forest path with me
> To where a Vision sleeps
> Bowered in a hawthorn tree.'
>
> So ran the whisper: but I turned
> Mine eyes into the world again,
> Seeing its rage of sorrow,
> Its innocence and pain.

The word 'innocence' is striking and unexpected. It seems to imply that the danger of corruption lies in turning away from the suffering of one's fellow human beings. What gives her poetry a dimension beyond its obvious musical qualities is this sharp awareness of duty which is at war with her world of dreams.

52

'All the solitary things'

One of her best and most characteristic poems in the collection is the Keatsian 'Ode on Tranquillity', a subject dear to her heart. A harsh critic might describe it as a mere pastiche of Keats, albeit an excellent one. While it is certainly true that Stella was influenced by Keats, and by no other poet to quite such an extent, it might be fairer to say that the poem expresses the extreme congruence of their tastes and sensibilities, despite their being divided by over a century. And there is a kind of mystical, passionately inward-looking quality which is not quite Keatsian, but is wholly Stella's. The poem concludes:

> The nearest mirror Earth can hold to this
> Is when the sky, blown blue from thinnest cloud,
> Roofs a green hill, and in that emptiness
> The white sheep wander and the wind blows loud
> Into the silence and away again
> While the grass ripples free –
> This is the mirror of the inner heaven
> Shadowed within thy name, Tranquillity.

One of Stella's most frequently anthologised poems from this collection is 'Coverings'. It is deservedly famous, as it successfully combines her feeling for nature with her satirical instincts. The first four stanzas describe the strange, savage beauty of a snake which has just shed its skin:

> With bar, curve, loop and whirling ring
> The patterned swathes, papyrus thin,
> Lay on the cage's sanded floor . . .

Contrasted with the snake is Mrs Fand, a rich, middle-aged lady with a fox fur around 'her wrinkled throat',

> He [the fox] was killed at dawn as he snarled his threat
> In a bracken brake where the mist lay wet.

The poem goes on to itemise her clothes, which consist chiefly of parts of slaughtered animals, and concludes:

And to make her card-case a lizard died.

Her detailed knowledge of clothes and fashion, sharpened in her years as a journalist, is in evidence. In the final stanza snake and woman are brought together:

> She watched the flickering counterplay
> As the snake reared up with tongue and eye
> Licking the air for newt or fly,
> And shook herself as she turned away
> With a tolerant movement of her head.
> 'The nasty, horrid thing!' she said.

Not surprisingly the poem has been recently anthologised by Richard Adams, the author of *Watership Down* and a leading animal rights campaigner. The same theme is explored in 'A Fat Woman in Bond Street' but with rather less subtlety.

Stella's ecological concerns were ahead of her time. In 'The Marriage of the Machine', a poem in her last collection, *The Lowland Venus* (1938), the subject of industrial pollution is tackled. The earliest of Stella's writing in manuscript that I have seen is a translation, dating from about 1924, of some stanzas of Alfred de Vigny's 'La Maison du Berger' which deal with the corruption of the industrial age, symbolised by the railway train:

> On this iron bull which smokes, puffs and bellows
> Man has mounted too soon . . .

Later come the lines which she translates:

> Everyone cries 'Forward!' but none is the master
> Of the dragon born of a scientist's [*savant*] knowledge . . .

They were prophetic words for 1924, and even more so for 1845 when they were originally written.

Her environmental concerns sprang from the solace she found in natural objects, but also because she felt that they had a life in themselves which was worth preserving. Her beliefs in some poems, such as 'The Companion', seem to hover between polytheism and a vague apprehension of a unifying spirit:

> I speak to rocks and growing flowers,
> But the words are heard by One within
> Mine eyes, who sits and sees the world
> Float like a pageant under him.
>
> He hears the plea I make to clouds,
> Long emerald grass and nodding reed;
> He knows that if these failed, my heart
> Were desolate indeed.

The love poems in the collection, or the poems that deal with love, are mostly written from a distance. Unhappiness and 'love's cruel wars' are mentioned, but they are, with one notable exception to be quoted later, seen through the veil of metaphor and allusion.

This habit, Classical rather than Romantic in origin, of dealing with subjects at a distance, through a new interpretation of received images, occasionally makes Stella's work seem a little too cool. Sometimes, however, as with those poems which deal with angels and devils, heaven and hell, the effect is strangely powerful. Despite not being a conventional believer at this time Stella had a strong sense of good and evil, but she was aware of the difficulties involved in contemplating them in their absolute form. Fallen angels are likely to be more appealing to the human eye than risen ones. She saw how the same inner demon that made her father a monster at home also made him beloved by his many patients. The best poem in this vein is 'The Transformed Demon', in which the demon Azrafel 'slain in heaven's latest war' falls through space, and in finding solitude also finds redemption:

> For on a star whose gentle light
> Earth sees not on the clearest night,
> Where silver rays from a young sun
> Fall on the wandering rescued one –
> In a new guise that suits him well
> Dances the angel Azrafel.

> He swayed and sprang with conquering joy,
> Blowing his flute by Hell's cold brim:
> Sunlight, flowers, and flowing wind
> Danced in an ecstasy with him.

It may be that in these haunting and curious poems about demons she is working out her feelings about her father, and the fragment of demonic energy which he had planted in her.

One of the reasons why Stella's poetry has been so little regarded and (apart from 'Coverings' and the touching 'Lullaby for a Baby Toad') seldom anthologised is that it has been characterised as 'Georgian', a category which has come to be identified with minor, sentimental and backward-looking verse. And though it must be remembered that Stella's work was published in T. S. Eliot's *Criterion* and praised by Virginia Woolf, it is true that the superficial characteristics of Stella's verse are Georgian. The main accusation brought against the Georgians was, in the words of Edward Shanks (himself a Georgian), that their verse 'was not revolutionary, it made no innovation in technique or in diction or in subject-matter or in thought, but continued in the ways of poetry that had gone before it'. This is true, up to a point, but the best of the Georgians used the old techniques to express original ideas.

Leading modernists, such as Eliot and Auden (both of whom Stella admired), will remain undisputedly the major poets of their day. In the lesser modernists, such as Ezra Pound, Roy Campbell and the Sitwells, a striving after originality of image and effect often dominated at the expense of other qualities. Clarity, which is the courtesy of the writer towards the reader, was often entirely forgotten, as was musicality of expression, now a much under-rated poetic skill. Where Edith Sitwell was concerned, however, it was often all music and very little else.

J. C., later Sir John, Squire, who promoted and encouraged Stella's work, was one of the leaders of the Georgians. They included a number of writers who are still highly regarded – Wilfred Owen, Edward Thomas, Walter de la Mare (Stella's

favourite among them), Frances Cornford and many others –
but the beer-swilling, cricket-playing, Squirearchical image of the
movement as a whole has since been much caricatured. In fact the
London Mercury, of which Squire was the first editor, was a very
remarkable literary and artistic magazine which can still be read
with pleasure. Squire himself, far from being an arch-conservative,
was a Liberal who had been a socialist in his youth. Married early
to an ardent suffragette, he was also a keen promoter of women's
rights and in 1920 had edited the first serious modern anthology
of women's poetry for Oxford University Press.

In 1919 he founded the *London Mercury* as a non-political
monthly magazine dedicated to publishing all that was best in
contemporary writing, regardless of whether the writer belonged
to any particular school or none. It would also devote space
to consideration and criticism of the other arts. But Squire did
have a particular agenda: '... my entire purpose was, while
telling nobody about it, to give youth its opportunity'. Despite
its non-partisan approach, the *Mercury*'s style was shaped chiefly
by the tastes of its editor. Squire was not a modernist, and from the
outset he would not publish anything unintelligible. The magazine,
needless to say, attracted the hostility of the Sitwells who were
always spoiling for a literary scrap, and Squire, log-roller-in-chief
of the Georgians, became their particular enemy.

Though it is true that Squire set his face against modernist poetry
in the shape of Pound, Eliot and the Sitwells, he recognised the
merits of Joyce and Lawrence. And even his review of Eliot's *Waste
Land* contains a grudging acceptance that here was a major talent at
work. Stella's opinion was similar. She found the work as a whole
hard to take, but admired parts of it, in particular the passage at
the beginning of 'A Game of Chess' which ends with a line she
considered exquisite: 'In which sad light a carvèd dolphin swam.'

It is a passage which shows that Eliot was capable of the kind
of Keatsian verbal music that Stella most admired and strove
to emulate. Her attitude towards modernist poetry was not so
much hostile as uncomprehending. She once quoted to me from
a review of a volume of poetry in which the critic had spoken
with approval of a passage in which a swan's neck was likened
to a question mark. 'Yes, it's arresting, ingenious certainly,' she
said, 'but what's it *for*?'

Squire himself was not a great poet, but he was, occasionally, a good one, and poems of his such as 'The Stockyard' – a vivid and harsh evocation of a Chicago slaughterhouse, and about as far from the received image of Georgianism as one can imagine – deserve to be better known. Stella was not a whole-hearted admirer of Squire's verse, which lacked for her the 'distinctive voice' that she looked for. In her copy of his *Poems in One Volume* she wrote marginal comments in pencil, a habit of hers. She liked some of the descriptive pieces such as 'Late Snow' and was particularly fond of 'The Discovery', a skilful sonnet which offers an American Indian's first impression of Columbus's landing. This seeing of the familiar through strange eyes she used in one of her own favourite poems, 'The Giraffes'. But against Squire's rather absurd poem about a fall from a cliff which begins: 'Why would you climb down the cliff, little maid?', she has written '*Really!!*', a characteristic note of half-amused exasperation.

Squire published Stella's verse in the *London Mercury* for the first time in January 1928, as well as in a number of anthologies with which he was connected. He was an adviser to the publisher Robert Longman and persuaded him to publish *The Mountain Beast* on the grounds that Stella would, in time, write successful novels for the firm.

Stella may have come to the attention of Squire and the *London Mercury* through the poet and novelist Gwen Clear, a friend of hers whom Squire had been publishing since 1924. Or it may have been Squire's assistant, Edward Shanks, who first noticed Stella's work. They certainly knew each other before Squire published Stella's poetry and probably met when she was working at the *Evening Standard*, to which Shanks contributed frequent articles. A letter to Stella from Max Beerbohm, dated 20 July 1927, is in response to a letter of introduction to him from Shanks. Stella was staying in Italy at Santa Margherita Ligure, a few miles away from Beerbohm's residence, the Villino Chiaro at Rapallo. Unfortunately the two never met: Max and his wife were about to take a trip into the Ligurian mountains for their health. Stella admired his minor but finely honed talents, but there was something about Beerbohm's approach to life – amiably disposed, but essentially narcissistic – which did not appeal to her.

*   *   *

When *The Mountain Beast* came out in 1930, Stella's poetry attracted considerable attention. Her champion Edward Shanks called it 'the best first book of verse I have read since Blunden's *Waggoner*', while an article in *John O'London's Weekly* was headed 'Two Young Poets of Genius: Mr Roy Campbell and Miss Stella Gibbons'. Campbell's modernist *Adamastor* and Stella's more traditional book had been published within a day of one another.

The reviewer, Frank Whitaker, wrote: 'Miss Gibbons, a London Journalist, works in a different medium. If Mr Campbell traffics in thunder and lightning, her best verse is shot with the cold beauty of moonlight. His world is the world about us; hers is the world of the Greek Gods – of mountain air, the swift chase, heraldic beasts and the shy life of the woods. She has Pan's gusty contempt for humans, and Pan's delights in Nature's sports. . . .' Whitaker here gives an impression that the poems are imbued with the kind of arch neo-paganism sometimes found in minor *fin de siècle* versifiers. This is far from the case, and he was nearer the mark when he wrote: 'Miss Gibbons is impelled not so much by experience as by a deep-rooted instinct which would present an interesting problem to a psycho-analyst. She is more at home with fauns and unicorns than in writing about desolate lovers. One or two of her poems of experience, such as "The Lie", approach the commonplace, and "Death of a Heart" contains both Sitwellian and Meredithian echoes.' The Sitwellian echo occurs in the uncharacteristic refrain: 'So come, make moan with saxophone, and hollow bell.' 'But these are details,' Whitaker went on, 'which can be forgotten in gratitude for such conceptions as "The Giraffes", "The Legend of the Mountain Beast", "The Cunning Huntress" and "Artemis Married". These four and others beside have the delicate beauty of a Persian Manuscript.'

Stella's poems are musical, well-crafted and easily understood, but their real merits lie beyond those superficial characteristics. She found her own voice, and used it to explore themes and ideas peculiar to herself, but perhaps her work is not quite distinctive enough entirely to escape the stigma of Georgianism. Her verse will receive the attention it deserves only when she is recognised as belonging to a separate tradition, as valid as modernism, and not a kind of literary backwater.

As to her career as a prose writer, Stella had done little more than publish one or two stories in newspapers and obscure magazines. But an incident occurred in 1926 which, indirectly, was to serve this side of her genius. It came about through an error in calculation which sent a tremor through the financial markets of the world.

CHAPTER 3

The *Standard* and the *Lady*

Stella gave various versions of her contribution to the world's financial instability in 1926, and her inability to remember the precise details was symptomatic of what caused the problem in the first place. It was one of her daily duties at British United Press to convert the French franc rate into dollars, then into pounds sterling, and send the result around the world. The franc was volatile at that time, and she made a miscalculation while converting it from dollars into sterling. In the version of the story she gave to Libby Purves in 1981 she omitted the decimal point altogether. 'In those days the dollar was calculated at seven to the pound, but of course when you were doing a story on the stock market, you would have had to work it out to decimal points. Well, I never was any good at arithmetic anyway, so I just worked it out at seven to the pound, down came the stock market and a lot of people were ruined, I think.'

What seems to have happened, according to an earlier and less florid version, is that, as a result of her error, the franc appeared to have fallen to an even greater degree than normal. She went on: 'The manager of British United Press was quite understandably very annoyed about it, rumpled his hair and said, "Miss Gibbons, things can't go on like this around here, and I've promised the evening papers who've published this story that the person who did it will be sacked." So I was sacked.' Through the influence of good friends and some 'very kind but not very true' letters of commendation from her former employers she was taken on as secretary to the editor of the London *Evening Standard*.

In 1926 the paper was owned by Lord Beaverbrook and edited by E. R. Thompson, 'a delightful editor, and a most delightful man', according to Stella. The paper was lively, and only occasionally reflected its proprietor's prejudices. It had a strong interest in the arts, particularly literature. Arnold Bennett contributed a famous book page and there were regular serialisations of popular books of the day, including two, in Stella's time there, by Bennett himself. Less regular pieces were solicited from a wide range of eminent contributors, from Robert Graves and Evelyn Waugh to Dean Inge and Benito Mussolini. One of Mussolini's articles offers an example of the curious paradoxes thrown up by changing attitudes. In writing about women in Italy he stated that: 'We have abolished the beauty contest in Italy', not on feminist grounds, but because they were unbecoming to the modesty of women whose proper place was in the home. He considered the modern woman 'an abomination', and no doubt this estimation was reciprocated.

Leading stories tended towards the domestic and non-political. Society divorce cases, financial scandals and murders (particularly poisonings) were favoured. Wimbledon and the Test Match nearly always found their way on to the front page in their season. There was a time during the slump when hardly a day went by without another disgraced financier or missing banker.

It was soon evident that Stella's talents were not being exercised in the role of secretary. By her own admission she was positively inefficient, so she was put to writing stories of female interest, mostly on the Home Page, under its editor John Adcock. However, it was not until late in 1928 that any of her articles carried a byline to indicate her authorship.

In an interview conducted for her old school magazine in November 1933 she was asked what kind of journalism she had done. She replied that her work covered practically everything from dramatic criticism to sub-editing.

'And enjoyed it all?'
'Yes, all of it, except the reporting. It's such exhausting work, you have to dash all over the place; and the change of mood is so tiring. In the morning you have to report the wedding of a famous tennis player; in the afternoon interview the heroine of some tragedy, and I remember once riding down on a paper wagon to report a fire. On the whole English newspapers are very good about sending women out late. The paper I worked

on never sent me out later than half past nine. . . . I'd like to say to anyone who is thinking of taking it up, if you go in for journalism you can really have hardly any life of your own. You just have to sell yourself to your paper for the time being.'

She recalled to a friend of hers, the writer Suzanne Goodwin, that when she began reporting she had to fill out an expenses sheet. As she sat down in the *Evening Standard* offices to perform this task for the first time she was surprised, and initially flattered, to find the male reporters gathering round to watch her. She soon discovered the reason: they wanted to make sure that she was not giving too modest and accurate an account. She was, of course, being far too honest and they remonstrated with her. Stella was amused rather than shocked by their attitude, but never told Suzanne whether she subsequently conformed to their ways or not.

As a reporter she earned the National Union of Journalists' rate of nine guineas (£9.45) a week, a good salary for those days. She told Libby Purves in 1981 that the men on the staff did not resent her earning as much as them once they found out that she was not living at home with her parents and earning pin money, but supporting herself and, occasionally, her brothers. Much of the writing she had to do was mere hack work, though some of this was to play a significant role in the genesis of *Cold Comfort Farm*.

In 1928 the novels of a writer called Mary Webb had suddenly become fashionable. When she had died the previous year her passing was not much noticed in the press, in spite of the fact that she had won the prestigious French *Fémina-Vie Heureuse* Prize for her last book, *Precious Bane*. But in April 1928 Stanley Baldwin, then Prime Minister, spoke at a dinner of the Royal Literary Fund, mentioning her in glowing terms and castigating the press for the undeserved oblivion into which she had fallen. Baldwin was a cousin of Rudyard Kipling and a man with some literary pretensions of his own, so his words were heeded. *Precious Bane* was republished that year with an introduction by Baldwin, and a Mary Webb revival began. In his regular book page in the *Evening Standard* Arnold Bennett wrote on 3 May:

The resuscitation of books out of a state of suspended vitality is a fine game. Mr Stanley Baldwin has just been playing at it – with the novels of the late Mary Webb. I receive with polite reserve the pronouncements of Prime Ministers about imaginative literature. As a rule, either their taste has been distorted by terrible experiences in public schools, and resembles a bicycle after it has been run over by a motor lorry, or they have been too busy conscientiously misguiding the destiny of fifty million human beings properly to nourish their taste. . . . But Mr Stanley Baldwin has made no mistake about Mary Webb. I have read only one of her novels, *Precious Bane* – and I admit that I would not have read even that had it not been forced upon me with violence by an enthusiast for the distinguished unappreciated. *Precious Bane*, however, can scarcely count among those of Mary Webb's novels which are in a state of suspended vitality. It has been re-printed every year since its original publication. . . . Mary Webb has power; she could create beauty; and she is truthful concerning human nature. All I would say against her is that her writing is somewhat mannered. If Mr Baldwin's remark has a sequel in the shape of a uniform edition of the Webb novels he may go down to posterity.

Always eager to jump on a bandwagon, even a literary one, the *Evening Standard* decided to take Bennett's hint and began to serialise an earlier novel of Webb's, *The Golden Arrow*, on 9 June. On the 8th there was a long article about her on the Home Page which ended: 'The one great disappointment of her life was that success did not come. It is the irony of fate that it should have come so quickly after her death. Today her books are selling in the thousands. "If that had happened only a year ago, she would have been in seventh heaven," her husband said. "That is what makes me feel bitter, that it should come now when it is too late. And the bigger the success, the more bitter I shall feel."' The lack of recognition for her great gifts had been something of an obsession with Mary Webb, and may well have contributed to her early death at the age of forty-six. ('*When* I have succeeded in getting paid fairly by the British Public,' she once wrote to a friend, 'I shall naturally have the best treatment I can get [for her illness].')

Stella would have found such an attitude tiresomely egotistical. Once, when we were discussing the comparative lack of success of her works other than *Cold Comfort Farm*, Stella said to me: 'Of course most writers have this secret resentment against the world for neglecting their work; but most writers have the sense to realise that the world sometimes has more important things to do than worry about their novels.'

The Golden Arrow, published in 1916, was the first of Webb's six novels. It was, as P. G. Wodehouse would have said, ripe stuff, and it so happened that one of Stella's tasks was to summarise the plot for readers who were joining the serialisation late. The Story So Far was always full of incident: 'Eli becomes enraged with his daughter because she has decked herself out with cheap finery for the benefit of Joe and in his fury cuts off Lily's long golden hair. She fires at him with a rook rifle, but misses. . . .'

The task of précis is not calculated to endear one to any novel, even a novel to which one is sympathetically disposed – and Stella did not find *The Golden Arrow* sympathetic. She found it ridiculous. 'The large agonised faces in Mary Webb's book annoyed me,' she wrote in 1966 in a *Punch* article entitled 'Genesis of a Novel'; 'they were over life-size (no blame to her for that; she was writing fiction) but they were also silly, and I did not believe people were any more despairing and passionate in Herefordshire [*sic* Mary Webb actually wrote about Shropshire] than they were in Camden Town.' She knew, from personal experience, how despairing and passionate they could be in Camden Town; and Mary Webb might have known it too, because she had written her last three novels while living in Hampstead.

The world of Webb's novels, and especially *The Golden Arrow*, was peculiarly confined. Little or nothing of life beyond the Shropshire countryside intruded. There are some writers who make a virtue of this narrow field of vision: Jane Austen is often cited as an example; but Austen's 'little bit (two inches wide) of ivory' – as she herself described her literary scope in a letter of 1816 – seems like a continent by comparison with Webb's territory. What makes it suffocating is that Webb is using landscape almost exclusively as a metaphor for her own passions and aspirations. Hers, as Michèle Barale says in *Daughters and*

Lovers: The Life and Writing of Mary Webb, 'is the geography of desire and not of fact'. Stella began to wonder how the grim, outlandish characters of Webb's suffocating rural milieu might fare if confronted by a brisk, smart, sensible young lady from London. This was the germ of *Cold Comfort Farm*.

Since the age of sixteen, as she recalled in an interview published in *Leader* magazine on 28 April 1945, Stella had been carrying in her head a story about one sane and balanced person living in a family of melodramatic neurotics. All she needed was a setting in which an essentially autobiographical notion could take flight on the wings of imagination. Webb had presented her with it.

The serialisation of *The Golden Arrow* continued until the middle of August. Webb's poems regularly appeared on the Home Page and there were articles in the paper about the writer and her work. In July her name was coupled with that of 'another discouraged *Fémina* prize winner', Constance Holme. She too was the author of rural fiction, such as *Crump Folk Going Home* and *The Lonely Plough*. She had won the *Fémina* prize in 1920 for *The Splendid Fairing*, and the *Evening Standard* informed its readers that 'outside her work her hobbies are sheepdogs and music'. Her work is now quite forgotten.

This concerted campaign by the *Evening Standard* in favour of neglected female ruralists – and it should be noted that another of them, Sheila Kaye-Smith, was a frequent contributor to the *Standard* throughout this period – resulted in a number of writers sending in novels of a similar character in the hope of having them serialised, or at least reviewed. It was one of Stella's jobs to read them and deliver a verdict. While Webb's work, for all its occasional absurdity, possesses genuine literary merit, it can safely be assumed that the work of these epigoni did not. Stella's heart was further hardened against the genre. When *The Golden Arrow* concluded it was succeeded by the serialisation of a novel by Edith Wharton, a writer of an entirely different stamp. Meanwhile, Stella was beginning to make her mark on the Home Page.

The Women's Page was monopolised by 'Corisande', a Miss Hogg who wrote society gossip and fashion notes. Opposite Corisande, the Home Page covered a wider range of issues with a female and domestic slant. There were verses for children, columns of advice and humorous pieces. Sometimes the page would be taken up with an entire feature, and it was here that Stella's byline first appeared. On 28 November 1928 the Home Page was devoted entirely to a short story of Stella's called 'To Love and to Cherish', a rather downbeat but effective study of a frustrated suburban marriage. It was to be republished twelve years later, with minor improvements, in her second collection of short stories, *Christmas at Cold Comfort Farm*.

On 1 April 1929 a second short story of Stella's appeared: 'Lost Children This Way', a bank holiday story. A female Hampstead writer named Anne – 'Critics were beginning to speak of her as a second, more poetic Jane Austen' – is distracted by the traditional bank holiday fair on the Heath and finds that some cockney children have found their way into her garden. They have been diverted by an odiously masterful young man called Hugh Welsh – somehow the perfect name for such a character – who has put a sign on her gate: 'Lost Children This Way'.

> 'Well, you could have filled your garden with nice quiet clean children of your own if you'd married me when I asked you to,' said Hugh Welsh brutally. 'And if you want to know who put the notice there, I put it there, and I'd put a cocoa-nut shy in your bedroom and a hoop-la in your study if I thought they would stop you turning into a silly, fussy, childless old maid!'
>
> 'But, Hugh, what about my work?' she protested, making a last stand for freedom.
>
> 'You won't miss it with me and your own children to look after,' he said decidedly. 'If you have to shut yourself away from reality in order to write good books, you won't want to write again when you begin to live a real life yourself.'
>
> And, at the risk of offending all the people who believe in Art for Art's sake, I must admit that she never did.

One looks in vain for a note of irony in this fairly repulsive story, but Stella must have turned against it too because, though she thriftily reprinted most of her short stories in book form, 'Lost Children This Way' was – happily – never seen again.

There was a side to Stella, expressed in 'Lost Children This Way', which believed that domestic happiness was an achievement which transcended all others. 'I am, as you know, *always* pleased when people marry,' she wrote to me once in a letter, '(except Hitler and Eva Braun, I suppose, though I think even that was a good final idea, and showed some better feeling.)' Perhaps Stella's longing for marriage was so violently and irrationally expressed because it had only recently been dealt a blow by the ending of her affair with Walter Beck.

At some time in 1928 Stella broke off her engagement to Walter, 'the young man', as she put it to Libby Purves in 1981, 'who caused all the trouble'. Her verdict was that he was 'very beautiful, but shallow'. She said in the same interview: 'I knew what I wanted in that I didn't like what I was getting. . . . There were two young men, one when I was very young and one when I was in my early twenties, who were making me very unhappy, and when they got to a point of behaviour which I regarded as beyond the pale, I dropped them absolutely cold.'

The reason for the break-up was essentially profound incompatibility. Stella was someone for whom marriage was a complete commitment; Walter, fond as he was of her, wanted – or perhaps needed – to keep something back for himself. She described him in *Bassett* as 'a very nervous, complex and over-civilised young man, moody as a cat, knowing next to nothing about his own deeper motives, living by impulse and by a daily ritual which soothed his nerves and which his deepest instincts were against breaking'. The intensity of Stella's devotion must have seemed suffocating and stultifying to him.

The actual circumstances of the rupture are not known, and it would be foolish to look for them in a novel. However, the psychological outlines can reasonably be inferred from *Bassett* since they are so convincingly specific. Walter was unfaithful to Stella, if not in body, then certainly in spirit. Stella, who could recognise that from his point of view she was 'possessive and over-earnest, over-affectionate, wickedly jealous', decided the affair must end and acted promptly.

Her most poignant comment on the Walter affair is the poem 'To a Deserted Girl', published in *The Mountain Beast*. It is written apparently from the man's point of view:

Know, when your thought returns to me at night
And being hungry, would be fully fed,
That I am lying with my arms wrapped round
Some stranger-woman, in an unknown bed.

That carelessly I give her what I gave
To you, and use the same words that I said,
And that her fairer breast is soft to kiss,
Whiter, and sweeter to a young man's head.

Think of this always. There shall come a day
When your starved love, defeated, turns away.

Knowing the sex of the writer adds a dimension to the poem that
it otherwise might not have. Stella wrote to me once: 'Very good
writers are nearly always detached; the absolute tip-top ones –
Proust, for instance – manage to convey agonies of personal
involvement *and* remain detached – don't ask me how it's done,
but I do know it has to be paid for.' She often achieved this kind
of detachment in her writing, notably in this poem and in the
account of her affair with Beck in *Bassett*. To be able to tear
oneself away from an emotionally painful situation and, instead
of trying to forget it, to stare at it without giving way to self-pity,
requires courage. Stella believedthat such a capacity 'has to be paid
for', not only in pain at the time, but also in a certain subsequent
hardness of heart. That is why she emphasised the word 'writers':
she was differentiating between very good writers and very good
human beings.

For all that, Stella could not dismiss Beck from her mind. In
her misery she looked with an even more harshly satirical eye at
the fictional miseries of Mary Webb's characters in *The Golden
Arrow*. The quotation from *Mansfield Park* which is the epigraph
to *Cold Comfort Farm* summed up her attitude: 'Let other pens
dwell on guilt and misery.' There was enough real guilt and misery
in her own life at the time without having it foisted on her in the
form of a novel. After coming into the *Evening Standard* office
in tears over the break-up with Walter, she had to sit down and
summarise a turgid, doom-laden romance like *The Golden Arrow*.
It was not fair on her; in the end it was perhaps not entirely fair on
Mary Webb either.

Despite these personal agonies her career was flourishing. The year 1929 marks the high point of Stella's bylined contributions to the *Evening Standard*. There were articles on the Home Page on 'Dressing to Match Your Rooms' ('thunder blue' was the fashionable colour) and 'Scarves and How to Wear Them': 'Few women wear a scarf well. The most common mistake is to wear a parti-coloured scarf under a coat with a fur collar, thus making a confused, broken line effect at the neck, the one place in a woman's dress where a simple, becoming line is essential. . . .' There was little to distinguish these pieces except a certain crisp authority – rather remarkable for a woman in her mid-twenties at that time. Her pen pictures of seasonal events have a period charm: 'Wimbledon is developing the Ascot touch. The women who go to watch Helen Wills and Tilden and Betty Nuthall wear frocks of fragile beauty worthy of the paddock and the Royal Enclosure. For at Wimbledon under a cloudless sky I saw blue, green and rose parasols that floated like brilliant bubbles over their heads. . . .'

Throughout her life Stella remained deeply interested in clothes and knowledgeable about them. In 1929 she began to write for the *Standard* an occasional series which became popular, entitled 'Unusual Women: Pen Pictures of Some London Types'. In these articles she would describe, sometimes critically, the well or expensively dressed women that she saw around London. They were not profound pieces, but they were elegantly written and the little touches of character drawing that she introduced gave them an edge. Here is one not quite typical example from 21 February 1929:

> The most attractive woman I saw this week was unusually tall, strikingly fair skinned and gracious in manner. Her grey hair, worn high on her head, shows her ears which are large, with single diamond earrings, and was dressed in many small close waves. The gold and silver threads in her toque of soft and twisted metal tissue matched the gold threads woven into her long dark blue coat. Her low-heeled shoes were beautifully cut and were made of dark brown suede. Her eyes were serious and observant, but her mouth was easily moved to smiling. When she laughed she just caught the top of her lower lip with her small

teeth which gave an unexpectedly girlish look to her beautiful face. Her gestures were very quick, and she used her hands to point and emphasise her remarks more than the average woman does. I saw her twice. On the first occasion her coat, which was so long that it touched her ankles, was of rich dark brown cloth closely woven with gold thread with a brown fur collar; and the second time her coat was of exactly the same pattern and material, but dark blue instead of brown. She evidently liked the material so much she had two coats made alike, but of different colours. On the second day her diamond drop earrings were replaced by large single pearls. She also wore a large shoulder knot of shaded pink velvet flowers caught with a single bar brooch of diamonds and three large pearls. Her beautifully fine grained skin has natural, healthy beauty. Fresh air, a quiet and regular home life, and many interests at home and abroad had evidently conspired with Nature to make a complexion that any grandchild would love to kiss.

It was Queen Mary.

Stella's later novels are notable for their very exact descriptions of clothes and interiors, which are used with quiet subtlety to indicate character and atmosphere. They can be traced back to the professional habits of observation acquired on the *Evening Standard*. So, it has to be said, can their occasionally excessive attention to detail.

The 'Unusual Women' series was sufficiently well thought of for the editor to send Stella to Vienna to write some impressions of the women of that city. Eleven years later, in an article in *St Martin's Review* in May 1940, she recalled a small incident which demonstrates another of her qualities as a writer, an intuitive feeling for the spirit of the times:

In 1929 Vienna was a sad city. It was as lovely and friendly as a charming woman, but (as if she were having a run of cruel luck) it was also melancholy. I loved it. I walked about the streets, grey as our own streets in London, but unstained by smoke, and lunched on *wiener schnitzel* at Sachers, the once fashionable and still famous restaurant.

In the evening I went to one of the open-air concerts of

classical music that are held in the parks of Vienna, just as our military bands play Gilbert and Sullivan and *The Bronze Horse* to strolling Londoners in our parks on Sunday evenings.

At ten o'clock the concert was over, and I set out on the walk back to my hotel. The streets were almost deserted. The only sound was the occasional distant hoot of a taxi horn and sometimes the subdued voices of people going home. I was crossing a huge dimly-lit square, closed in on three sides by these glorious ancient palaces, when I suddenly became conscious of a new sound – a loud defiant sound.

Footsteps. Someone was marching through the deserted square, past the fantastic chancelleries and barracks whose stones echoed to that impatient vigorous tread.

I looked across to the far side of the square and there, passing under the faint glow of a street lamp, was a human figure.

It was dressed in the breeches and short coat and heavy boots (the nails gave that defiant ring to the step) of a mountaineer, and on the shoulders was a heavy rucksack. It was someone who was very young; youth showed in the eager way the figure pressed forward over the cobbled stones and in the swing of the arms and in the proud yet natural lift of the hatless head.

I was almost sure that it was a girl – but symbols are sometimes without sex – and here (I thought then) is the very Spirit of the New Europe; archetype of the Youth Movements that are marching forward past the hoary cathedrals and palaces of the past into the future. The figure strode on and vanished under a dark arch, and gradually – though they have rung on in my imagination for eleven years – the footsteps died away.

Very occasionally Stella's articles in the *Standard* were more personally revealing. On 22 May 1929 the Home Page printed a piece entitled 'Three Women I Would Like to Be When I Am Forty, the Confessions of a Woman of Twenty-seven'. It has no byline, but it is unquestionably Stella. She was indeed twenty-seven, and there surely could not have been two twenty-seven-year-old women in England, let alone writing for the *Evening Standard*, whose favourite authors included Keats, Mrs Hungerford and Herman Melville.

When I am forty, which will be thirteen years from now, I want

to be like one of the three imaginary women who have been
growing up beside me like invisible sisters during the last three
years. I suppose they represent three sides of my character, but
this is doubtful.

The first one, whom I think I like best, is the clearest figure
of the three. She is married, and she lives in a large happy
house in the country with six sons and a husband. She is in
love with her husband, and he with her. They are not 'good
comrades' nor 'sensible' nor resigned to putting up with each
other. They are romantically in love. They still like to look at one
another and to be with one another more than anyone else they
know. They have many common interests. The woman loves
the yearly festivals: Christmas, birthdays, anniversaries and the
various speech days and prizegiving days of her six sons. She
likes doing the same happy peaceful thing year in year out. She
is usually up to her eyes in work because she and her husband
have little money and she loves it. She loves laughter and she is
tender-hearted. She loves the open air, and music, and dogs, and
all the country sights and smells and colours. She loves a good
gossip and clothes (though her beauty is natural and is more
the beauty of character than the beauty of body). She reads
enormously and indiscriminately, and likes the oddest mixture:
Keats and Berta Ruck, Mrs Hungerford and Herman Melville.
She likes being alone so that she can think about the country
and what perfect lambs her six sons and husband are . . . though
she knows they are very far from perfect. She is never bored,
though she is often angry and puzzled at cruelty. She can always
laugh. She is outwardly casual of her standards of conduct, but
inwardly strict with herself. She hates gush and false snobbery
and false romance, pompousness and spinstery 'good taste'. She
is as happy as a flower growing in the right soil.

The second woman is only a shadow. I am afraid she will
never grow up. She knows men as she knows the palm of her
hand which is always manicured. She is fastidious, reserved and
disillusioned. She never betrays a friend or a confidence. She
dislikes gossip and noise, and back-slapping human beings. Her
manners are perfect. She never treats her servants as human
beings, but she is kind to them. She is married too and in love
with her husband, and he with her. He adores her beauty and

so does she. I don't think they have any children. If she is not married, she has many men friends whom she has known for years, and she is rather a mystery to them. They fall in love with her and are wistful about her because she is so aloof in spite of her kindness. She is a little amused at life, never very deeply moved by it. She has experienced much and so fully that she is a little tired. She has perfect clothes and extracts from her personality the last grain of charm, but she is a ghost beside the third.

The third is a nice old muddle. She only knows two things: she cares (or thinks she cares) about what is beautiful and she can be faithful to people she loves. Beauty to this woman excuses ANYTHING. She knows this is all wrong and she has stopped trying to fight her own weakness. She loves to watch life spinning past like an insane and gorgeous dream. She hates being involved in it: it is too painful. She is utterly happy by herself in a foreign country with a map which she can't read, and absorbing sounds and colours and scents and people. She is hopelessly lazy; she does not fall in love easily. Sometimes she looks lovely; sometimes she looks awful. She is passionately interested in every blessed thing in the wide world. She gets tired easily and is always trying to be well-balanced and sensible, heaven help her. She likes men, and has numerous men friends, but they are not all in love with her. She is most hopelessly romantic, and she has a sense of humour which I hope saves her. I doubt if she will be there when I have reached forty. She will probably have got herself killed watching something interesting and beautiful. A crane will fall on her, I expect. It will be rather exhausting to be like her when I am forty, but I am afraid she will be strong enough to defeat the other two. Confound her!

The first is by far the most removed from the real Stella Gibbons, though she has similar tastes and inclinations, particularly literary ones. She represents the sort of person Stella thought she would like to be. Many of the heroines of Stella's later novels – and even, to a certain extent, Flora Poste – are in the process of becoming this contented if unexciting paragon. The second represents the sharp, sophisticated side of Stella's character which she liked to keep in abeyance, but which occasionally peeped through her natural modesty. The third figure is most recognisably Stella as I knew her, and shows how clearly she saw her own faults and foibles.

As her journalistic reputation grew, Stella began to be put on to all kinds of stories. She saw Mary Pickford's first talkie and reported on its effects: 'By the way, have you ever looked at yourself in your handbag mirror after a good satisfying cry when the lights go up?' She also interviewed a number of celebrities, one of the first being a former mistress of King Edward VII.

On 13 October 1928 Lillie Langtry, by then Lady de Bathe, was paying one of her last visits to London. It was the Jersey Lily's seventy-fourth birthday. Inevitably Stella asked her what she thought of 'the Modern Girl' – interviewees were always being asked what they thought of 'the Modern Girl' in those days – and her subject gave a muted if favourable response. She said little of interest, except in reply to a question about Oscar Wilde. Was he lovable? 'No. He could be extraordinarily amusing and a good companion. But lovable, no. I could never get over the fact that his nails were dirty.'

The unpleasant impression left by this remark was confirmed by Stella's recollections. Writing in the *Lady* a few years later, she remembered that 'though her manner was that of a woman used to appearing before great crowds, and therefore had something regal about it, she certainly was not a vivid personality. The world famous blue eyes, however, were undimmed and the legendary complexion clear as a young girl's.' She did not find her beautiful, because her face 'lacked spirituality'. On the subject of complexions, Stella recalled to me that in the course of the interview the Jersey Lily made some pointed remarks to her on young girls' deplorable habit of using make-up. It became clear that she suspected her interviewer, who had an unusually good skin and very red lips, of employing cosmetics. Stella took a clean handkerchief out of her pocket and, without a word, firmly wiped her lips and cheeks with it, then presented the result to the Jersey Lily. It was still pristine, innocent even of powder.

More to her taste were the parents of the aviator Amy Johnson. The piece she did on them, half interview half profile, shows her sympathies for 'ordinary' people.

At first glance Mr and Mrs Johnson look like any other prosperous, provincial couple. She small, dark and prettily dressed in a flowered crepe de chine frock, small black hat, good shoes, and stockings of unusually fine grey silk, nicely kept hands. He, slow of speech with a broad humorous face and an imperturbably calm manner. She wore no make-up, but looked young to be the mother of a grown-up daughter. . . . Life is seen in plain black or white by Mrs Johnson; there are no subtle, bewildering intermediate shades of grey. She has many interests: rotary clubs, girl guides, her daughters, her home. She is a woman of strong likes and dislikes. . . . Mr Johnson has a typically masculine reaction to his daughter's achievement; enormous pride concealed under a mask of tolerant approval.

Another interviewee was Hugh Walpole, then a highly esteemed and successful writer. Stella told Libby Purves in 1981: 'Poor Hugh Walpole . . . I went to interview him at his flat in Piccadilly overlooking Green Park and I thought he was pompous and very vain. He had a special edition of his books bound in ivory vellum, that kind of thing. I thought it was all awfully affected, though in later years I came to think of it as pathetic.' In later years she herself possessed a set of her novels bound in tooled leather. 'Poor Hugh Walpole' became Anthony Pookworthy of the dedicatory letter in *Cold Comfort Farm*. She saw in him not only an over-rated writer with an unduly high opinion of himself, but the representative of a smug, self-congratulatory literary establishment. The initials A.B.S and L.L.R after Pookworthy's name stand for Associate Back Scratcher and Licensed Log Roller.

A version of Walpole appears in *My American* (1939). The young editorial assistant and would-be writer Amy Lee visits Mr Antrobus, a popular and successful old writer, at his flat overlooking the park. He engages her in conversation, not because he is interested in her but because he is pumping her for material, assuming her to be a representative example of the average young office typist. 'Mr Antrobus . . . had reached that stage in his career when he was too busy, too popular, too dignified, too well known to go and sit behind *The Evening News* in Lyons Corner House and listen to typists for himself.' As an already published young poet, Stella would have found such an approach peculiarly galling.

Beginning in March 1930, one of Walpole's novels was serialised in the *Evening Standard*. It was *Murder in Piccadilly*, which became *Death Above the Circus* and was finally published in book form as *Above the Dark Circus*. It was intended as a study of the nature of good and evil, a theme which always fascinated him. Unfortunately he had nothing of interest to say on the subject, and the result is a shallow, verbose thriller which unthinkingly reflects the prejudices of its age. The hero is a gentleman, the villain whom he murders decidedly not, and so on. If Stella was asked to write the synopsis, as she had been for Webb's *The Golden Arrow*, it could only have increased her irritation with Walpole.

In August 1930 Stella was sacked from the *Evening Standard*. 'I have always liked, and tried, to believe that this was due to one of Lord Beaverbrook's periodical fits of economy,' she wrote much later in 'Genesis of a Novel', 'and only the years have brought a suspicion that there may have been other causes.' These causes she enumerated in an interview as dreaminess in the office and crying over her unhappy love affair with Walter. By that time, of course, her affair with Walter Beck had ended and she had met her future husband, Allan; but she never entirely got over Walter.

Six years after the affair had ended, the mention of Walter's name could still make Stella lose her customary self-control. In April 1934, her sister-in-law Renée recorded in her diary that while she was at a sherry party at Stella's 'Araminta . . . made Stella furious by talking about a young man called Jim [i.e. Walter] (the origin of 'George' in *Bassett*) with whom S[tella] once had an unhappy love affair. This tactlessness did indeed annoy S so much that she afterwards referred to Araminta as a "nasty little semi-prostitute". "She *isn't*!" I declared indignantly. "Of course she isn't," said Lewis, adding thoughtfully, "She's an entire prostitute."'

One of the curious aspects of the Beck situation, as Ida Graves remarked to me, was that Ida now remained friendly with Stella's former lover, Walter, while in due course Stella would remain friendly with Ida's former lover, Eric Schilsky, who had a distinguished artistic career and became a Royal Academician. Stella was to become godmother to Schilsky's daughter, Clare.

By 1929 Ida's husband, Herbert Marks, was beginning to form

an attachment with Isobel Powys, daughter of A. R. Powys and niece of the famous literary Powys brothers J. C. and T. F. According to Ida, the scene recalled by Mybug in *Cold Comfort Farm* when 'a whole lot of us bathed in the river and afterwards little Harriet Belmont sat naked on the grass and played to us on the flute' was based on an actual incident, and Harriet Belmont was Isobel Powys.

Meanwhile Ida was still passionately involved with her sculptor. Whenever she wanted to visit Schilsky she would say that she was visiting Stella at Vale Cottage. The obvious solution was for Ida to divorce Marks. But while this would have been perfectly acceptable in bohemian circles, Marks's position as accountant to the United Jewish Synagogues would be in jeopardy if he were regarded as the guilty party in a divorce case, especially as he had already broken ranks by marrying a Gentile. Yet if Ida ran away with Schilsky, the courts would make her lose the children. As a result she was in an agony of indecision and kept him waiting.

Stella and Schilsky would go for walks on Hampstead Heath and confide in each other. From these conversations, Stella formed the impression that Ida was treating Schilsky very badly. She may well have projected some of her grievances with Walter on to the Ida/Eric situation and thereby misconstrued it. As it is, only Ida's version of events survives. She recalled to me:

> One day [some time in 1929] Stella came to tea. She knew I wasn't a wicked mother. Herbert by that time had gone off with Isobel Powys. I was delighted. I said to Stella would she say I was a good mother – which I was. She was then on the *Evening Standard*. And d'you know, she wouldn't? She was my friend, but she wouldn't sign an affidavit to help me get custody of the children. She said if she was found to be involved in the divorce case and had to stand up in court she might lose her job.

It is more than likely that the reason Stella gave for not signing the affidavit was an excuse, and that for disinterested, though perhaps misguided, motives she was trying to break up Ida's liaison with Eric. If this is the case, she succeeded. Ida realised that she could not keep Schilsky waiting while she sorted out the custody of her children. She and Eric parted, Ida said, with great regret and by mutual consent. Stella, however, continued to believe that Ida had been a bad influence on Schilsky, though she and Ida went on seeing each other from time to time. They finally parted company altogether, according to Ida, through a misunderstanding:

Later on [in the early 1930s] I'd parted from Eric while Stella remained friends with him. Meanwhile I'd made an attachment to Blair [Hughes-Stanton, the engraver]. He was still married, though he never stopped being friendly with his wife [the artist Gertrude Hermes] – almost annoyingly so. I was in Wales, and now and again I came to London. On one of these occasions I came up from Wales, where I was completely cut off from people, and I wanted to see Stella. So I rang her up for a date and we agreed to meet, but I got a cold so I rang her and said could I come next Tuesday when my cold was better? Then Stella got into a tizzy and rang me up to say I was not to come on Tuesday because Eric was coming and she was perfectly certain that I'd known, and that I'd put off the meeting before so that I could meet Eric. I said I was innocent. She wouldn't believe me.

It was over forty years before they communicated again. When Ida finally wrote to Stella in May 1977 it was to inform her of Walter Beck's death. She wrote: 'Suddenly, one morning a few years ago, a happy face peered sideways into my window, and I shouted "Walter!!!" He was to die in about a year's time (as from Torquay) [Walter Beck died at Torquay in December 1973] and was on a last tour to see his friends. . . . Walter spoke of you very affectionately, and I was to send/give you his warm greetings if and when I could find you.' On receiving this letter Stella wrote to the Superintendent Registrar at Torquay requesting a copy of Beck's death certificate. This certificate, together with Ida's letter, she placed in the envelope with the letter 'W' scrawled on it which I found among Stella's papers. Her friend Suzanne Goodwin told me that Stella actually visited Torquay after Walter's death in search of further information and to visit Walter's grave.

Stella's sending for the death certificate was not an act of morbidity or vindictiveness, merely a reflection of one of the principles that guided her life. It is summed up by something she said to Renée in 1934 and which Renée recorded in her diary: 'Stella says that it is sometimes better to love someone who does not love one than to have nothing of that sort in one's life at all. She says one can build one's life round them.'

After their bitter misunderstanding, Ida had not been disposed to renew the acquaintance, and she only wrote to Stella four years after Walter's death because, quite by chance, her daughter had visited Stella's house in connection with a piece of furniture she had repaired for her. It was an opportunity, Ida felt, for further repairs to be made and so she wrote to her old friend, beginning her letter characteristically with the words: 'Dear Paddy, Ida speaking!' When Stella replied to Ida's letter in June 1977 her letter was friendly and chatty, but it ended: 'I can't sign *truly* "with love" – I love so few people – so I'll use the word you use of Walter – Yours affectionately, for old time's sake – Paddy.'

There is a certain chilly integrity here, very characteristic of one aspect of Stella's nature. She had still not quite forgiven Ida for what she saw as Ida's shabby treatment of Eric Schilsky.

In the same letter to Ida Stella had written: 'I shall always be grateful to Walter for having taught me to love music.' When I interviewed Ida in 1997 she gave me some further details about Beck:

When Walter was getting quite ancient, he did a rather pathetic journey with his chauffeur to visit all his friends. He knew he was dying. He went all over England. I said to him: 'Walter, why did you break with Stella?' Because I'd never known. And he said: 'She was hopelessly depressive. She could be so silent and moody.' ['Be not too wildly amorous of the far,' he had written in the volume of Yeats he had given her.] That was complete news to me, though I did realise there was a great difference between Stella and me.

After the break with Stella, Ida went on,

He married a very beautiful American girl called Dorothea. She was very shy. They had no children, but they were a perfect couple. They had a beautiful house in Hampstead, complete with central heating, not a thing out of place. I was their first visitor. They got a maid called Maud. She was perfect too. She watered the flowers every day with a special little watering can, kept the place beautifully. I couldn't sleep there when I stayed because the place was too perfect. Walter went to the office every day, saw his mother, came back again. Dorothea had exquisite clothes, and this went on for many years. Perfect harmony. Then very gradually Maud, the maid, took over. It would make a magnificent story *à la* Henry James – one of curious and sinister possession, and I think she must have been secretly in love with Walter. Their lives were ordered by her. She would say she was going out, so Walter and Dorothea would arrange to have dinner at a restaurant. Then they moved to a very expensive flat in St John's Wood. I called on them one day. I rang the bell and there was a long pause before Dorothea answered. I knew there was something wrong. On the top of a chest of drawers I spied a full glass. She had become an alcoholic. Another time I went to supper and Walter more or less admitted it. She died of cancer a few years before he did.

Ida's story offers independent proof that Stella's assessment of Walter's life in her novel *Bassett* as 'elegant' but 'empty' had some truth to it.

One further footnote may be added. While researching for this biography I bought a copy of Stella's first volume of poetry, *The Mountain Beast*, from a book dealer. On the inside cover it is inscribed: 'To my dear Dorothea from Walter 30/8/30'. The 'Walter' is undoubtedly Beck, because the handwriting is identical to his inscription to Stella in the Yeats volume: 'To dear Paddy from Lord Jim'. In the same handwriting (but presumably later than 1930 because some of it is in red ballpoint) there are notes and corrections against a few of the poems. The 'corrections' seem to be from previous versions of the poems because the variant supplied by the writer is never an improvement on the printed version. It is always clumsier or more florid, the kind of thing that a careful writer would eliminate on mature consideration. Confirmation can be found in the table of contents, where against one poem, 'The Golden Age', Walter has written: 'originally "An Enchanted Garden".'

These annotations show that he remained interested in Stella and was not so 'shallow' as to be quite indifferent to her poetry. On the other hand, to give one's present fiancée a volume of poetry written by one's previous one shows a certain lack of sensitivity.

Ida finally left Herbert Marks in 1931 and went to live with Blair Hughes-Stanton. They lived first in Wales, then in the house at Stratford St Mary in Essex where I interviewed her. Herbert Marks took up with Isobel Powys on a permanent basis. It was a suitable match, considering that the Powys brothers were among Stella's targets in *Cold Comfort Farm*. J. C. Powys approved of Marks, saying in his letters that he was 'a very decent chap' and 'as leftist as anyone'. Marks had two children with Isobel, Stephen and Tamar. Mr Mybug had found his Rennet.

Within a month of being sacked from the *Standard* in 1930 Stella had a better job. 'As a result of kind endeavours on the part of older people who were interested in me,' she wrote in 'Genesis of a Novel', 'I went as editorial assistant to *The Lady*.'

The *Lady*, 'a magazine for gentlewomen', had been founded in 1885 as a society weekly which was also read by the aspiring middle classes. Since the First World War it had been struggling to adapt to changing social conditions, in particular to the increasing scarcity of domestic help, often referred to as 'the servant problem'. When Stella joined the staff in 1930 the magazine, then edited by Nora Heald, bore an aspect of genteel dowdiness. The fashion plates had a certain period charm but were not of the best. Photographs of recently engaged aristocrats in tweeds adorned its pages. Recipes (by Mrs C. S. Peel) were dull, sometimes nauseatingly so (Minced Cabbage with Scrambled Eggs, 'an ideal supper dish'). There were practical domestic articles (on, for example, 'Embroidered Luncheon Mats'), columns of advice, light articles and the occasional short story. In addition, it contained theatre and book reviews and pages of small advertisements for property and domestic staff.

In 'Genesis of a Novel' Stella wrote:

The Lady is, and always has been a gentle and civilised magazine. There, I had a *very* nice time. There were three of us on the editorial side; young women working under a wise and gay woman editor; K. [Kathleen Goddard], who had brown curls and was prettier and much more useful than Kafka's K. and, to my awed amazement, bought her clothes on a carefully planned budget; Elizabeth Coxhead, just down from Oxford and the future biographer of Lady Gregory; and myself. Between us, we covered the sub-editing, the new goods likely to interest ladies (there were ladies in those days) in the peaceful pleasant shops of the late 'twenties, and the cinema, while for me there was occasionally a play to criticise or a clutch of novels to review. It was one plum of a job.

When she became editorial assistant on the *Lady* Stella applied her versatility to writing every kind of article with the exception of cookery, the province of the egregious Mrs Peel. But in some administrative tasks she was less than able. There was one column called 'How to Live' which she describes fictionally in *Bassett* as 'a column entitled *The Helping Hand*':

Underneath this heading there were given details about partner-ships, described by a lady who signed herself 'Phoebe,' and who conducted this column from an obscure side-street in Holborn. She it was who put, by letter, untrained but willing spinsters in touch with energetic gentlewomen with some capital; and set them off on some glorious career of breeding chickens in St Ives or running an arts and crafts shop in Newcastle-on-Tyne. Nor did she ever hear (except sometimes indirectly and long years afterwards) whether the partnership had been a success, or whether the ladies had slit each other's throats within the first half hour of meeting. She sowed ruin and rapture among her readers, but herself remained (perhaps wisely) invisible and anonymous.

On more than one occasion, she told her sister-in-law Renée, Stella carelessly mixed up the letters and put the wrong people in touch with each other: prospective chicken farmers were receiving letters from handicraft enthusiasts, and vice versa.

In her capacity as drama critic she was usually sent to the less glamorous first nights, and turned in work that was no more than competent. One suspects that her heart was not in it, except perhaps when she was able to deliver a favourable verdict on a light opera (*The Piper* or *Tantivy Towers*) in which her new fiancé Allan was appearing. She told me that on more than one occasion she would write her copy on the basis of the first act alone and leave early. 'I was young and frivolous,' she said. She was also bright enough to get away with it.

Exhaustion at the end of a long day, rather than frivolity, was perhaps more often the cause of uninspired work. Renée remembers going with Stella to review an all-star production of *Julius Caesar* (Godfrey Tearle, Oscar Asche, Basil Gill, Baliol Holloway) at His Majesty's in 1931. To her indignation, Stella fell asleep during Tearle's 'Friends, Romans, countrymen. . . .' A note of pained astonishment still enters Renée's voice as she recalls it. Stella was worked hard at the *Lady*, she often had to attend four or five first nights a week, she was 'ghosting' articles for Lady Muriel Beckwith, and she was beginning to write *Cold Comfort Farm*.

It was on the book pages that Stella turned in excellent work and raised the tone of the magazine. Before her time reviews appeared under the banal heading 'Books to Read', and consisted of random notices of the week's publications. But Stella soon appropriated a whole page and produced a feature article, deftly linking two or three books with a single theme, or building a piece around a particularly important one. She told me that she took a special pride in this. From these pages emerges the authentic voice of Stella Gibbons, witty, provocative and extremely well informed.

Her first signed article in the *Lady* appeared on 23 October 1930: appropriately titled 'A Poet's Prose', it was concerned mainly with a new collection of Walter de la Mare's short stories. She brought a poet's sensibility to her criticism. On de la Mare's use of adjectives she wrote: 'He sets them in the frame of a sentence like jewels; and there they perform their proper task and shine. They are not made to do the work of all the other parts of speech, and to give colour and strength to a sentence as well.' But her enthusiasm for him as a writer did not blind her to the fact that this was an inferior collection of stories. In the same article she hailed the early work of a much less personally congenial writer, Dorothy Parker. On her collection of sketches and stories *Laments for the Living* she commented astutely: 'Miss Parker's talent (which will not develop its range, I prophesy) is perfect of its type.'

The majority of books Stella was given to read were second-rate, sometimes to the point of absurdity. Ironically, it was these which stimulated her to write *Cold Comfort Farm*. How little exaggeration its parody contains is brought out by her brief assessments of books like '*Gay Agony* by H. A. Manhood (Jonathan Cape 7/6). This is about a young man called Micah Born in a place called Thrust. There is someone else called Shaphan Ask and a girl called Drusilla Rue. What's in a name? A violent style and distorted grammar will make some people label this book a work of genius.' Or Soviet romances like Alexandra Kollontai's *Free Love* ('Passion had entangled her with Petia Raggulov of the Machinery Depot.') Or passages like this in Edward Charles's *Sand and the Blue Moss*, in which 'the influence of the late D. H. Lawrence is obvious': 'Go out, my lad – go out, my lad – turn your face to the sun and when it's brown and the girls can love you, love them all, and the sun be with you. They'll have children every one, and bless you and love you. They'll have children every one, and bless you and love you so long as you leave 'em alone in the sun – in the sun.' Stella added: 'We are only too willing to leave 'em alone.'

Sometimes more considerable writers were grist to her mill. In February 1931 she reviewed J. C. Powys's *In Defence of Sensuality*:

> Mr Cowper Powys proposes a remedy for the unhappiness that torments the human race. We are to run away from modern life 'that turns our human life into a galvanised ant heap' by 'stepping sideways out of the human-consciousness groove into the backward-consciousness of animal-vegetable life, and into the forward consciousness of unrealised godlike life. . . .'
>
> The glaring flaw in the book is our old friend the Pathetic Fallacy; that is, the endowment of animals, trees and rocks with human attributes. No man can know how a viper feels, or a beetroot, or a quartz crystal. They have their worlds and we have ours; and when this has been said, there is no more to be said.

She added: 'D. H. Lawrence found our age so unbearable that he told the human race to run back into the savage night of sex-worship; to become natural as animals. But it is too late.' It was the ideas of Lawrence and Powys which were the most serious targets of Stella's satire in *Cold Comfort Farm*. In their backward-looking neo-primitivism, there was much that connected them to fascist ideas. Bertrand Russell once said that Lawrence's beliefs 'led straight to Auschwitz'.

Many of Stella's views on the novel emerged in an article entitled 'Do Women Write Novels?' (On the opposite page Mrs Peel had a full-page article on 'How to Fry Potatoes'.) Her answer to the question she had posed herself was ambiguous.

> The brutal fact is that anyone who has been educated and has read much can write a good novel. I could. You could. In fact we both do. But the other brutal fact is still true as well; novelists like poets are born not made. And it is still doubtful that many more true novelists among women were born twenty-five years ago than were born fifty years ago. A sex does not change its mental characteristics in two generations.

She noted that women had 'just been made free of all avenues of experience', and yet their outlook is all too often morbid and unadventurous ('Oh how miserable they are!'). Rosamond Lehmann, for example, she characterised as belonging to the '*What are we here for?* school'.

> How the heart sinks as one reads the opening lines of *A Note In Music*:
> 'She was dressing for dinner. Next door she heard Tom splashing in his bath and singing over and over again the refrain of one of his three tunes.'
> Coarse brute! And for 318 pages just nothing happens at all, except that we meet a number of miserable people who are all utterly true to life. Well, who wants them to be true when such a life as theirs is without vitality or beauty? Only genius, like that of the late D. H. Lawrence, can reverently set them alight with the mystery belonging to all living creatures. Good novelists are too earnest; they cannot.

The '*What are we here for?* school' is still with us.

The point she was making in this and other articles was that if we are going to be cast into the depths of gloom by a work of art, it had better be a great one. Minor artists are there to divert us, to cheer us up – for what in a great writer can look like a brave stare into the cosmic void may seem like whining self-pity in a lesser one.

Her view of contemporary women novelists was uncompromising. While she could welcome the rising talent of a new writer like Elizabeth Jenkins (later a friend), she could be hard on more established figures. Of Rose Macaulay she wrote that 'her range is miniature and her outlook virginal' and 'her mind seems to lack both a kind of simplicity, and a spider sensitive subtlety. One of these two qualities is needed for the writing of novels; they are found perfectly expressed in the work of Tolstoy and of Proust. This of course is to make a comparison with male giants; so let us say George Eliot and Virginia Woolf. (Women *can* do it, you see, when they are born novelists.)'

Elsewhere she was more severe on Virginia Woolf. In her review of *The Waves* she wrote:

> . . . a drop of grease on a soiled restaurant table has as much significance for her as the fall of an empire or a woman's dead body. This keeps her work at one pitch of intensity which is exhausting and blurs the clarity of her discoveries. Her work is curiously generalised; she writes 'a woman', 'a girl', 'an old man sitting in the sun' . . . as though she saw everything from the window of a railway train rushing through the country at fifty miles an hour.

Stella's conclusion to 'Do Women Write Novels?' ran: 'Adolescent is the word for the woman writer of good novels. She must mature before this century begins to produce more born novelists who are also, and incidentally, women.'

Male writers fared no better, particularly when Stella felt that they had been too highly regarded. In reviewing *Judith Paris*, one of Hugh Walpole's Herries Chronicles, she wrote: 'We have found that readers are either enthusiastically Mr Walpole's slaves, or else they are curiously impatient with his work; and we must confess to being in the second category.' Walpole became 'My Dear Tony' of the dedicatory letter in *Cold Comfort Farm*, which is surely modelled on the absurdly pompous 'prefatory letter' in *Judith Paris* to J. B. Priestley ('My Dear Jack').

Walpole, who was abnormally sensitive to criticism even for a writer, was fortunate not to see this notice. He had written in his diary of the *Judith Paris* reviews that they were 'all splendid. Not one unfavourable one.' He was fortunate too not to have realised that he was Pookworthy in *Cold Comfort Farm*. When *Cakes and Ale* came out in 1930 he recognised Somerset Maugham's caricature of him as Alroy Kear and was deeply hurt by it.

Another inflated reputation to be punctured by Stella with even greater savagery was that of Charles Morgan, whose *The Fountain* she found offensive as well as wearisome. Morgan too was to find his way into one of her books, as the appalling Gerard Challis in *Westwood* (1946). Time has confirmed Stella's verdict on both Morgan and Walpole.

Her reviews also reveal who were her literary heroes and heroines. Proust is often mentioned, though very much as if she admired him despite a certain temperamental aversion. Reviewing a novel by Sylvia Thomson, she wrote: 'The assumption that everyone in the book has a right to be poetically disgruntled makes it depressing. . . . When people are comfortably off, and can dine at smart restaurants, visit Paris and live in a pleasant country house, it is only a genius like Marcel Proust who can make their discontents moving.' He remained her ideal of fine writing to the end of her life. She had an early edition of the C. K. Scott Moncrieff translation on her shelves and reread it regularly. Her early acquaintance with Proust may have come about on the recommendation of J. C. Squire, a promoter of Moncrieff whose minor Georgian verse was published in the *London Mercury*.

Though Stella tried to emulate Proust's capacity to be both detached and emotionally sensitive, he seems to have had little stylistic influence on her work. Writers of talent rarely try to imitate the superficial characteristics of the writers they most admire; they are more likely to be directly inspired by lesser writers in whom there is something unfulfilled which can be brought to fruition.

Stella's capacity for cool, elegant prose, for example at the beginning of *Cold Comfort Farm*, has an obvious antecedent in Jane Austen. The depth of her identification with Austen can be gauged from her review in the *Lady* of a biography of the novelist:

> Whenever a reader thinks of those passionate, suffering creatures, Emily Brontë, Emily Dickinson, Christina Rossetti, and wonders, a little despondently perhaps, whether happiness must be sacrificed by women artists to produce good work, this same reader can open her *Persuasion* with a contented little sigh, remembering that at least one woman artist, and one of the most exquisite, enjoyed life, flirted, and dearly loved her sister.

Persuasion evidently meant most to Stella of all Austen's books. In *Cold Comfort Farm* Flora says that when she is fifty-three she would like 'to write a novel as good as *Persuasion*'. It is curious, though, that she should single it out to contrast with the world of Emily Brontë et al, because, despite its blissful ending, it is perhaps the darkest of Austen's six major works. It would be natural, however, that Anne Elliot's happiness won in the face of a mean and oppressive father would have a personal significance and satisfaction for Stella. Happiness, of a serene, unruffled, domesticated kind, was the lodestar of Stella's life, and it pleased her to imagine that Austen had found it. 'Jane Austen solved the problem of happiness rather than conquered it by her pleasure in the small, pleasant things of life. . . . The delighted acceptance of man's foibles, a type of impish intellectual revelling in detail, combined with a calm acceptance of beauty made Jane Austen a happier woman.'

But she could never entirely identify with Jane Austen. The poet in Stella, mystical, deeply entranced by the world of nature, was more akin to Christina Rossetti, a far less placid figure. Jane Austen, she noted in the same essay, 'had no sense of wonder'. In her introduction to a 1957 American edition of *Sense and Sensibility* Stella wrote of Austen being 'an almost excessively detached novelist. . . . There is no poetry in her writing, nor any mystery beyond that of plot, nor is there any religious feeling; there are no gulfs and no heights.' When, in her early *Evening Standard* story 'Lost Children This Way', Stella said of her writer heroine that 'critics were beginning to speak of her as a second, more poetic Jane Austen', she was describing her own aspirations.

There was, as it were, an Elfine as well as a Flora Poste side to Stella Gibbons – Sensibility as well as Sense – which is what gives *Cold Comfort Farm* its exquisite comic balance. The Flora in her mocks Elfine; but there are also significant moments in the novel when the Elfine in her mocks Flora Poste.

If *Cold Comfort Farm* belongs to any genre, it is to the 'fantastic satirical' novel of the twenties and thirties. Novels such as David Garnett's *Lady into Fox* and *A Man in the Zoo*, and Sylvia Townsend Warner's *Lolly Willowes*, have all survived rather better than more reputable mainstream novels, and are appreciated for their quirkish observations of society. It is interesting that Stella favourably reviews John Collier's *His Monkey Wife*, another entertaining example of the genre – now, along with Sandy Wilson's delightful musical of the same name, scarcely remembered. All these novels pitch an outlandish character – a chimpanzee who is almost human, a woman who turns into a fox, a witch – against society. There is a similar contrast in *Cold Comfort Farm* between the farouche, almost bestial Starkadders and various representatives of society, county, bohemian and genteel. In *Cold Comfort Farm* these encounters are touched with a vein of fantasy; but most of Stella's later novels are also based upon the collision between representatives of mutually uncomprehending strata of society.

Stella had begun to write *Cold Comfort Farm* not long after moving from the *Standard* to the *Lady*. 'One day,' she wrote in 'Genesis of a Novel',

> I scrabbled about at home until I found four little sheets of writing paper in a box or somewhere and wrote something about Flora Poste's birth and education.
>
> But I was not satisfied with what I had written. It was mannered, and affected, modelled on a style which I vaguely supposed to be a pastiche of an 'eighteenth century' one. I was trying to write, instead of writing.
>
> So tearing up the four little sheets, which I yet remember with affection, I started again – carelessly, this time. . . .
>
> The book seemed to write itself. That is true. It dashed itself onto paper; sometimes on the backs of some of those envelopes which have played their part in many writers' lives; sometimes

on office paper, in office time, in a dark little den at the back of
The Lady premises, to which I had been gently relegated because
I made the other two in the main office laugh so much that we
couldn't work; sometimes while I was on my way to work or
coming home in the Underground; in those days there were quite
often men sitting down who offered a girl a seat. (There was also
room for them to get up and offer it.) Thus protected, I wrote;
using a little suitcase or the back of my library book as a desk,
and often laughing to myself.

She would often go out with her friends from the *Lady*, Kathleen
Goddard and Elizabeth Coxhead.

We used to go to Honeydew, a café vanished with our youth,
and lunch there, while I read the latest bit of *Cold Comfort Farm*
aloud to the other two.
   We used to stuff our round young faces with hot dogs, newly
sprung upon London by the Canadian proprietor, and choke
with laughter. I suppose the other customers must have noticed
us; the proprietor certainly did, because he used to hover round
our table in a state, and more than once asked us to please *go*,
as other people were waiting for our seats. . . . I used to get
back from lunch drunk on orange juice and my power to make
people laugh.

Elizabeth Coxhead, later a distinguished novelist and biographer,
and a lifelong friend of Stella's, was to have a small but significant
effect on the novel. In 1975, when my father was compiling Stella's
obituary for the *Times*, she wrote to him in answer to a query about
the title of *Cold Comfort Farm*:

It was on the first day of my first job, as secretary to Nora
Heald at *The Lady*, in January of 1931. I was replacing Stella
who moved up to chief (only) reporter, and who had neglected
her duties disgracefully because she was writing her masterpiece
in the little room at the end of the passage. To make amends for
the vast pile of MSS I had to return to their authors she took
me out to lunch, and began with what was then her favourite
gambit: 'Let's have a long, cosy chat all about me. I am a genius.

I am writing a book which is to be a take-off of all the grim farm novels. It is to be called Curse God Farm.'

At which point I, even in those days the little interferer, said: 'I don't think that's a very good name, why don't you call it Cold Comfort?' She stared at me and said, 'Where did you get that marvellous name?' and I said, 'Well, my father is Headmaster of a very old country Grammar School in the Midlands (Hinckley) which has property left to it in Puritan days, and C. C. F. is one of its farms, and deserves its name because tenant after tenant has gone bankrupt and had to emigrate to Canada.' And she said, 'Nature always goes one better than art – do you think the present tenants would mind if I took the name?' And I said, 'You may be quite certain they'll never read the book,' and so she did.

Cold Comfort Farm was an inspired choice, of course, but Curse God Farm is more in keeping with its Gibbons roots. Coxhead continued:

I can't pretend to have influenced the masterpiece in any other way, but I did have enormous fun hearing her read aloud each day the bit she'd composed the night before, and laughing myself sick, and then seeing her 'awake one morning and find herself famous,' the Fémina-Vie Heureuse Prize and all the rest. And of course I fondly imagined that one day the same thing would happen to me – little realising that such a success is a once-in-a-million affair.

A rather charming sequel, which delighted [the actor] Kenneth Williams when I wrote to congratulate him on his remarkable reading [on BBC radio], was that some years afterwards the Hinckley Times . . . had an item about the then tenant of C. C. F. being fined 7s.6d. for riding his bicycle without lights. I cut it out and sent it to Stella, who wrote back how strange it seemed to her to see the name in print and know it wasn't hers.

A further sequel appeared in the correspondence columns of the Times on 22 December 1989, shortly after Stella's death. A Mr J. K. Waterlow wrote from Hinckley: 'The late Stella Gibbons's Cold Comfort Farm is in our locality and is now

Comfort Farm, a "greenhouse effect", no doubt.' The change of name is understandable, but it is to be hoped that some future owner who knows of the farm's honourable literary pedigree will restore its Cold.

On 16 March 1931 Grandfather Gibbons died from coronary thrombosis at his daughter Louise's house. The previous day he had finished rereading Sir James Jeans's *The Universe Around Us* which, he had told his daughter, was 'one of the most wonderful books he had ever read'. His copy was eventually passed on to Stella and there are pencil annotations in the hands of both grandfather and granddaughter, separated by almost fifty years. Both were advanced in years when they read the book; both had a passion for cosmology. The one was an atheist, the other by 1981 a devout believer, but the sense of wonder was identical.

CHAPTER 4

Courtship and
Cold Comfort Farm

On 24 May 1929 a young man of twenty-two recorded in his diary that he went down for the weekend to Tunbridge Wells to stay with his cousins. The next day he wrote: 'Played tennis again. Met two girls who are on the staff of *The Evening Standard* (by far the best evening paper), Marjorie Scott-Johnston and Stella Gibbons. I was most attracted by Stella Gibbons. She had just interviewed Epstein, the famous sculptor.' The following day the three of them travelled back together to London by train. 'The third-class carriages were impossible, so we got into first-class carriages and even they were uncomfortably full. Stella was working at a poem.' By the time they reached Charing Cross he had arranged for all three of them to go to the theatre. 'M S-J then went off by bus and Stella and I went part of the way together by tube.'

The poem she was writing was very possibly 'The First Nightingale' which in her collection *The Mountain Beast* has 'Ecault 19th May 1929' below it. It describes how, alone on holiday 'in a green pine-grown vale', she had heard a nightingale for the first time in her life:

> Breaking with frenzied crying the calm light
> Thrown by a young spring moon into the night!

The next day the young man wrote to Stella and read her interview with Epstein in the *Standard* which concerned some mild controversy stirred up by the appearance of Epstein's *Night* outside St James's Park tube station. The newspaper had first canvassed the opinions of two 'members of the public', and got satisfactory responses. '"That's what I call downright crude. Just like a schoolboy's first attempt," said a postman. "I think it's hideous. It's not my idea of beauty," said a policeman.'

Stella's interview with Epstein is skilfully self-effacing, but the figure cut by the sculptor is not entirely sympathetic:

I reminded him that *Night* is in a prominent position in a busy London street on a public building and therefore more likely to be seen by many thousands of ordinary people than most works of art. Mr Epstein says: 'Nature does not appear to the artist as he does to the ordinary non-creative man. In all beauty there is an element of strangeness and unfamiliarity which ordinary, non-creative people find alarming.'

'Few people would care to have an Egyptian statue in the house.'

'Non-creative people have muddled ideas about what is beautiful. Millions of them have confused their own senti-mental personal human ideas with the abstract idea of beauty. Unfamiliar beauty frightens them.'

Stella, who tended to side with the views of the ordinary 'non-creative' person, must have found his attitude unpleasantly arrogant. Nevertheless she admired his work, whose Egyptian echoes appealed to her: 'I remarked that this figure of *Night* seemed beautifully calm. . . . I quoted from *Macbeth* "Sleep that knits up the ravelled sleeve of care", and he agreed that this also applied to *Night*.' The sculpture was tarred and feathered not long afterwards. Nowadays it attracts little attention, favourable or otherwise, but it remains an impressive piece of work.

The day after the interview appeared Stella wrote back to her new friend, and on 29 May the following entry was made in his diary:

Mrs Stopford Green, widow of the historian J. R. Green, and herself an historical and political writer, has died at the age of 84.

Took Stella Gibbons and Marjorie Scott-Johnston to dinner in Soho and afterwards to *The Sacred Flame*. Marjorie is a charming girl and most intelligent and with that I dismiss her.

> Stella was lovely. Her eyes and her smile and her personality
> have made me her slave. If only I were less inadequate!

There followed a rather banal criticism of Maugham's play before
the entry concluded with: 'I am falling in love with Stella.' Four
years later they were to marry.

The inadequate young man of twenty-two was a student at the
Webber-Douglas School of Singing – then more of an academy
for opera singers than a drama school – and his name was Allan
Charles Webb. There is no doubt that he did feel inadequate – his
words were no ritual gesture of humility in the face of beauty. He
had often felt so, but with little apparent reason. Allan had been
born into a loving and united family; he was not unintelligent; he
had a talent for singing and acting; he played a decent game of
cricket; he was six foot tall and strikingly good-looking. Throughout his diary, however, he exhibited self-doubt and a sometimes
shaky sense of his own identity. The opening of the entry for 29
May, with its reference to the death of a comparatively obscure
public figure with whom he had no connection whatsoever, is
entirely typical.

The diary itself has been carefully edited and copied out from
now destroyed volumes by Allan himself and it ends – neatly on the
final page of the single hard-backed exercise book – with the con-
cluding words of that entry for 29 May: 'I am falling in love with
Stella.' The text is littered with the deaths of notables, sporting stat-
istics and the like. Some of Allan's books also contain similar annotations on the fly leaves. For example, his copy of Allardyce Nicoll's
An Introduction to Dramatic Theory not only contains pictures of
himself cut from the theatrical directory *Spotlight* pasted into the
inside cover, but a long hand-written list of names, beginning with
Ellen Terry and ending with Julie Andrews, under the heading: 'A
selection of some of the greatest or most famous actors, actresses
and singers, dancers and comedians I have seen on the stage.' It is
as if he feels that association with well-known people and events
can somehow bolster a distinctly shaky sense of self-worth.

Some of his more introspective diary entries confirm this. On
16 May of the same year he wrote:

> I wonder whether I shall ever be successful at anything. I can

write, yet somehow nothing is written. I can act, yet I am awkward and seemingly uninspired. There seems to be a powerful inner me, and a dull, unattractive and incompetent outer me, and there is no bridge between. There is the fire, imagination and understanding for love, ambition and adventure; but the perseverance and stamina, which would bridge the gulf and pour forth my armies on the world, are lacking. The dormant me might be extinct for all it would ever achieve. Will it ever shoot forth its flames? One glorious eruption would satisfy me!

Other entries show glimpses of some decidedly odd thought processes: for example, on 24 August 1927 he had written: 'My imagination must be controlled, for MY world is becoming more real to me than the world in which the Canadian Government has just announced the death of 1655 sea-lions by machine-gun fire!'

Allan's family was, in terms of the time, socially more respectable than Stella's, but not much better off. He was the son of a clergyman, the Rev. Charles J. B. Webb, and was named after his paternal grandfather, the Rev. Allan Becher Webb. Allan Becher Webb had been a remarkable man: appointed Bishop of Bloemfontein in South Africa in 1870 at the age of thirty-one, he was later Bishop of Grahamstown and ended his days back in England as Dean of Salisbury, where there is a memorial window to him in the cathedral's north-east transept. Like many great and energetic figures, he cast a shadow of guilt and inadequacy over succeeding and less impressive generations.

Allan was brought up in a succession of country vicarages, in straitened but not wholly impoverished circumstances. His father was a man of frustrated ambitions. Like Allan he was a fine cricketer – he had played for Middlesex – and had a talent for acting. This was his passion, but he was persuaded by his formidable mother that the stage was no occupation for the son of a bishop. After he had failed at his first chosen profession, schoolmastering, his mother offered him a financial inducement to take holy orders. Being weak and lacking in confidence, he chose the respectability and safety of the Church rather than the risk and raffishness of the theatre. But he was never entirely happy as a clergyman: hence his restless moves from parish to parish, and his early retirement. He satisfied his love of acting with amateur theatricals in which his wife Jessie, his son Allan and daughter Renée were also involved. Jessie, also from a clerical family, was a more robust character than her husband. She was a gifted amateur painter and musician and a close friend of the feminist Cecily Hamilton, who wrote the words to the composer Ethel Smyth's *The March of the Women*. Family letters show Charles and Jessie's relationship to have been deep and lasting.

Allan had inherited many of his father's talents, but also his crippling lack of confidence and fear of responsibility. His diary is mainly that of an ordinary educated young man of the time: full of cricket scores, books read and, above all, films seen. He was an avid filmgoer all his life, an enthusiasm Stella shared to some extent. The occasional revealing entry surfaces in the record of his schooldays at Radley, such as: 'All through the term I had periodical attacks of nerves, lasting for several days, during which I could do nothing.' Stella told me that some kind of crisis occurred at school which prevented Allan from taking, as he saw it, his rightful place in the first eleven at cricket. This had deeply affected him, she said, and she could never quite understand why. His daughter told me that he hated school because he was badly bullied. He vividly recalled to her many years later having his head banged against desks and being made to drink ink. His nature, openly affectionate, sensitive and vulnerable, was one least likely to flourish in an early twentieth-century British public school. In addition, his obvious good looks may have caused trouble. In some ways girls of the same class had a better deal: his sister Renée was able to insist on being educated mostly at home by a succession of governesses, an option not open to young gentlemen.

From Radley Allan went on to Worcester College, Oxford. He was there at the time of the General Strike in 1926 and, like many undergraduates at the time, he went up to London to do his bit for the establishment. In spite of being under twenty, and therefore not old enough for the office, he enrolled as a Special Constable. An exciting if unreflective account of events ends with the words: 'I am sorry it is over, it was quite good fun.' But he has the grace to add in parentheses: 'I am afraid Youth is entirely selfish on these occasions!' This attitude of boyish adventure towards the Strike was shared by many of Allan's class and generation, and by many such as J. C. Squire who were older than him and had more experience of the world.

While at Oxford Allan published at his own expense some poems in pamphlet form under the title *Night Clouds.* They are a fairly typical example of undergraduate verse of that period and reveal a moody, introspective young man much preoccupied with dreams and death.

In his last year at university, 1928, Allan had fallen in love, violently and almost at sight, with his sister Renée's French governess (also called Renée). This affair was broken off by his parents with much anguish on all sides. His sister Renée's diaries reveal that their mother was the main agent of dissolution, having somehow discovered that the governess had another attachment. The unpleasantness of the situation was aggravated by the disapproval of interfering relatives, in particular Allan's Uncle Cyprian (Charles Webb's elder brother), who wrote the family long letters of rambling admonishment. Uncle Cyprian loomed large in Webb family affairs, being rich, well-connected and childless.

On leaving Oxford, with a moderate degree and no ideas about what to do beyond vaguely artistic aspirations, Allan opted, like so many in his situation, for teaching at a preparatory school. Family connections secured him a post at Winton House, Winchester; by the end of his first week there he had bolted. No explanation is given for this action. He wrote in his diary:

I was mad with worry and lack of sleep. I must have been half crazy, I acted quite incredibly. At the end of the day's work I went out, just as I was, without hat or coat, and said I was going out to get a breath of fresh air. I walked along the Andover Road (about 5.30 p.m. on September 25th.) I struck off across country. Came out into another road. I was then thoroughly unbalanced and just went on walking. I walked on; the roads were lonely; it got dark; I was out on the plains. I bought some chocolate in Stockbridge which I ate as I went along. It was bitterly cold. I had almost stopped thinking. Altogether I walked for about ten hours. How much can one think in ten minutes! But in ten hours! Yet I can remember practically nothing. Alone and walking in the dark, on and on. Once I lay flat on my back in the middle of the road. For several hours now I had been utterly exhausted, and yet I walked on. I came to some cross-roads, four miles or so from Amesbury. Those four miles seemed like forty. Perhaps

I had read wrong. I staggered on. Lights to the right. Darkness ahead. Should I turn off? It would be safer to go on. Miles and miles, and then what appeared to be a deserted country village. No sound. I tried to make myself heard. It was about 3.30 a.m. on September the 26th. At last I got someone to direct me to the Police Station. The Superintendent was very kind. He told me I must have walked about 30 miles. He found a lodging for me. Later in the morning he rang up home and also Winchester. My mother and father fetched me in the car. I went to bed and slept. The next day I saw the doctor. He said I must have a rest and give up Winton House. The following day I got up. I shall start on my novel.

In her diary his sister Renée, then thirteen years old, attributed the breakdown to his disappointed love for the French governess. ('What a rotten sought [*sic*] of little thing love is when considered from a practical point of view,' she wrote on the day Allan returned from Winton House.) Her analysis may have been correct, because in February 1929 her diary revealed that the affair had continued clandestinely and they had once more become engaged. His parents – in particular his mother – saw to it that the relationship was again broken off, permanently this time. In April of that year his sister noted in her diary that Allan 'seems to have forgotten' her.

The novel referred to by Allan in his diary was never published and is now lost. It was called *Incompetence Writes*, an unpromising title. In January 1929 he enrolled at Kensington College to study book-keeping and shorthand. Entries in his diary for that period are almost entirely a record of plays and films seen. With great excitement he recorded going to his first 'talkie' (*Interference* with Clive Brook and William Powell) and remarked solemnly: 'The talking film certainly has possibilities.' Stella may have been gently mocking his passion for the cinema in the talkie-obsessed character of Seth in *Cold Comfort Farm*.

Allan was still uncertain about the profession he should adopt, but Jessie decided that, with his natural advantages, he should fulfil both her husband's, and to a certain extent her own, frustrated ambitions and go on the stage. By the end of February she had persuaded Allan to take singing lessons to develop his pleasing baritone voice. In April he was accepted as a student at the Webber-Douglas, and in May he met Stella.

The physical attraction was mutual. Years later Stella referred in a letter to Allan's 'beautiful broad shoulders' which her grandson had inherited. In addition each clearly found in the other a refuge from the harshness of life and from unsatisfactory love affairs in the not too distant past. Allan saw in Stella the mature, confident, talented individual which he aspired to be; while Stella rejoiced in the warm, comparatively stable family background which Allan enjoyed. In *Cold Comfort Farm* the hero who marries Flora Poste is modelled on Allan, but he is a clergyman called Charles, like Allan's father. The hero Charles's surname, Fairford, derives from the village not far from Kempsford in Gloucestershire where Allan's father was vicar. The church at Fairford, famous for its stained glass, was the subject of a wartime poem, the last in Stella's volume of *Collected Poems*.

It was through Allan that Stella eventually found the faith which sustained her when he died in 1959. The world they shared was one above all of the imagination: some would describe their attitude as escapist, others as merely unworldly. Both descriptions have their validity.

The relationship developed quickly, and already in the late summer of 1929 Allan was taking Stella down to visit his parents at Kempsford. The first photograph of them together is at the ruins of the nearby Roman Villa at Chedworth. In September Allan wrote to his father:

> About the girls! I have no wish to become entangled, and there is no danger so long as I have someone young and intelligent and attractive like Stella to talk to and go about with occasionally. I do hope you aren't nervous about *her*!
>
> She is entirely engrossed in her work, and I *know* she has not the smallest intention of getting married to anybody. She has a very great number of friends of all ages and sexes, and she goes about with them and stays with them in a way which a past generation would call highly compromising! She is very fond of her younger brother and has every intention of keeping house for him until he marries.
>
> It is very good for me to have a well-balanced and interesting friend of whom I can be very fond without any unfortunate messes and scenes.

Both of us are content and happy to keep the friendship within water-tight limits, and are both quite determined that nothing in the way of an entanglement shall interfere with either of our careers.

Please read or report all this to mother.

I am rather worried about your worrying about me, and I don't want to have any worries of that kind!

Please set my mind at rest. Surely you can see that a friendship with a sensible person like Stella is about the most excellent thing I could have, and that it reduces the dangers of sex and entanglements to a minimum or to all intents and purposes to nil.

Though the letter is less than honest about his feelings towards Stella, it is probably true that she was not contemplating marriage at that time. The break-up with Walter Beck had affected her deeply, and long afterwards she told her daughter Laura that she found it difficult to trust any man for some years after it.

Allan's ambitions to be a writer were never fulfilled, except perhaps vicariously through Stella, though he did publish some more poetry. A sequence of poems printed in pamphlet form by the National Poetry Circle in 1931 survives. It is entitled *Far and Deep: A Dream Life*, and in its rhythms and use of language it bears a striking resemblance to Stella's verse. On 9 February that year he wrote to his parents:

I am sending you my farewell literary effort! A present (50 copies for £1.9.0) to myself to mark the beginning of my theatrical career, and a tombstone to mark the end of that period of one's life when all is hope and one's only happiness dreams!

Now that all the excitements, joys and disasters (probably) and happy ups and downs (certainly) have begun I can bury the old life of dreams. But I could not help erecting a small monument on the grave, and I send it to you who have had most to do with me during the most tiresome and least interesting time of my life.

The best that can be said for *Far and Deep: A Dream Life* is that it is not embarrassing. One passage, however, provides an insight into the intense and rather inward-looking nature of his relationship with Stella:

> At last we are out of the world,
> You and I, here in the dark,
> With the fear and the worry behind.
> Treading the pavement of love,
> Beneath canopied tenderness, we
> Are secure from the future and past.
> All present, and the present is joy,
> Peace infinite, infinite joy,
> And forgetfulness wrapping us round. . . .

I once mentioned *Far and Deep* to Stella. She professed no recollection of it and did not seem interested in discussing it. On the inside cover of one copy Allan had written: 'Yours Stella, my darling wife, because you changed the gloomy writer of this poem into the happy Allan I now am.'

In another copy of *Far and Deep* he had added in manuscript:

> Cold of a moor wind,
> Shiver of shaken trees,
> Heat of a lion's breath,
> Swiftness of bumble bees,
> Leap of a salmon,
> Voice of a turtle dove,
> Thrust of a serpent,
> Range of the sky above –
> Yes, I'm in love.

On 6 March 1931 Allan wrote to his parents again:

I don't intend to marry for at least two years (when I am 26), but I am afraid that I must break the news to you that for some months I have been quite decided that when I do I am going to marry Stella.

I hope this won't be a terrible shock to you; but I am afraid you will be rather upset, as I know you think I am too young to come to an understanding with anyone, and if I did you would rather it was someone else than Stella.

However there it is. This time anyway it is deep 'respect and admiration' (which you say is the proper basis!) as well as romantic attraction – and of a year's standing and intimacy, and acquaintance with her friends (some of them – the acquaintances – awful, but her real friends people that one likes and respects the more one sees them).

Perhaps the thing that will hurt you most is that I have not owned to it before. You have every right to be hurt and angry. But my excuse is that I felt that at the early stages you would feel it was for my good to dissuade me. My mind was made up, and I was not going to allow a series of painful scenes to interfere with our (yours and mine) happiness and work.

The time before [referring to the affair with his sister's French governess] there was no particular respect and no long standing intimacy, only very young though rather violent romance. You were quite right and I am a damned nuisance. Even now you may feel you ought to try and dissuade me. I do beg of you not to. It is not an affair that argument could change. It would only make all of us desperately unhappy. And you can surely see that a happy, sensible background is far better for my work than the continually disturbed and depressed state of mind I had from the time I went to Radley until I got to know Stella properly. . . .

I should of course keep the engagement entirely secret from the relations who would write reams if they knew or who would be fussed and interfering – lovable though they are in their own spheres!

I am afraid I am a secret and independent person, perhaps also selfish and conceited, as regards wishing to settle my life entirely myself. So please try not to be hurt and remember I do love you very, very much.

V.M.L.

Allan

The Count in Figaro is getting on very well.

Almaviva in *The Marriage of Figaro* was to be Allan's most acclaimed stage role. He sang it in a number of productions, notably in the famous 1946 Sadlers Wells season which included the first production of Benjamin Britten's *Peter Grimes*.

As Allan had expected, the announcement of his engagement to Stella was not received with great joy. His father was easy-going, but Jessie was an altogether more severe character. Despite her friendship with the feminist campaigner Cecily Hamilton, she remained a Victorian at heart. (Renée's diary notes that in 1935 her mother was still capable of being shocked on hearing that a prominent actor and actress were 'living together'.) It was not the age difference between Allan and Stella to which she objected – she herself was four years older than her husband – so much as Stella's position. Her son's fiancée was a mature, sophisticated woman with a career while he was just beginning in one of the most insecure of professions, one that Jessie's own husband had funked. Such a discrepancy might further injure the fragile confidence of a man like Allan. Moreover Stella was, as the Victorians would say, 'a woman with a past'.

There was also a difference in class, slight perhaps by modern standards but significant for the time. Stella's father and grandfather had belonged to the professional classes, but could not claim descent from the landed gentry. Allan's parents were conventional enough to think that this mattered. Their relations, particularly Allan's deeply snobbish Uncle Cyprian, a wealthy, childless lawyer married to a brainless Scottish aristocrat, would have minded even more. And whenever a family crisis occurred Uncle Cyprian had a habit of writing ponderous, disapproving letters which, though ridiculed in secret, were also dreaded.

One of the few benefits which Stella's upbringing had conferred on her was an absence of class feelings, either of superiority or inferiority. Her father had moved freely and without condescension among his working-class patients: he preferred them as his drinking and card-playing companions, or for closer liaisons. His three children had inherited this open, conventionless approach to their fellow human beings. In consequence Lewis, and Gerald particularly, made a bad impression on the more privileged, and therefore hidebound, Webbs. The entry in Renée's diary for 23 January 1932 reads:

> This afternoon Stella brought her brothers Gerald and Lewis to tea. Gerald has a good nose, blue eyes and a dimple in his chin. He is unfortunately rather fat and has cultivated a little moustache which gives him a faux air of my military cousin Alexander Bennett, and is rather unmagnetic. Like Stella he is

more attractive when talking or laughing. Lewis is very plain but nice – they are both nice, I like them and hope to see more of them; though I doubt if I shall as Mother and Daddy think them not in the least like gentlemen and when I murmured something about Uncle Cyprian meeting them, Mother exclaimed, 'Heaven forbid that they should ever meet!' It seems a pity that – but I will say no more.

The phrase 'not . . . like gentlemen' is significant. The Webb parents were prepared to concede that Gerald and Lewis were technically gentlemen because their father was a doctor and they had been to minor public schools, but their manner had put them beyond the pale.

Allan, as he himself admitted, had an impulsiveness in love which had caused trouble before, and his parents felt that he was still not old or mature enough to marry. But perhaps a greater obstacle to the marriage in his parents' eyes was that Stella at that time was neither a regular churchgoer nor even a conventional Christian believer. Charles and Jessie were deeply involved with the Church of England – he after all, was a clergyman, and both were the offspring of clergy. Their faith had deep atavistic, if not spiritual, roots. Stella, with her career in journalism and her 'fast' artistic friends, came from a very different world. In an undated letter to his parents – probably just before or after the announcement of his engagement – Allan tried to allay their fears: 'I will go to Church with you during the week you are up [in London], or during Holy Week by myself if you are not up then! But it's not poor Stella's fault that I am not a regular churchgoer!'

There was also the problem of money. When Stella and he became engaged Allan had just begun his professional career with a job in the chorus of *Tantivy Towers*, which transferred successfully to the New (now the Albery) Theatre from the Lyric, Hammersmith. He had taken the stage name of Allan Bourne Webb to distinguish him from one Alan Webb who was already a highly regarded West End actor. Allan's modest wage was augmented by a very small private income. The combined amount would not have been sufficient for both of them to live on comfortably, and did not compare with Stella's salary of nine guineas and upwards per week. The idea of Stella being the principal breadwinner was not thought to be quite proper, and journalism ranked, if anything, somewhat below the stage as a profession. When Allan took Stella to dinner at Uncle Cyprian's, his wife Rachel asked Stella if her editor would release her from her journalistic obligations in the evening if she had been asked to attend a social function. When Stella said no, Rachel expressed both surprise and disapproval. Aunt Rachel's life had belonged entirely to the aristocratic cycle of house parties and London seasons, and her mind could comprehend very little beyond it. Allan used to say that he and Stella were the lowest on the social scale that Cyprian and his wife ever met.

On 16 March 1931, ten days after Allan had announced their engagement to his parents, Stella wrote to her future mother-in-law, Jessie Webb. The letter was in her usual neat, evenly spaced handwriting, though even neater and more evenly spaced than usual, and was written from her flat at 54 Fitzjohn's Avenue, Hampstead. Although its tone might suggest to modern readers that Allan was already living with Stella, this was not the case.

Dear Mrs Webb,

Thank you very much for your letter. This one is very difficult to write, as I am sure you will realise, as I do so want to tell you that we are very happy, and that I will always love Allan and try to look after him and make him happy.

I should very much like to see you soon; perhaps if you could have me, I could come down to Kempsford, as you suggest, and then we could discuss some of the things which are difficult to write, and look all stiff and formal on paper.

I do think, even putting the case quite impartially, that we have every chance of being happy, because apart from loving each other and wanting to take care of each other and share things, we have the same tastes – bookish, and domesticated and liking the country and happy, peaceful things. And I do realise that he isn't very strong, and has to be looked after, and I *will*.

I do hope you will get to love me a little too, because I did like you both so much, and I love Renée.

Thank you both again for your letter.

With love
Stella.

Though his parents' concern for Allan's mental and physical stability was justified, it is also true that the relationship with Stella had had a steadying and strengthening effect on him. Indeed, by the middle of 1931 Allan was writing to his father and mother:

> Thank you very much for your letters in which you both talked a lot of nonsense about not having made a success of your lives. If you took the trouble, you could find quite a number of excellent achievements to your credit. Besides, nobody makes the most of themselves!
>
> There are some things which are not done;
> To do the best one can is one.
>
> is a motto that one learns early and shakes off late!

The influence of Stella's 'Higher Common Sense' can be detected in these wise words. Charles Webb was at that moment on the point of giving up his parish in Kempsford and going into semi-retirement at the age of fifty-seven. A local paper recorded – curiously to our modern eyes – that: 'Unfortunately, the Cotswold air does not suit him and so, for health reasons, he is to move to London.' One of the reasons Charles and Jessie moved to London was, according to Renée, 'to make a home for Allan', another indication of their somewhat over-protective attitude towards him, and their distrust of Stella.

A rather less formal letter than the one to Allan's mother was sent by Stella on 27 March to his sister Renée, then a few days away from her sixteenth birthday and at boarding school. It was written on headed notepaper from the editorial department of the *Lady*. Allan had written to Renée a few days earlier to announce the engagement, and she had noted in her diary that she was 'glad but not surprised'. Stella wrote:

> Very many thanks for your congratulatory note. I thought I detected a note of reserve in it, but whether this was due to a) indignation or b) sisterly anxiety for Allan's welfare, I could not decide!
> In fact, I did not tell you when I saw you because we had only just told your family, and I was not sure whether they

would like it kept secret or not. I asked Allan if I could tell you, but he thought not, until we had the family's verdict. But I was *pining* to tell you, and felt something of a serpent while we talked about other things!

We are going to be very happy. There isn't any question of that at all. And if we have any place large enough for even a mouse to sleep in you must come and stay with us for nice long gossiping (I am never sure about those two 'p's'?) visits, and we will invite

a) a beautiful young man

or

b) prosperous middle aged ones

or

c) learned old ones

to meet you. Or else we will ask mad artists and people to provide you with the lurid 'copy' for all your best-sellers which will (we hope) keep us in our old age in comfort.

Allan says when he is *quite* old he intends to keep a book shop to sell my books and yours and 'a little tiny pile of copies of "Far and Deep".' Also we shall have an annexe where we shall sell the work of a sculptor friend of mine and a painter.

I am lunching with Allan and your Mother on Sunday at his digs. I wish you could be there too. . . .

I hope your End-of-Term will go off pleasantly. I think you are well cast as Mercutio! oh, I beg your pardon – it's Malvolio! (no offence meant!)

with much love
Stella

Renée's aspirations to write best-sellers were not fulfilled, despite Stella's support and encouragement. Like her brother Allan, she abandoned literature for the stage and followed him to the Webber-Douglas Academy after a brief flirtation with London University life at Bedford College. Her abandonment of Bedford had provoked the inevitable letter of reproach from Uncle Cyprian. The sculptor and painter Stella referred to were Eric Schilsky and Gerald Trice Martin, later a successful portrait painter.

Stella very soon established a rapport with Renée which developed into a lifelong friendship. When Stella came to stay with her parents soon after the engagement was announced, Renée wrote in her diary: 'We talked a great deal and went for a long walk. She understands what one really means, however badly one expresses oneself, better than anyone I know.' This gift of sympathy, especially with the young, remained one of Stella's most striking character traits throughout her life. People felt they could tell her anything, and did. In *Conference at Cold Comfort Farm* (1949) Stella wrote that 'years and years of listening to people had taught her [Flora Poste] that if she just kept quiet and sipped or sewed and never looked shocked, there was literally no limit – *no limit at all* – to what people would tell her'. On one of the last occasions that I saw Stella before she became seriously ill she said to me, just as I was leaving: 'This morning I had a long talk with a young man who told me all about rent boys.' Her tone was one of mild amusement and even milder interest. It is not every eighty-five-year-old lady to whom one feels one can talk about rent boys, but Stella was one of them.

In the same letter to Renée, Stella wrote: 'I am going away by myself for 4 days at Easter to a place called Alfriston in Sussex, where I hope I shall be able to write a lot of my novel *Cold Comfort Farm*. I have started it again and it is going very well. It ought to be ready in about three months from now. I am enjoying writing it immensely. If only it amuses the British Public as much as it is amusing me it should do well.' Stella's stay at Alfriston was remembered by Mrs Frida Shaw Jones, who wrote to her over fifty years later:

I, plus two children and a new baby, were staying at Alfriston, actually with Mrs Comfort, when you were writing *Cold Comfort Farm*. After the ghastly suppers that were provided, you used to read the latest chapters to us, to our great joy. Those awful meals! The very first evening we arrived we sat hopefully down to enjoy what we expected to be a farm high tea. A large dish was slapped down in front of us holding a huge congealing cod's head – eyes and all – and some watery potatoes. This was followed, I think, by tapioca pudding or something equally nasty! We stuck it out for the week in order to follow the progress of the Starkadders, but after that we gave in and went home.

It is a curious coincidence that a Mrs Comfort should have been dispensing such cold comfort to her at a farm in Sussex. I doubt if Stella went down to Alfriston deliberately in search of local colour, but the letter shows an early instance of her working methods. Throughout her life she would feel the need to take herself away to the country to be alone and work – not an uncommon impulse in writers. Not so common was her practice of reading out work in progress to an audience. Her daughter Laura remembers from an early age having the latest chapter of a new novel read to her by Stella, and being aware that this was somehow a necessary part of her mother's creative process. Novel writing was inextricably connected in her mind with story-telling. There is an obvious connection between these readings and the fantastic tales she used to weave for her brothers in the attic room at Malden Crescent.

Stella was reassured by the response of those to whom she read her novel, but she always claimed that what gave her greatest confidence in it were the typists. 'I knew it was going to be a success because the girls who typed my manuscript were laughing at it,' she told Libby Purves in 1981. Armed with this remarkable endorsement, she presented it to her publisher Robert Longman in February 1932. Longman was alarmed by the book's oddity and told her that she would have to hawk it about on a wheelbarrow before she sold any copies. However, on the advice of J. C. Squire, who persuaded him that she would follow *Cold Comfort Farm* with novels of a more conventional stamp, Longman paid her an advance of £30. On 12 April 1932 Renée noted in her diary that 'Stella seems to be on the verge of getting her book printed.'

Cold Comfort Farm was published on 8 September that year, priced at 7s.6d. (37½p), and was an immediate success. There was, however, some incredulity expressed that a mere journalist, and a woman at that, could have produced such an accomplished work. One reviewer even saw in Stella Gibbons a pseudonym of Evelyn Waugh.

Stella attributed much of the success of *Cold Comfort Farm* to 'coming at exactly the right time'. There is some truth in this. Most of the reviews suggest that the vogue for the rural novel had run its course and that the genre was ripe for mockery. Stanley Baldwin, who had done so much to boost the posthumous reputation of Mary Webb, was no longer Prime Minister; besides, the British public never respects the opinions of its leaders for long. *Punch* wrote:

> We have suffered too long from that school of novelists whose roots run so deep into the sad soil that their thoughts have grown consequently limited to the inevitability of gloom and reproduction; but at last we are revenged by Miss STELLA GIBBONS, who has arisen to mock with devilish skill at 'a certain type of much read, earthy passionate novel – the kind of story in which peasants have babies in cowsheds and push each other down wells'.

The *Times Literary Supplement* concluded: 'It is quite time that the earthy and passionate novel was parodied.'

The grandparent of the 'Loam and Lovechild School of Fiction' as Gerald Gould called these novels, was Thomas Hardy, and they had some notable exponents. This school was in itself a reaction against the effete pastoralism of the eighteenth century and the idealising nature worship of the Romantics. Tennyson's notion of nature being 'red in tooth and claw' became a commonplace in the mid-nineteenth century, and the idea that the violence of nature is mirrored in the emotional violence of its inhabitants was first expressed in Emily Brontë's *Wuthering Heights*. As T. R. Heilpern notes in her dissertation on the sources of *Cold Comfort Farm*, Brontë makes use of 'Our old friend the Pathetic Fallacy' in reverse: instead of imbuing aspects of nature with human characteristics, she imbues human beings with natural ones. Charlotte Brontë underlines this in her preface to *Wuthering Heights*, which she characterises as 'rustic all through. It is moorish, and wild, and knotty as a root of heather.' J. C. Powys and Lawrence were later to convert this Apathetic Fallacy into a philosophy.

It was Hardy who introduced the atmosphere of doom-laden struggle against impossible odds into the country. The use of Old Testament names for many of his characters, though no doubt reflecting what people were actually called in rural areas, also enhances the mood of these works. The deity that these characters serve is as vindictive and arbitrary as the Jehovah of the Old Testament, and the religion which they practise is correspondingly gloomy and oppressive.

Grandfather Gibbons in the
1920s: a combination of Amos
and Seth Starkadder with the
features of an elderly satyr.

Stella's father,
Dr Telford Gibbons,
'a bad man but a good
doctor' who had a
fanatical preoccupation
with fresh air.

The three-year-old Stella.

On holiday at Clacton about 1912: Maudie with Gerald at the wheel, Lewis plus teddy bear on her lap, and Stella wielding the starting handle.

Maudie and her younger
son, Lewis, about 1913.

Auntie Ru
(Ruby Williams),
Maudie's sister, on
Hampstead Heath
during World War I.

North London Collegiate School, 1919: seventeen-year-old Stella is in the centre, left of the girl not in uniform, with Stevie Smith on the far right of the same row.

The budding poet and journalist in 1927.

'They trip along hatless and gay...so unlike the Englishwoman of to-day,' began Stella's 1929 *Evening Standard* article on Viennese women.

Ida Graves and her first husband, Herbert Marks, the prototype for Mybug in *Cold Comfort Farm*, introduced Stella to a coterie of thirties' bohemian intellectuals. 'The men used…to try to kiss me and…talk to me about sex, like Mr Mybug does,' she recalled.

The good-looking, gifted sculptor Eric Schilsky had a passionate affair with Ida Graves, and became a lifelong platonic friend of Stella's.

Renée Webb, Stella's actress sister-in-law, as a young woman. She and Stella were to become close companions.

Stella first met Allan Bourne Webb in 1929, but they were unable to marry for four years. This picture was taken in spring 1932, the year *Cold Comfort Farm* was published, on Stella's beloved Hampstead Heath.

Allan in costume in a sketch called 'The Bandit's Opera' from the revue *Moonshine*, staged at London's Vaudeville Theatre in 1940.

Stella in the 1940s, a portrait that reveals both her toughness and her vulnerability. (Note the resemblance to her father.)

Allan in uniform, Egypt 1944.

In 1944 Stella took
eight-year-old Laura
away from the bombs
of London to rural
Gloucestershire.
The central figure is
Beth Draw.

After the war: Stella and
Laura in 1945.

Writer Charles Morgan
and the established poet
and novelist, both
photographed in the early
fifties by Mark Gerson.

On holiday at Roscoff in Brittany in 1955 with nephews Charlie
(next to Stella) and Reggie.

Proud parents Stella and Allan at Laura's wedding to Joe Richardson in June 1957.

Stella in the 1980s. Although she had given up writing herself, her sharp eye and trenchant mind still enabled her to keep a commonplace book of examples of bad writing by others.

Mary Webb had a mind of a more conventional stamp than Hardy's. She was a Christian with a strong vein of nature mysticism, derived from reading Wordsworth and Richard Jefferies. Many of her most high-flown passages are expressions of this mysticism. Here is John Arden talking to his daughter Deb in *The Golden Arrow*: '"See you Deb! The flockmaster goes westering; and the brown water and the blue wind above the cloud and the kestrels and you and me all go after the shippen with the starry door. Hear you Deb, what a noise o' little leaves clapping in the far coppy! Tis he, that shakes the bits of leaves and the bits of worlds, and sends love like forkit lightning – him as the stars fall before like white 'ool at sheep shearing. . . ."'

Arden is as keen on his sheep as Adam Lambsbreath is on his cows. The authentic tones of Adam are found in Arden's rebuke to Eli Huntbach, who has just laid a stick on his sheep: '"Dunna clout 'em, Eli! . . . I'd liefer they'd come round me than find the pot of gold under the rainbow. They be my friends, as you know well, and they'm not speechless from emptiness of heart. No, sorrowful and loving they be."'

Though intensely mystical, Webb is very down on conventional religion and chapel bigotry. The religious bigot is a frequently recurring character in her work and in the genre of rural fiction generally. Eli Huntbach in *The Golden Arrow* and Mrs Darke in *The House in Dormer Forest*, with their oppressive, Old Testament faith, are both prototypes of Amos Starkadder, and they themselves are descended from Joseph in *Wuthering Heights*. Stella exploits the stock theme of religious bigotry to glorious effect in the Quivering Brethren, and the scene in their chapel, like 'an unusually large dog kennel', is one of the high spots of the book. Interestingly enough, Amos himself is a much more convincing character than his fictional forebears. Stella humanises him by revealing the underlying vanity of the man and the sheer pleasure he secretly derives from practising his craft as a preacher ('. . . the man was an artist'). One of the subtlest pieces of comedy in the book comes in the passage where Flora plays on Amos's vanity to woo him away from Cold Comfort Farm to go on a preaching tour 'in one o' they Ford vans'. This perception, that inside even the most doom-laden of preachers exists an actor delighting in his own rodomontade, is derived from Stella's recognition of the secret pleasure that her Gibbons relatives took in making scenes.

Webb's best-known work, *Precious Bane*, is told in retrospect by an old countrywoman with a hare lip, Prue Sarn. Though its plot and characterisation find no echo in *Cold Comfort Farm*, it is full of rhapsodic description and bizarre incident. At one point Prue, naked save for some muslin over her head to cover her deformity, is hoisted through a trapdoor by a fake magician who hopes thereby to persuade Squire Camperdine that he can raise Venus. Unknown to her, the man she loves, Kester Woodseaves, is also present. The book is a repository of rustic dialect and words such as 'winnocked' ('Mother winnocked a bit to hear I was off to Plash'), 'canbottlins', 'lantun-puff', 'snoffle', 'daggly' and 'yarbs'.

Stella's invention of parody rural words ('scranlet', 'sukebind', 'cletter', 'hoot piece', 'mollocking' and so on) has often been imitated. Rambling Sid Rumpo of the classic radio comedy programme *Round the Horne*, with his repertoire of moolies, gander-bags and nadgerings, was obviously a near relative of the Starkadders. He was a great favourite of Stella's, and she was delighted when she heard that Kenneth Williams (the voice of Rumpo) was going to read *Cold Comfort Farm* on the radio.

There are, as T. R. Heilpern points out, some powerful similarities between *Cold Comfort Farm* and Mary Webb's third novel, *The House in Dormer Forest*; and Dorothy Wrenn in her biography of Webb confidently proclaims it to be the model for *Cold Comfort Farm*. Both the House and the Farm are ancient, rambling buildings, inhabited for several generations by one family and brooded over by an ageing matriarch. In the case of *The House in Dormer Forest* this is Mrs Velindre, whose description could equally apply to Aunt Ada Doom who 'saw something nasty in the woodshed'.

> There was a ghost hiding in Mrs Velindre's eyes – a cadaverous grisly thing which had looked at her out of other people's eyes when she was a child; slowly possessing her in womanhood, finally absorbing her whole personality – eating into it like a worm into a rotten fruit. . . . Mrs Velindre, who was the oracle of the family, never used either intellect or intuition in giving her verdicts. She simply echoed her ancestors. If anything occurred without precedent in her tradition, she was flustered and incompetent until she had found some text which could be made to bear on the question. Then she would give her ultimatum.

In Mrs Velindre's case the texts were biblical, while Ada Doom got by on two gnomic sayings: the one about the woodshed, of course, and 'There've always been Starkadders at Cold Comfort Farm.' Where Ada Doom threatens to 'go mad' if crossed, Mrs Velindre threatens to die. But while Ada is revealed as a manipulative, but ultimately quite sane, old creature with a hearty appetite, Mrs Velindre remains a shadowy figure. Under them, they have thwarted, withdrawn married women in the shape of Judith Starkadder and Rachel Darke respectively.

Adam Lambsbreath, the half-mad retainer, has something in common with Enoch Gale, the servant in *The House in Dormer Forest*. Both are impossibly in love with young girls, both are close to animals. With Adam it is cows, with Enoch birds: 'In dew-dark summer mornings Enoch loved to be among them as one kin to them, and, at the first shrilling of the summer chorus when each beast was startled (walking at ease with its soul) by its sudden shadow flung blue before it by the early ray, Enoch also went as three – his broad and sturdy body, his half tamed soul, and his pansy tinted shadow.' There is even a parallel with Flora Poste in Catherine Velindre, 'a distant relation' and a paying guest at the House, like Flora a smart, intelligent and interfering outsider. She is, however, a wholly malign character. For all its excesses, and its 'pansy tinted shadows', *The House in Dormer Forest* is an interesting novel by a remarkable if uneven writer, and is not without touches of humour.

Enthusiasts for Mary Webb's work – and there are still many, especially in America – have tried to deny the connection between it and *Cold Comfort Farm*. Yet unquestionably it exists. Stella once expressed her regret to the writer Michael Pick that she had parodied Mary Webb, 'because she had such an unhappy life'. This was perhaps over-sensitive. Webb had, after all, died five years before the publication of *Cold Comfort Farm*. Her life, though dogged by illness and depression, was by no means without happiness, and her childhood, compared with Stella's, had been idyllic.

One of the roots of Stella's objections to Webb can be found in the two writers' poetry. Stella would have known Webb's verse because, while *The Golden Arrow* was being serialised in the *Evening Standard*, some of it was appearing on the Home Page.

Like Stella's, it has a genuine sense of beauty and a profound feeling for nature, but it is shapeless and often descends into cliché-ridden banality. Out of Stella's poetry emerges a distinctive voice: passionate, but shaped and crafted. Webb's verse, by comparison, is, to use a phrase of Stella's, 'attempted literature'; some of the samples which appeared on the Home Page were little better than doggerel. The difference between Mary Webb and Stella Gibbons as poets is that between a gifted amateur and a talented professional. While the sensibilities were remarkably similar, Stella's was tempered by style, wit and a greater sense of humour.

There was more than a little silliness about Mary Webb, as exemplified by an anecdote quoted in Dorothy Wrenn's biography. When Webb lived in Shropshire she would walk to a nearby farm to buy butter. One morning, after a heavy dew, she arrived soaked to the knees and bedraggled. On being asked by the farmer's wife the cause of her condition, she replied: 'The tall corn called me, and I had to walk through it,' a remark worthy of Elfine Starkadder. Whether the farmer appreciated his crops being vandalised is not recorded. When the mood took her she would shower the local children with unsuitable and unwanted gifts – baby's bootees for a child of six, three hats of the same size for three children of different ages. Stella would not have felt so guilty about her mockery of Webb had she remembered an article by a Mrs Nicholson in the *Evening Standard* of 19 July 1928. When Mrs Nicholson, a fervent admirer of Webb's work, kindly suggested a remedy for one of her recurring ailments, the writer replied grandly: 'You have intruded into a poet's reserve and sorrows. In that wilderness you have no guide – and there you are lost.' One is reminded of Judith Starkadder's: 'Curtains! . . . Child, child, it is many years since such trifles broke across the web of my solitude.'

When, in 1943, Stella was invited by the Bristol University Literary Society to talk about Mary Webb, she cautioned in her letter of acceptance: 'You don't want me to try to be funny about Mary Webb, do you? I hope not.' Too late; she had been.

Mary Webb was, however, by no means the only object of Stella's parody. Stella told me that she was also aiming at lesser writers in the same mould, and in particular Sheila Kaye-Smith.

A curious figure, Kaye-Smith was, like Webb, a Christian with a mystical bent. Married to an Anglo-Catholic clergyman, she later converted to Catholicism and set up a kind of commune in the country. Also, somewhat improbably, she was a friend of Noël Coward's and a lesbian. Her many novels were mostly set in Sussex (the location which Stella borrowed for *Cold Comfort Farm*) and bore titles such as *Shepherds in Sackcloth*. In April 1931 in the *Lady* Stella reviewed her *Susan Spray*, a study of religious mania in a rural setting, and found it 'curiously flat in treatment' compared to Kaye-Smith's earlier novels with which she was obviously familiar. Her novels are remarkably similar to Webb's, but lack that spark of genuine poetry which informs Webb's work.

Perhaps Kaye-Smith's most famous book was *Sussex Gorse*. Published in 1916, it was one of her earliest rural novels and was reprinted many times. It is difficult now to account for its former popularity: the novel is as hard, uncompromising and humourless a read as its hero, Reuben Backfield. Reuben is, of course, 'close to the earth' and surprisingly tough ('he did not in the least mind being flogged'). The process by which he attains a certain piece of land, Boarzell Moor, is relentlessly charted: 'He coveted Boarzell only, virgin of tool and brick. . . . He must be ruthless as the wind that blustered over it, hard as the stones that covered it, wiry as the gorse-roots that twisted in its marl.' In this respect he is not dissimilar to Reuben Starkadder, whose one ambition is to run and possess Cold Comfort Farm; though Stella's Reuben is a more rounded and humane character than Kaye-Smith's.

Hugh Walpole does not quite belong to this school, but his Herries Chronicles, set in the Lake District and full of melo-dramatic incident, have a sufficient family resemblance to the work of Webb, Kaye-Smith, Holme and others for him to stand as their representative in the guise of Pookworthy. Stella was not so much satirising his writing, which she nevertheless considered to be flatulent, mediocre stuff, as attacking his status. Pookworthy, like Walpole's other fictional manifestation Alroy Kear, is a pat-ronising, vain elder statesman of the literary world. He is also, as the letters after his name would suggest – Associate Back Scratcher, Licensed Log Roller – in a subtle way corrupt.

Though the Loam and Lovechild School is Stella's most overt and obvious target, she is also attacking the ideas and, to some extent, style of a much more considerable writer, D. H. Lawrence.

As Michèle Barale observes in *Daughters and Lovers*, Webb's outlook is in some ways similar to Lawrence: 'Both authors invest sexuality with mystical power and both view the sexual union of man and woman and the union of the human with the natural world as the catalysts of transcendence.'

Lawrence was not alone among writers of genius in thinking that his gifts as a creative artist entitled him to assume the mantle of preacher and prophet. He had a taste for power and took his messianic role seriously. The problem was that his philosophy was, by its very nature, inarticulate. He summed it up in a letter to his friend Ernest Collings in January 1913: 'My great religion is a belief in the blood, the flesh, as being wiser than the intellect. We can go wrong in our minds. But what our blood feels and believes and says is always true. . . . All I want is to answer to my blood, direct, without fribbling intervention of mind, or moral, or what-not.'

To many readers today the repeated calls to follow the blood have a disturbingly fascist ring, but this was not what exercised Stella. She had found from her experience with the Herbert Marks set in Golders Green that this Lawrentian philosophy – if it can be dignified by that name – offered men a perfect excuse to behave badly. They were only obeying the blood and the flesh when they tried to seduce her; and Stella was being sexually repressed when she rejected their advances.

Mr Mybug, an amalgam of all that was unpleasant and absurd about the Golders Green men, is forever striking Lawrentian attitudes. His walks with Flora Poste are an endless game of Hunt the Phallic Symbol. 'He pointed out to Flora that he and she were walking on seeds which were germinating in the womb of the earth. He said it made him feel as if he were trampling on the body of a great brown woman.' The pathetic fallacies of his conversation come straight from Lawrence's account of the Brangwens in *The Rainbow*: 'They knew the intercourse between heaven and earth, sunshine drawn into the breast and bowels, the rain sucked up in the daytime, nakedness that comes under the wind in autumn. . . . Their life and interrelations were such; feeling the pulse and body of the soil, that opened to their furrow for the grain, and became smooth and supple after their ploughing, and clung to their feet with a weight that pulled like desire. . . .'

Mybug, as a human being is, of course, far from being a

Lawrentian ideal. In the first place he is an intellectual, a breed Lawrence may have relied upon to promote his works but which he also thoroughly despised. In the second place, he is physically unappealing. 'I cannot help feeling . . . rather sorry for Mr Mybug,' says Flora. 'You see he is rather fat. I always feel sorry for people who are fat. And I haven't the heart to tell him that's why I won't let him kiss me. He thinks it's because I'm inhibited.' This humanises Mr Mybug, so that he becomes more than a mere collection of intellectual foibles, and the reader rejoices when he finds and marries Rennet at the end of the book.

Musing on the subject of marriage, Mybug actually refers to Lawrence by name: 'He said that, by God, D. H. Lawrence was right when he had said there must be a dumb, dark, dull, bitter belly-tension between a man and a woman, and how else could this be achieved save in the long monotony of marriage?' The first part of this sentence sounds like authentic Lawrence (though I can find no exact echo of it in his work), while the second part is pure Mybug. The splendid irony is that he is using Lawrence to excuse his lapse into a very unbohemian respectability.

The comic intellectual was, of course, a stock figure in the middlebrow English fiction of that period. In *Punch* drawings of the time he appears, often dressed anachronistically as an 1890s' aesthete with a floppy bow tie and a fedora hat, gazing raptly at a Cubist painting. What differentiates Mybug from these stereotypes is that Stella had experienced him at first hand and was drawing from life. She was not a philistine, nor an anti-intellectual. What she objected to in Mybug was shallowness and lack of intellectual rigour. Mybug was trying to make a name for himself by writing a book which attempted to prove, on the flimsiest of grounds, that Bramwell Brontë had written *Wuthering Heights*. Works of grotesque literary speculation are with us today in even greater numbers than they were in 1932. I remember telling Stella that a feminist critic had come up with the idea that the Brontë sisters had lesbian tendencies. She responded: 'Well, really! Apart from anything else, it's so *ignorant*. And I suppose she thinks that Anne Brontë wrote *The Tenant of Radclyffe Hall*.'

The animal sensuality of Seth Starkadder comes much closer to Lawrence's idea of perfect manhood than Mybug. Interestingly, he shares with many of Lawrence's men a fear of being possessed and diminished by women. In his bizarre late essay 'Matriarchy' Lawrence wrote: 'Man is not afraid of being petticoat ruled. He is afraid of being swamped, turned into a mere accessory of bare-limbed swooping women. Swamped by her numbers, swamped by her devouring energy. He talks . . . feebly about man being master again. He knows perfectly well that he will never be master again.' Seth's ruminations run along similar lines: 'Women are all alike – ay fussin' over their fal-lals and bedazin' a man's eyes, when all they really want is man's blood and his heart out of his body and his soul and his pride. . . .' His mother Judith is possessively and semi-incestuously in love with him, an example of what Lawrence called the 'Woman who selects her sons as lovers.'

As with Mybug, however, Stella humanises Seth. He ceases to be a mere symbol of Lawrentian manhood when the reader discovers that he is obsessed by the talking pictures. Lawrence would not have approved of Seth's relegation to the artificial existence of a Hollywood star, let alone his whole-hearted enjoyment of it. Yet this is the kind of thing that happens in real life: human beings are odd and do not conform to type.

What gives the satire of *Cold Comfort Farm* its depth and lasting quality is that Stella is not merely mocking the superficial failings of a literary genre, but attacking its underlying assumptions. She takes some of the stereotypical characters of the rural novel – the tyrannical matriarch, the religious bigot, the mystic simpleton, the farmyard Don Juan – and, by revealing unexpected sides to their characters, imbues them with life.

In connection with *Cold Comfort Farm* critics have often used words such as 'wicked', 'malicious', 'irreverent', 'sharp' and even 'cruel'. But if this is all that could be said of it, the book would not have lasted as it has done. 'Nothing dates like hate,' wrote Cyril Connolly, 'and in literature a little of it goes a very long way.' What is striking about the comedy of *Cold Comfort Farm* is that, while maintaining a keen satirical edge and making few concessions to sentimentality, its values are essentially humane.

Lawrence, the Powys brothers, Hugh Walpole, the rural novel in general: these would seem to be enough targets for one satirical novel, but the list is longer. It includes Freudian psychology, avant-garde foreign films, Hollywood (affectionate mockery, this), county society, arts and crafts movements, and the 1930s' equivalent of Fringe Theatre. *Cold Comfort Farm* is a comic encyclopaedia of the fads and fancies of the period, and it is remarkable how many of them are still with us.

Many readers have been puzzled by the fact that Stella set the action of the book at some time in the future (around 1950, perhaps, since the minor character Claud Hart-Harris 'served in the Anglo-Nicaraguan wars of '46'). I regret that I never asked her precisely why she did this. Perhaps it was a means of giving her satirical invention a freer rein – she could exaggerate current tendencies without straining the reader's credulity. The result is that the book is quite prophetic in a number of small ways: London residential districts south of the Thames *have* become fashionable; there *are* in effect 'state psycho-analysts' (i.e. available on the National Health); and one may only have to live a little longer to see air postal services and video telephones in England. Moreover, at least two writers, Daphne du Maurier and Winifred Gérin, followed Mr Mybug's example and wrote biographical studies of Bramwell Brontë. Like her idea of putting Baedeker stars against the purple patches to separate her parodic manner from her authentic authorial voice, setting *Cold Comfort Farm* in the future was a technical device which was both amusing in itself and imaginatively stimulating.

Perhaps Stella's most profound feat of comic invention revolves round the famous phrase 'something nasty in the woodshed'. Aunt Ada Doom uses the fact that she saw something nasty in the woodshed when she was 'no bigger than a titty wren' to tyrannise the Starkadder family. Stella would never say what that 'something nasty' was. Sometimes she would say that she knew what it was, but would not tell; once she told me that actually she did not know herself. As a result, it stands for every childhood trauma, real or imagined, which is used by its supposed victims to excuse their selfish or erratic behaviour. Stella had as good a claim as any to have seen something nasty in the woodshed of her childhood, but she refused to allow the guilt and misery of the past to colour the present. Having seen how her father had handed on the misery of his childhood to her own, she was determined to break the cycle and lift the curse. Her own liberation came through laughter, which can be a braver and a more radical therapy than any obtained through psychoanalysis or counselling.

Since Stella's day, the culture of victimhood has grown. Its wilder excrescences, such as the so-called 'recovered memory syndrome', have given the phrase 'something nasty in the woodshed' a more extended and sinister resonance. In her 1981 interview with Libby Purves, Stella said: 'I think, quite without meaning to, I presented a kind of weapon to people against melodrama and the over-emphasising of disorder and disharmony, and especially the people who rather enjoy it. . . . I think it could teach people not to take them seriously, and therefore perhaps avoid being hurt by them.'

In 1991 I saw a stage version of *Cold Comfort Farm* by Paul Doust at the Watermill Theatre, Newbury. It was a skilful and well-staged adaptation, but by far the most telling moment of the evening came from one of Stella's simplest lines. Towards the end Flora invites the American film producer Earl P. Neck to Cold Comfort Farm to meet Seth, the film-mad and sexually rampant young Starkadder. As Neck is carrying Seth off to America and Hollywood stardom Ada Doom tries to stop him with 'I saw something nasty in the woodshed!', to which Neck replies: 'Did it see you?' In the theatre there was a great burst of laughter at this rejoinder and a round of applause. The laughter had that deep, satisfying note that only comes from recognition. Neck (and Stella) on behalf of the audience were thumbing their noses at all those people – often relatives – who use emotional blackmail to make others pay for their own problems. In John Schlesinger's film version of 1995, the simplicity of the original dialogue was not adhered to and the effect was marred.

Stella's subsequent relationship with *Cold Comfort Farm* was difficult because the book eclipsed her other literary achievements. There were times when she did not even like to mention it by name, and it was referred to as 'That Book' or 'You-Know-What', even at times 'Hmm hmm hmm', a sort of lugubrious hum made with the lips tightly closed. In 1981 she wrote to someone who had written expressing admiration for two of her later novels, *Westwood* and *Enbury Heath*: 'I always love hearing from a reader who has enjoyed my other books as well as that *wretched* CCF. (I know this sounds ungrateful, but honestly, I do get rather browned off with having it tagged onto me – or rather, me tagged onto it.)'

In 1966, in 'Genesis of a Novel', she wrote:

A very successful book leaves a lifelong mark on its writer.

Cold Comfort Farm is a member of my family; he is like some unignorable old uncle, to whom you have to be grateful because he makes you a handsome allowance, but who is often an embarrassment and a bore; skipping about, and reminding you of the days when you were a bright young thing. To him, and to his admirers, you have never grown up.

The old monster has also over-lain all my other books, and if I do happen to glance at him occasionally, I am filled by an incredulous wonder that I could once have been so light-hearted – but so light-hearted.

CHAPTER 5

'Let other pens dwell on guilt and misery'

The above quotation from *Mansfield Park* placed on the dedication page of *Cold Comfort Farm* was for Stella something more than a swipe against those writers whose pens dwelt (and still dwell) on little else; it was almost a manifesto. This does not mean that she believed guilt and misery should not play an essential role in a novel – simply that they should not be *dwelt* on. She wanted contentment, serenity and calm in her own life, and she wanted it in the lives of others, so she deliberately set out to dispense it in her fiction. For a writer, such an intention was as radically unfashionable in 1932 as it is now.

In all forms of art criticism the word 'disturbing' has become a term of approbation; and the frequent implication is that if a work does not disturb it is not important as art. It is a valid function of art to subvert and question; but not all disturbing art is great and not all great art is disturbing. Great art can also amuse, elevate, inspire, even comfort. Stella's gentle powers were more suited to these artistic functions. Her attitude towards the human race was, on the whole, warm and optimistic: she actually liked its silly face. In this she went against the grain of modernism, under so much of which there lies a solid foundation of misanthropy.

Towards the end of her 1949 novel *The Matchmaker* Stella mentions in passing the death, in sordid circumstances, of the son of a comparatively minor character (Emilio, an Italian prisoner of war). The details of his death, Stella wrote, 'will not be told here, for we agree with that philosopher of the Ancient World who said that the death of a young child is the only grief which is insupportable'. This minor incident demonstrates some of Stella's faults and virtues as a novelist. A lesser writer would have omitted the distressing episode altogether, but for Stella the death of Emilio's son was somehow a small but essential part of the pattern of her novel. She had the integrity to touch on guilt and misery when necessary; but she should have had the courage to do so without coyness.

In that same novel Stella wrote:

> The mighty George Eliot once commented with acerbity upon those readers who 'demand adultery, murder and ermine tippets on every page,' and we ourselves, confronted whenever we open a volume of contemporary fiction by explosions, lust, perversion and despair in every line, join our feeble voice to hers. Though often tempted to show that we, too, know all about That – yes *and* That, to say nothing of the Anglo-Saxon Words (all nine of them), we refuse to be bounced into what we do not enjoy writing. Our themes are gentle, it is true, but
>
> > We do but sing because we must
> > And pipe but as the linnets do,
>
> and our final decision is that enough is going on everywhere without our starting in.

This defence is not entirely satisfactory: there is a certain archness in its expression, and Stella seems to contradict herself. Her poetic quotation suggests that she is writing what she must; the rest of the passage implies that she is writing what she chooses. It seems more likely that she placed herself under something of a self-denying ordinance, albeit not a very onerous one.

Of her novels after *Cold Comfort Farm* at least four are of outstanding merit, and are as good in their way as her most famous book. But the quality of sustained comic inspiration that we find in *Cold Comfort Farm* is never found again. 'That book' was the only one which wrote itself, but what she lost in spontaneity she gained in maturity. Her work from then on was generally more relaxed and less motivated, but there is a great deal to be said in its favour. Stella's 'other' books have always had a substantial and dedicated following. All her novels sold well, few of them have ever gathered dust in public libraries, and their appearance on the shelves of second-hand bookshops are rare and brief.

Quite suddenly in 1932 Stella found that she was famous. Celebrity bewildered her, and throughout her life she was indifferent, occasionally even hostile, to it. Though, later on, she enjoyed the mild distinction that a Fellowship of the Royal Society of Literature conferred, she never courted honours or publicity, and on at least one occasion she turned down the opportunity to appear on television. She did not even greatly care for the chances fame offered for her to meet other famous people. Interviewing for the *Evening Standard* had perhaps inured her to their glamour. Soon after her success with *Cold Comfort Farm* she was introduced to J. B. Priestley, possibly through J. C. Squire who had helped him in his early years. 'Well, J. B. Priestley took me out to lunch once,' she said in an interview with Jill Neville in 1985. 'He asked me what I liked doing and I said I liked going for walks on Hampstead Heath. He said, "Oh, nonsense, you just see yourself walking on Hampstead Heath," and I thought, oh, well, if you know more about me than I do myself I haven't much time for you. He was extremely rude and seemed rather unhappy.'

When *Cold Comfort Farm* became a success Stella found a literary agent, the firm of Pearn, Pollinger and Higham. One of the first matters on which she consulted them was whether she could hope for a regular and respectable income from writing novels. The agency told her she could. So she resigned from the *Lady* and told Allan's parents what the agents had said. Satisfied that Allan and she would not starve, Charles and Jessie Webb gave the match their approval.

Allan and Stella were married on 1 April 1933 at St Matthew's, Bayswater. Charles Webb, who was a curate there, conducted the ceremony. A choir recruited from Allan's friends at the Webber-Douglas sang; Ina Dornan and Stella's brother Gerald were witnesses, and a party for about seventy people was held in the garden of Charles and Jessie's rented house in nearby St Petersburgh Place.

Allan and Stella set up home in Belsize Park at 30 Upper Park Road. The marriage by this time had even received the blessing of the bridegroom's stiff and snobbish uncle. On 17 August 1933 Allan's sister Renée recorded in her diary: 'This evening Uncle

Cyprian came to dinner and we drove him over to the flat to have coffee with Allan and Stella. He admired everything very much although he seemed a bit embarrassed at being taken into the kitchen. Stella remarked afterwards that one felt he was saying "Nice kitchen! Nice kitchen!" like a person propitiating a large, fierce dog.'

Stella had become fully absorbed into Allan's family, even to the point of taking part on one occasion in their amateur theatricals. Though relations with her mother-in-law were not always easy, she was deeply attached to Renée, now eighteen. In September 1933 she went on holiday with Renée and her parents-in-law to Trevone in Cornwall while Allan was rehearsing with a touring opera company in London. Renée recorded in her diary:

Stella and I bathed with nothing on, a great triumph for both of us. We are always deploring the prudery which makes it impossible in most sea-side places. This was in the afternoon; in the morning we went for a walk and found a ruined tower on the edge of the cliff like the tower in Stella's story *Roaring Tower* [the title story of her first short story collection]. It really *does* roar when the wind blows through it. . . .

The following day:

There was a nasty, depressing sermon in church this morning, all about there being a scientific explanation for everything. Stella and I, therefore, went down on the beach and watched some winkles in a pool and S wrote on the sand with her finger; 'Fearfully and wonderfully made.' . . . After tea S and I went up the cliff and lay on our stomachs on the edge, talking. I remember she said something about my being more sensible about love and those sort of things than she had been at my age and I said didn't the idea of being in love strike her as being terribly funny? and I laughed – not a 'bitter, mirthless laugh' (I don't believe there is such a thing) but quite an ordinary sort of laugh, and Stella laughed too, and said I had such a funny little face.

Renée was also spending much time in the company of Stella's friends. She was painted by Stella's artist friend Gerald Trice Martin, and met Eric Schilsky with whom she fell instantly and quite hopelessly in love. This lasted until she went to drama school in 1934 – at the Webber-Douglas she fell instantly and equally hopelessly in love with the young Stewart Granger (then called Jimmy Stewart). She frequented the flat in Leinster Mews where Gerald and Lewis lived in a perpetual fog of debt, drink and parties. They were just around the corner from the Leinster Arms, from which bottles of gin and other beverages were brought in at all hours. A floating population of young men and women, most of them connected loosely with the theatre, flowed in and out, drank too much and made scenes. It was the kind of milieu Stella detested and had done her best to escape. Once, when Renée went to tea there, 'Lewis informed me that two ladies of easy virtue brought by Reggie Hammerstein (brother of Oscar Hammerstein) had smashed some of the gramophone records.' Stella finally warned her sister-in-law gently not to spend too much time there. Both Stella's brothers were flirting with Renée in a desultory way. Relations with Lewis almost became serious at one point, and Gerald proposed to her; but he was drunk at the time and she was too sensible to pay much attention to his advances.

Gerald finally gave up the stage in 1936, at about the time when Renée was starting her career on it. He gave her one piece of advice about the theatrical world which, she said, was the only remotely intelligent thing she ever heard him say. It was: 'Never interfere in a quarrel between queers; they have the strength of men and the courage of women.'

After a brief and inevitably unsuccessful attempt to run a night club in Regent Street, Gerald took a job in the Post Office. One day in 1937 Renée recorded in her diary that she had received an urgent telephone call from him asking for thirty shillings 'to save him from gaol'. She was in the middle of a dress rehearsal at Brixton at the time, but summoned him down to the theatre and gave him the money. She heard later that he had taken some cash from the Post Office till and then found that he could not repay it.

On numerous other occasions it had been Stella who bailed him out, and it was only when the war came that she felt she could stop worrying about him. She remarkked sardonically to Renée on one occasion that the one good thing about the Hitler Crisis was that for its duration there would not be a Gerald Crisis. She was right. Throughout the Second World War he was gainfully and honourably occupied in the Fire Service.

Stella won the *Prix Etranger* of the *Prix Fémina-Vie Heureuse* of 1933 for *Cold Comfort Farm*, and was presented with the £40 prize in May 1934. Seven years previously it had been won by *Precious Bane*. In one of those coincidences that some people call stranger than fiction, a second Mrs Webb was winning the prize for a parody of the first Mrs Webb to win it.

The *Prix Fémina-Vie Heureuse* was founded in 1904 by a Madame de Broutelles and has a jury consisting of twelve distinguished women of letters. It owes its name to its female founder and all-woman jury, and is still awarded annually. The prize has two categories, one for a novel in French, and the *Prix Etranger* for a work of fiction translated from another language. (The French version of *Cold Comfort Farm* was entitled *La Ferme de Froid Accueil*.) Though many women have won the prize, it is open to both sexes. In 1930, for example, it was won by one of Stella's *bêtes noires*, Charles Morgan, for *Portrait in a Mirror*.

On receiving the award at the Institut Français in London Stella had to make a ten-minute speech, which she detested doing. Yet though she disliked making an exhibition of herself, she did speak in public with distinction and charm. She was often asked to speak by university societies, and occasionally accepted. The writer Richard Adams remembers enjoying an address by her to the English Society at Oxford in 1938 on the life of a professional writer. She even spoke to the Royal Society of Literature in 1954 on the subject of *Cold Comfort Farm*. She was also, unlike many poets, a good reader of her own verse. Her voice, though not loud, was clear and pleasing.

The award did not meet with universal approval. Virginia Woolf wrote to Elizabeth Bowen, another contender, on 16 May 1934: 'I was enraged to see they gave the £40 to Gibbons; still now you and Rosamund [Lehmann] can join in blaming her. Who is she? What is this book? And so you can't buy your carpet.'

Woolf had for the moment forgotten that this was the Gibbons whose poem seven years previously both she and Bowen had admired in *Criterion*, and who had been considered for inclusion in the Hogarth Living Poets series. By the time she wrote to Bowen again on the 20th she had remembered, but she still insisted that Bowen and Lehmann 'had a better claim' to the prize. Woolf had won in 1928 with *To the Lighthouse* and had assumed a proprietorial attitude to the award, which she considered suitable only for writers in the same mould as herself.

Elizabeth Bowen never showed any resentment at being deprived of her hoped for carpet. She reviewed many of Stella's later books generously and appreciatively and was on excellent terms with Stella herself, who, though she disliked literary parties, attended Bowen's. It was at one of these that she met and befriended the distinguished novelist and biographer Elizabeth Jenkins, who won the *Fémina* prize herself in 1935 for her novel *Harriet*.

In the light of all this, it is ironical that the only two *Fémina* prize-winning novels of the inter-war years which are still generally read and regularly reprinted happen to be *To the Lighthouse* and *Cold Comfort Farm*. Though utterly dissimilar in almost every way, the two books performed comparable functions in their authors' lives. Both were in some sense exorcisms of family life. Of her parents Woolf wrote in her diary in November 1928 that 'The Lighthouse laid them in my mind.' And again in *Sketch of the Past* she wrote that she had been obsessed by her mother until she wrote the book, then: 'I suppose I did for myself what psychoanalysts do for their patients. I expressed some very long and deeply felt emotions. And in expressing it I explained it and then laid it to rest.' In neither Stella's nor Woolf's case, however, was the laying to rest quite as simple or final as that. Creative minds thrive on revisiting the past; but they often do so (subconsciously perhaps) so that the past will not revisit them.

In the same year, 1934, Stella's second novel, *Bassett*, appeared. While it was, as Robert Longman had hoped, quite conventional in overall conception, it possessed a number of distinctive and unusual qualities. Though less brilliant than its predecessor, it has a depth of characterisation and insight which one might not necessarily expect from the author of *Cold Comfort Farm*. The book deals with the nature of relationships, sexual and non-sexual. Two people of the same sex, apparently quite incompatible, find fulfilment together, while two young lovers do not. Linking both stories is the paradox that those who recognise their need for another are frequently more fulfilled and mature than the seemingly self-sufficient. Stella shows a firm grasp of narrative and handles her two interlocking storylines with great technical assurance, though it suffers from the shortcoming of such double narratives in that one plot strand is rather less interesting than the other.

The first, and slighter, story concerns Miss Baker, a London working-class woman who is sacked from her job in a dress factory and goes to Bassett, a Buckinghamshire village, to help run a boarding house with a decayed gentlewoman called Miss Padsoe. Miss Baker is far from being the stereotyped comic cockney of so much fiction of the period, but a closely observed and fully rounded character. Much excellent, understated comedy is derived from the initial antipathy of these two characters whom necessity has thrown together: 'Miss Baker thought Miss Padsoe looked as balmy [*sic*] as her letters, if not balmier; and Miss Padsoe, who had been vaguely hoping that Miss Baker was not going to look like *her* letters, found that she did.' From *Cold Comfort Farm* onwards it is the little misunderstandings that exist between people of different classes and social worlds that are the source of Stella's best comedy.

The main plotline concerns Queenie Catton, the rather serious daughter of a socialist dentist, who goes to Bassett to act as companion to Mrs Shelling, a rich widow, who lives with her unmarried son and daughter, George and Bell. Queenie, like so many of Stella's heroines, is 'just the kind of woman for whom marriage, as a holy order, was ordained'. She falls in love with the charming George Shelling and he, for a brief while, with her. She goes away for the weekend with George to a hotel where they sign the register in time-honoured fashion as man and wife, an incident based on Stella's own experience with Walter Beck. But George cannot sustain the depth and intensity which Queenie requires of him. The disintegration of their relationship is charted painfully but even-handedly.

In her interview with Jill Neville for the *Independent Magazine* in 1985 Stella makes it sound as if her characterisation of George Shelling in *Bassett* was a straightforward act of writer's revenge on her former lover. But this is not the case. A lesser writer would have made him simply a heartless if charming seducer, but the character of George that emerges is complex, believable and even, up to a point, sympathetic. He feels guilt and remorse at his treatment of Queenie, but the guilt is not enough to change his essential nature, and he offers the fact that he is what he is as a half excuse for his conduct. At the same time, with some justification, he blames his mother for making him what he is. Like Freddie Page in Terence Rattigan's *The Deep Blue Sea* he is too shallow to cope with a demanding relationship, but sufficiently mature to be aware that this is a failing.

If the portrayal of George is an act of revenge, it is revenge of the subtlest kind, done in the knowledge that pity can be more wounding than hatred. While compassion is sometimes only contempt in the vestments of moral superiority, it is not, I think, so in this instance.

There are some incidental delights, in particular the portrait of Christopher Mildmay who is, though quite different in character, the book's Mr Mybug. Once again Stella is satirising those who write about the country, but of a quite different kind from the Webbs and Kaye-Smiths. Mildmay is 'Mohican', a somewhat Georgian belle-lettrist who produces whimsical books and articles about nature and the countryside. He is 'the exact opposite of the Continental Travel Snob . . . Mr Mildmay specialised in buried Essex Inns and almost extinct but incredibly potent brands of ale.' He comes to Bassett to write a book about badgers called *Brother Brock*, and his expertise in country matters is, of course, quite bogus. Without resorting to caricature Stella observes Mildmay with just the right degree of judicious malice.

The comic highlight of the book is the incident where the Shellings, accompanied by Queenie, go on a disastrous badger-watching expedition with Mildmay. Into it is cunningly inter-polated a little snatch of dialogue which indicates to Queenie that George has betrayed her in thought as well as in deed. There are echoes here of the Box Hill picnic in *Emma* at which Emma Woodhouse's rudeness to Miss Bates suddenly injects a sour and serious note into a relatively light-hearted episode. Stella may well have had the book fresh in her mind, as *Bassett* contains a reference to *Emma* and a quotation from it faces the opening page.

Written in 1933, *Bassett* shows a surprisingly early awareness of the evil of Hitler and the Nazis: 'Mrs Shelling decided to . . . pay a visit to Auntie Katt in Innsbruck, hoping to see her once more alive before those Nazis got hold of her, as they seemed to do, in the long run, of anyone who could read, write, and think for themselves.' *Bassett* was published in mid-1934, barely eighteen months after Hitler had become Chancellor and before the death of Hindenburg allowed him to assume absolute power. Female novelists have often been accused of writing within a narrow domestic compass closed off from events in the world outside, but this was never the case with Stella's books. The roar of earth-shaking events is always heard in the distance, like the rumble of London traffic that reaches up incessantly to the ears of walkers on Hampstead Heath.

Bassett bears signs of the carelessness over small details which characterised her fiction. She misuses words: 'careened' is persistently abused in both her prose and poetry; and she mis-spells. Mrs Baker is always calling people 'balmy' when she presumably means 'barmy'. Stella never mastered the simple fact that the possessive pronoun 'its' does not take an apostrophe. Moments of action are sometimes unsatisfactorily described: for example, Mrs Baker at one point negotiates her way through a small broken window without so much as a scratch. (This tendency would persist. Her sister-in-law Renée found in the manuscript of *Starlight*, published in 1967, a hopeless confusion between Mary Tudor and Mary Queen of Scots which fortunately she was able to correct in time.) In addition, and curiously for a poet, Stella sometimes uses unattractive locutions such as 'silverily'. These errors, together with occasional bouts of over-writing, could and should have been corrected by diligent editors and proofreaders.

Though the reviews generally expressed some regret that *Bassett* lacked the inspired brilliance of *Cold Comfort Farm*, there was general recognition that this was a work of solid merits. The *Times Literary Supplement* wrote that 'readers who hope for a repetition of the composite parody of *Cold Comfort Farm* will be surprised to find a straightforward story of village life' but that 'No-one will be disappointed.' The *Times* remarked that her 'wit and sense of fun are as ready as ever'. James Agate, always a fan, wrote that 'her character drawing is perfection, and her sense of fun too subtle to permit quotation'.

Stella used to say that there were two qualities which distinguished the good writer from the merely efficient popular one: the
authentic, individual authorial voice; and a sense of detachment.
She certainly showed that she had found, for better or worse, her
own voice: shrewd, ironic, kindly, but sometimes (in the earlier
books) maddeningly intrusive. As to detachment, it is intermit-
tently achieved in Stella's novels, as she herself acknowledged, but
it is well sustained in *Bassett*.

The novelist Anthony Powell once wrote that one of the essential
attributes of popular fiction is self-pity. It is a characteristic of
best-sellers that the reader is granted the luxury of a kind of
vicarious egoism, by only being permitted to see things from
the point of view of the hero or heroine. Other characters are
assessed entirely in terms of how they act on the protagonist,
who tends to begin as victim and end as victor. Stella never, even
in her worst novels, descended to that level of literary solipsism.
She maintained a degree of irony and detachment even – perhaps
especially – in her self-portraits, such as Sophia in *Enbury Heath*,
and she seldom if ever forgot that there is no such thing as an
unmixed motive. Though she wrote books which she sometimes
called 'romances' she never quite abandoned the integrity of her
irony, which accounts perhaps for the modesty of their success.

In the same year Longmans also published *The Priestess*, her
second collection of poems. After *The Mountain Beast* in 1930
Stella had continued to publish poetry in journals such as the
London Mercury, Time and Tide and *Country Life*, as well as
a number of anthologies. The themes and style of her poems are
not markedly different from her first collection, but many of them
reflect her newly found happiness and its necessary companion,
awareness of its transience. The tone in consequence is more
melancholy and elegiac than that of her first book. Characteristic
of this mood is 'The Secret' which, Renée recorded in her diary,
'is all about us (Stella, Allan, the boys, myself and our friends)
walking on the heath. We all die in the end which is very sad.'

> I know an open secret.
> I hear the music play
> So sweetly! but with a meaning
> Calm and plain as day.

> I know toward what ending
> The evenings turn like a bow;
> And into what silent winter
> I and my dear ones go.

The title poem of the collection is a mysterious, hypnotic piece concerning a priestess of love. She tends a deep inner world of the imagination which is also that of an enduring relationship.

> The world rolls away,
> Wars break in blood and pass.
> Pride, power and glory
> Are shadows on the grass;
> A legend, a story,
> In the cry of the sea.
> Sweetly tends the priestess
> Her dove by night and day.

In this and other poems in the collection, such as 'Worlds' and 'A Birthday', Stella was able to convey something of the intense inwardness of her relationship with Allan without giving away any of its secrets:

> Sea to moonlight,
> Bee to flower throat,
> Bud to sunlight,
> Thou to me.
>
> Seed in earth peace,
> Sight in slumber,
> Sound in silence,
> I in thee.

On 22 January 1935 Renée wrote in her diary that 'Stella was safely delivered of a daughter this morning', and on the 27th she wrote: 'Went to early church. Afterwards went to see Stella in the nursing home and my niece, Laura Caroline Bourne Webb. She seemed a remarkably plain child but she has a nice big mouth and is beautifully made.' Renée's judgement on her looks was soon to be revised. Laura was to become a most attractive and vivacious young girl, and Stella was devoted to her. When she was christened on 11 March the publisher Robert Longman and Allan's aristocratic Aunt Rachel were godparents.

Stella invited her mother's sister Ruby Williams to come and live with them at Upper Park Road. Known as 'Auntie Ru', she was unmarried and had been living in Sydenham. Her father had died in 1930 and Ru, uneducated and unmarriageable, had stayed on in the house which now belonged to Mr Williams's 'little house-keeper' Ethel Lester. Ru had apparently been treated very much as the poor relation by Ethel, though not by Ethel's daughter Nina who was kind to her. Ru told Stella that she was only allowed half a boiled egg at breakfast. Stella saw an opportunity to relieve her aunt's servitude and at the same time acquire an inexpensive nanny.

It was a mixed blessing. Ru was good with children but extremely possessive about both Stella and Laura. She succeeded, according to Renée, in creating bad blood between Stella and her mother-in-law when Allan's parents moved briefly into the flat above theirs in Upper Park Road. At some stage Ru acquired a marmalade cat, which was as jealous of its owner as Ru was of Stella. Ru lived with Stella and Allan until her death in 1954. Both she and her cat appear as Daisy Lister and Dandy in Stella's 1956 novel *Here Be Dragons*, and her young self, again called Daisy Lister, features in the short story 'Edwardian Afternoon'.

In August 1934 Stella's brother Lewis had become engaged to Enid Gawthorne, the sister of Ida Graves's school friend Jean, and in June the following year they married. Lewis's life now became more settled. Unable to fulfil his ambition to follow his father into the medical profession, he had taken a job in a company that sold surgical instruments, a business in which he remained (apart from the war, when he served in the Royal Army Medical Corps) until his retirement. Stella felt she no longer had to worry about him.

The bond between Stella and her brothers, despite their different personalities, remained powerful. The cement of a common suffering held them together, and one of the most interesting aspects of *Enbury Heath*, Stella's next novel, is how frankly she anatomises their relationship in it. The three main characters,

Sophia, Francis and Harry, are Stella, Lewis and Gerald to the life. Only the thinnest veil of fictional gauze covers raw experience and transforms the book into a novel.

This accounts for both its strengths and its weaknesses. There is very little plot: events occur, characters change and develop. It is a slice of life rather than a rounded narrative. At the same time, *Enbury Heath* is one of the bleakest and most vivid of all Stella's novels. The atmosphere of Hampstead (for 'Enbury' read Hampstead) and its less prosperous environs is hauntingly evoked.

The book suffers, as do so many of Stella's later novels, from an element of superfluity. Small incidents, and details of dress and decor, are described at times with unnecessary minuteness. There is a certain banality about some of her observations. Nobody needs to be told, for example, that 'being sick is one of the most disagreeable of the minor human afflictions'. On occasions Stella also employs that over-solicitous attitude to The Reader (once even apostrophised without ironic intention as 'gentle') found in Victorian novelists. Stella liked the amplitude of these writers, their cosy familiarity, and was deliberately imitating them. It is a matter of taste, of course, but on the whole what one can just about tolerate in Trollope and Brontë will not do in a novel of the 1930s.

The book begins with the death of Dr Garden (closely modelled on Telford Gibbons) and describes what happens to his three children, Sophia, Francis and Harry. The story is driven by the will which, produced by Francis at a family meeting, leaves the doctor's entire estate to the eldest son, Harry.

The Gardens' interfering relations are nicely drawn. To cover her tracks (very slightly) Stella has changed the sex of her models. Aunt Louise (the one who had painstakingly cut offending passages from Grandfather Gibbons's diaries) is turned into Uncle Preston, a man with a pathological need to fuss and interfere. The more louche figure of Uncle Arthur becomes Aunt Maxine, a quarrelsome old theatrical has-been, living alone in a malodorous, cat-infested apartment. The attempts of these relatives to invade the young Gardens' life are treated with amused sympathy by the mature Stella. Their efforts are met with stony, barely polite indifference from the children because the one thing all three of them want to do is get away from their miserable family background. The book charts the course of these escapes, and the theme of escape from the past is what gives the book its power. As in reality, the grimmer, more earnest – but more truly humorous – characters of Sophia and Francis (Stella and Lewis) succeed in making some kind of life for themselves. Harry, who, like Gerald, tries to blot out the past in a haze of gaiety and dissipation, never achieves anything and remains trapped in the woodshed of the past.

There are some moments of subtle comedy which are as good as anything Stella ever wrote. One of the best is the scene in which Sophia visits the parents of her younger brother's girlfriend. The father is a fireman and the family live in quarters above the fire station. Stella's gift for minute observation is seen at its best in this description of neat, confined lower middle-class respectability. The comedy derives not from mockery of these classes, but from the misunderstanding that exists between people from different worlds.

> 'Maysie tells me you write poetry,' said Mrs Kellett. 'Do have another tomato.'
> 'Yes,' murmured Sophia. 'No thank you.'
> 'That's very clever,' said Mrs Kellett, rather as a missionary might congratulate an aborigine on his skill in throwing the boomerang.

The book ends with the dissolution of the ménage which Sophia had set up for her brothers. Her attempts to control and discipline their lives have failed, and there is no prospect of her hopeless brother Harry redeeming himself, but the final note is one of optimism in the face of all odds. The possibility of tragedy looms, but youth is on their side, and its openness to adventure is freshly evoked in the closing pages.

In the book the ménage at the cottage in the Vale of Health survives for little more than a year, but in reality it lasted for nearly four years. Though Stella has condensed the time scale and changed the sex of some characters, *Enbury Heath* is, as she told one correspondent, the writer Joan Aiken, in a letter of 2 June 1981, substantially 'true from beginning to end'.

* * *

Renée describes Stella as a devoted mother, as much in love with the concept of motherhood as with her daughter. In a letter to her friend Suzanne Ebel (later Goodwin) in 1940, Stella called Laura 'my little masterpiece', deliberately giving her precedence over *Cold Comfort Farm* or any other work of hers. The distinguished Italian scholar Dr Barbara Reynolds remembers going to a party at Stella's in 1936. (Her father, Alfred Reynolds, composed the music for *1066 and All That*, in which Allan was appearing at the Strand Theatre.) She wrote to Stella some fifty years later: 'You took us upstairs to see your baby girl. She was just at the crawling stage and was sitting on the floor calmly when you opened the door. I was at the awkward age and shy with babies but for some reason she remained in my memory and so did the look of love you gave her.'

In October 1935, the year of Laura's birth, Stella brought out a book dedicated to her. *The Untidy Gnome*, Stella's only children's book, is a pleasing fairy tale set in her beloved Alpine landscape, with an exciting, well-paced narrative in the Hans Andersen vein. The book was elegantly designed by Longmans and, had the illustrations by William Townsend, a distinguished artist and art teacher, been less feeble, it would have done even better. Even so, for a number of people it was a favourite childhood book.

The story, like many of her poems, reflects Stella's ecological concerns. The woodcutter's daughter Gerda is kidnapped by the fairies because her father is cutting down too many trees. During her captivity she lodges with Kob, the untidy gnome of the title and, Flora-like, tidies him up. A familiar theme in Stella's books, the ordering of disorderly lives, is reworked in a pleasing minor key.

Kob, a gnome of letters, is a snobbish, self-absorbed character. His major work, *History of the Gnomes of Grünewald*, is so appallingly weighty that it has to be wheeled about his cave on a trolley (built on Gerda's instructions, of course). He can be added to Stella's extensive portrait gallery of inadequate literary types.

In March 1936 Mabel Constanduros's stage version of *Cold Comfort Farm*, which had been tried out at Brighton in June the previous year, was performed at the Arts Theatre. The cast, which included Felix Aylmer as Amos and Roger Livesey as Seth, was excellent. However, despite an enthusiastic reception from its first-night audience reviews in the papers the next day were lukewarm at best. It was the first of many adaptations, and suffered from the difficulty of transposing a work, the main aspect of whose humour is literary, into a non-literary medium. Other versions have tackled this problem with varying success: only Elizabeth Proud's radio adaptation of 1980 almost completely overcame it. The constraints of time had forced Constanduros, like some subsequent adapters of *Cold Comfort Farm* for the stage, to abandon two of the book's most entertaining characters, Mrs Smiling and Mr Mybug.

In April 1936 Renée's diary recorded the arrival of the first copies of *Miss Linsey and Pa*, Stella's new novel which Renée thought was 'the best yet'. As with *Enbury Heath* Stella had drawn upon her intimate knowledge of life in the poorer environs of Hampstead, but, because she was not bound by the constraints of semi-autobiography, this is a much more satisfactory book.

Pa Linsey is a small grocer driven out of business by the 1930s' equivalent of a supermarket, the Wholesale and Retail Fruiterers Ltd. Accompanied by his middle-aged unmarried daughter he comes to live near his brother-in-law Mr Petley, a tobacconist, and his son Len, a pleasant, weak-willed man still suffering from shell-shock after the First World War. Miss Linsey and Pa – a nicely observed study of genial selfishness – take lodgings in a dirty house owned by Mr Fell, a half-mad recluse, and his rackety wife. The other lodger, an enigmatic black man, works for a doctor who has been struck off the register. The atmosphere of this establishment is curiously Pinteresque.

All these characters – some damaged, some dangerous, some simply poor – are portrayed unsentimentally and on their own terms. Stella brings the force of her irony to bear on the way they are perceived by a smart, intelligent woman higher up the social scale:

> She noticed – for she had, it was generally conceded by her friends, an eye for detail – how mechanically he [Len] got out the packet, without interest, lifelessly. Like an automaton.
>
> But that was what their lives made of those victims of the economic system. They became automata: wireless-educated, cinema-thrilled, fed on tinned food, having no deep contact with Beauty, without which Life was only existence.

This is the kind of compassion that comes perilously close to contempt. It also signals one of the themes of the book, which is social class and attitudes towards it.

The character who is thinking these thoughts is Dorothy Hoad, the Bloomsbury lesbian to whom Miss Linsey goes as cook-housekeeper. Dorothy lives with a novelist, Edna Lassiter, for whom she feels a deep and possessive love. Edna is financially dependent on Dorothy and fond of her, but is not by nature a lesbian.

To be sure, Stella does not approve of Dorothy's lesbian passion, but less because of its sexual orientation than because it is solemn, over-intense and selfish. It may well be, as Nicola Beauman suggests in *A Very Great Profession*, that Stella is mocking the over-heated, miserable atmosphere of Radclyffe Hall's lesbian novel of 1928 *The Well of Loneliness*. The affair is chronicled with enough detail and conviction to suggest a fairly close acquaintance, not necessarily at first hand, with a certain kind of homosexual passion.

Edna is rescued by Billy Barton, a doctor, one of those hearty, over-masculine young heroes who occasionally crop up in Stella's fiction from her *Evening Standard* story 'Lost Children This Way' onwards. Stella seemed to approve of such men, even in real life, though she took care not to marry one of them. It was part of her passion for what she thought of as 'normality'; in other words, as different from the Gibbons family as possible.

After aiding and abetting the escape of Edna Lassiter into the arms of Billy, Miss Linsey goes to look after the child of one of Edna's friends, Perdita James. Perdita is a communist and when Miss Linsey first meets her she is reading J. C. Powys's *In Defence of Sensuality*, which Stella had reviewed rather disrespectfully in the *Lady* six years previously. Perdita is a study in modish silliness, with her guilt about a private income, her socialism (which does not prevent her behaving with upper-class condescension towards Miss Linsey) and her cranky ideas on child-rearing. Although very amusing, it makes some subtle and serious points about the misunderstandings that exist between classes. Miss Linsey's lower middle-class conservatism is seen for what it is: a product not so much of mental atrophy as of stony pragmatism.

Her sense is contrasted with the sensibility of the middle-class characters, who are progressive, liberal and intellectual, and who work for the BBC. The point is made that their abandonment of the shackles of convention has merely led them to adopt another set of shackles, all the more burdensome for being unacknowledged. Free love, in other words, proves to be exceedingly costly.

If the satire directed at them is at times heavy-handed, it is none the less based on experience. Four of the intellectuals spend a wife-swapping weekend in the country, which results in a series of farcical incidents with something of the vigour of *Cold Comfort Farm*. There is even a dash of parody thrown in. One of the characters, Tom, is writing a novel called *Work* about Yorkshire herring fishermen, and he insists on reading it aloud to his fellow weekenders: 'Ebor, his creased face poxed with nodules of frozen spray which the morning's thaw now dissolved, eased the mainsail a little, looking slantways at the slithering ruck of silver in the hold. . . .'

As with the starred passages in *Cold Comfort Farm*, the prose is almost genuinely evocative. But it gives the impression of a writer striving a little too hard, with rather too little genuine experience to draw upon, and that is what makes it comic. Stella's source of inspiration for *Work* was probably the self-consciously rugged prose of H. A. Manhood's *Gay Agony*, which she had reviewed for the *Lady* in 1930. Like *Work*, this is a novel written by a minor Bloomsburyite, and concerns the doings of fishermen and other rude folk with odd names such as Tobulus Steen, Obid Lanyon, Amos Toplady and Jesher Pouchall who live in a coastal village called Thrust. Stella's parody can seem like mere pastiche when set against passages in *Gay Agony* like this: 'Rain had come like a belated passion. Daylight seemed no more than a pale reflection surviving from some past day. The low, slow-moving clouds might have been ferns supported on the needle stems of rain. Hissing screens obscured the moor, breaking against the windows of the *Black Smock* with a sound suggestive of the birth of thorns.'

Besides the afflictions of inspissated prose, there is rain, a mad horse and too much washing up, all of which lead to unseemly scuffles and accusations of nymphomania. The couples, needless to say, never get to swap partners. The fiasco was inspired by goings on in Stella's friend Ina Dornan's cottage at Hockley where, according to Stella, it always rained.

'Let other pens dwell on guilt and misery'

Miss Linsey and Pa reaches a memorable and emblematic climax when Pa, who has befriended the deranged Mr Fell, decides he must release one of Fell's caged birds, a skylark, but is killed by Fell for having done so. His daughter has been the agent of freedom throughout the book, firstly of Edna Lassiter, then of Perdita James and her young daughter, then of her cousin Len Petley, much put upon by his stifling, cricket-loving father. Her mild, self-absorbed father's one attempt at an unselfish act is instantly punished. The scene at night in the mean streets just after the murder has an eerie, poetic quality about it:

> Someone had lit the gas, and the crude light poured on the two stooping figures in white coats, the red-clad negro towering over them and giving instructions which they heard with a quiet professional indifference: the form of Mrs Fell in the background weeping noisily and showing much white shoulder.
>
> A policeman had appeared from nowhere, asked some questions, looked at the huge figure of Mr Fell sitting on the stairs with his face in his hands, and gone away to fetch two more policemen. Now they were gently but inexorably taking Mr Fell to the station. Their deep voices rose and fell in a kind of soothing chorus as they urged, coaxed, brushed away the crowd like so many waterflies, and set off slowly with Mr Fell in their midst. They shut him in like a wall: each time he hung back, bewildered and frightened, he bumped against their iron arms.

If Stella's occasional tendency to moralise and to let her own personality intrude rather aggressively into the story can be tolerated, *Miss Linsey and Pa* has many rewards for the reader.

In November 1936 Allan and Stella bought 19 Oakshott Avenue off Highgate West Hill on the Holly Lodge Estate, not far from the Heath. It was a pleasant, undistinguished semi-detached house, of the kind once categorised by Osbert Lancaster as 'By-Pass Variegated'. There were two spacious reception rooms on the ground floor, one with a bow window looking on to Oakshott Avenue, the other at the back with French windows giving on to a long rectangular garden. Upstairs were three bedrooms and a small box room overlooking the front door, where Stella would write whenever possible from ten until lunchtime. Though a very ordinary house in many ways, the interior carried the clear imprint of Stella's personality. Neither the furniture, the pictures, nor the objects on display were very remarkable in themselves, but their arrangement was careful and harmonious. There was an air of orderly and idiosyncratic eclecticism about the decor – soft pinks and apricots on the walls – and, above all, of a kind of unforced serenity. Nearly everyone who entered the house remarked on the collection of shells on the hall table. No one individual shell was valuable, but each one had been carefully selected and positioned so that the overall effect was charming. It is evident from Stella's writing – in particular passages from her penultimate and unpublished novel *The Yellow Houses* – that these decorative effects were not unselfconscious effusions of her personality but deliberately achieved; they were a reaction against the chaotic gloom of her childhood home in Malden Crescent. Stella lived at Oakshott Avenue for the fifty-three years that remained to her.

Allan played Theseus in *A Midsummer Night's Dream* at Birmingham over the Christmas of 1936, then in 1937 returned to the West End as a footman in *Victoria Regina* at the Lyric. It was a lavish production, designed by Rex Whistler, which opened one hundred years to the day after Victoria's accession. Allan recalled to his sister long afterwards that this was one of the happiest of his professional engagements. The work was easy, pleasant and free from responsibility – most of his time was spent playing cards in the dressing room with his fellow small part players. Meanwhile, the more ambitious and self-confident Renée was playing leading roles in provincial repertory seasons.

With his attractive appearance and excellent singing voice, Allan was never out of work. After *Victoria Regina* he took leading parts in various touring opera productions which were followed in January 1939 by a small role in *Magyar Melody*, a sub-Novello-ish vehicle for Binnie Hale at His Majesty's (James Agate called it 'a mass of glitter and pretence, a costly wilderness in which nothing grows'). Then came Captain Frank Inglehurst VC in the extraordinary cult success *Young England* and a revue which occupied him until he enlisted in the army in July 1940. Reviews of his work were always complimentary, but never extravagantly enthusiastic. The old lack of confidence prevented Allan from scaling the heights, and his promise remained unfulfilled.

It was not that Allan did not care about his career. Meticulously he kept scrapbooks preserving programmes, press cuttings, even the odd contract. Letters from fans and from managements either engaging him, or releasing him from engagements, are also included. Scores of operas or copies of plays in which he appeared have cast lists and newspaper reviews pasted into the fly leaves. Allan was a man who was anxious to make his mark, but lacked the will to turn passive aspiration into active ambition.

Stella's book for 1937 was *Roaring Tower and Other Stories*. All but one of these stories, 'Single, St Alban's, First Class', had first been published in newspapers and magazines. Some of them, such as 'Sweet Peas of Paris' and 'Snowbound', very slight romantic tales that first appeared in the *Lady*, betray their ephemeral origin. All the stories are well crafted and deftly written; few are particularly original. The short story form did not suit Stella: her characters needed the longer maturation period of a novel in order to spring fully to life, and she rarely delivered a strong enough narrative punch at the end.

There are, however, some interesting and unexpected things in the collection. 'Saturday Afternoon', an account of a middle-aged working-class couple's day, surprises with a convincing and evocative account of a football match in the Chelsea ground at Stamford Bridge seen from a male point of view. 'Single, St Alban's, First Class' is a strange, rather memorable tale about an encounter with the Seven Deadly Sins in a railway carriage, while 'The Frowning Duchess' is a neat little story full of understated ironies about those who marry for money and position and those who condemn such acts, ostensibly from principle but actually out of envy.

'Roaring Tower' is the best story in the collection and has been anthologised several times, most recently in the *Virago Book of Women's Ghost Stories*. It takes the form of a pastiche Victorian ghost story and starts very much in the manner of Charlotte Brontë – all breathless emotional engagement – with a girl of nineteen's description of being sent away to Cornwall to be weaned off 'an unfortunate attachment'. She is drawn to a local landmark,

Roaring Tower, a ruined structure which emits a mysterious noise that both fascinates and terrifies the local inhabitants. In making contact with the spirit trapped in the tower and in feeling a grief other than her own she manages to release both the spirit and herself. Much is suggested, little explained; as a result of which the essential mystery and beauty of the story remain intact. There is something of the calculated reserve of M. R. James in the descriptions of the trapped spirit – a shadowy, half bear-like creature – and the noise it makes. In atmosphere and language the tale is nearer to Stella's poetry than to her prose. It is in the top class of supernatural stories and deserves to be better known.

The story in the collection that meant most to Stella was 'It Does Sometimes Happen'. In Renée's copy of *Roaring Tower* Stella has written the title of the story after an inscription to her sister-in-law. The story is set in theatreland, 'Grape Street' off Covent Garden. An over-the-hill actress, Dorothy Wood, meets a boxer, similarly on the slide, in a café, and they decide to run a pub together. Though slight, the story is told with great warmth and sincerity. It is a passionate affirmation of faith in her marriage to Allan: 'For out of a world ruled by cruelty, avarice and chance, where beauty may be a delusion and remorseless time rushes like the wind, a man and a woman will wrest happiness and hold it. Rare as an eclipse, rare as the flowering of the aloe, but it does sometimes happen.'

Though she came to conventional Christian belief later in life, Stella's most basic faith always resided in the possibility of happiness achievable through a close personal relationship and 'the holiness of the heart's affections'. A distinction must be drawn between faith and illusion, not always easy, but possible in Stella's case. She knew from experience that such happiness does not always happen, and that if it does it should not be taken for granted; but that 'it does sometimes happen'. This is faith. On the other hand she was under no illusions that Allan was a paragon, and was fully aware of his weaknesses when she married him.

Of all Stella's books after *Cold Comfort Farm*, the four which most deserve to be reprinted are *The Bachelor* (1944), *Westwood* (1946), *Starlight* (1967) and her next novel, *Nightingale Wood*, which was both a critical and commercial success when it appeared in 1938. It was serialised in *Good Housekeeping*, where it was billed as 'a romantic comedy'. Dedicated to her sister-in-law Renée and Ruth, a cousin by marriage, it is a lightly disguised and wittily ironic version of *Cinderella*. There is a handsome prince (a rich, unattached young businessman), who is indeed handsome but also more than a little absurd. There are two ugly sisters, but they are snobbish and thwarted rather than unpleasant; there is a Baron Hardup who is mean rather than poverty-stricken; there is a ball, but it is only the local charity ball; and Buttons (the chauffeur) runs off with one of the ugly sisters. Cinderella herself is an amiable, attractive, unimaginative young widow. Her fairy godmother is a worldly and 'common' friend who transforms her with a hairdo and a dress (by 'Rose-Berthe', the fashionable dressmaker) for the ball. She also gives the Cinderella character just the right advice for capturing her prince, who is also worldly and, if not exactly 'common', has more than a touch of brashness about him.

Nightingale Wood is *Cinderella* brought right up to date, and, like *Cold Comfort Farm*, a lexicon of contemporary fads and failings from dictators and developers to swing bands and psychological self-help books. The mood sustained throughout the book, again like *Cold Comfort Farm*, is of a slightly stylised, heightened reality, tempered by canny psychological subtlety.

The story is set in Essex and concerns the Withers, a stiflingly respectable family who have Viola, the young widow of the recently deceased son of the family, to live with them. She is a former shopgirl, emphatically not their class, and the book's Cinderella. The ugly sisters are the unmarried Wither daughters, both in their thirties. Madge is a twelve-stone golf-playing hearty; Tina is the thirties' equivalent of an anorexic, always dieting and reading books on psychology. Neither is particularly gifted or attractive. In their youth they had made half-hearted stabs at independence (working in kennels and attending art school respectively), but now they are stranded. Not gifted enough for an occupation, not attractive enough for marriage, they remain in the Wither home. Dim middle-class young men in those days could usually find some sort of employment, but for dim young women the prospects were dismal. Another character in the novel, Hetty, is richer and brighter than the Wither girls but suffers from the same sense of superfluity. She could conform and get married, but she is bookish and scornful of the amiable, vacuous young men-about-town who are cast in her direction. As Viola's fairy godmother Shirley puts it: 'That's about the ticket, darling. Vote, Marie [Stopes], perms and all, we still can't do anything.'

The household's stifling atmosphere is evoked with comedy, but its tragic aspects are only just beneath the surface. When, during one of the Withers' deadly meals, Madge, who 'Never Howls', tearfully blurts out her longing for a dog ('Colonel Phillips has just got three ripping Sealyham pups'), the effect is terrible and funny. It is absurd that Madge's happiness should rest on the possession of a Sealyham – *the* dog of the 1930s – and that Mr Wither out of sheer meanness should deny her one, but it is also desperately sad.

The problem lies not simply in old Wither's obsession with money, but in a condition of English society at the time. When Mrs Wither goes to persuade her husband to let Madge have a dog: 'She knew as a woman and as a mother that . . . what Madge needed was something to love. But it never entered her head to tell her husband so. Not only would he not have understood, but it would have been the kind of thing one does not say. There were ever so many things like that; most things, in fact.'

Mr Wither is a monster, and an enjoyably real one. As with many real-life monsters, his monstrosity is paradoxically all the more monstrous for being so petty. Stella observes him with gleeful malice as well as detached pity. He is a man who does not look up when his wife enters the room 'because he had seen her before'. He is obsessed by money, and I can remember more than once hearing Stella quote Mr Wither's catchphrase when she felt that she herself was becoming too preoccupied with financial matters. She would sigh: ' "Money: a little word but a very important one!", as old Mr Wither used to say.' In his obsession with wealth, his snobbery, his desiccated respectability and his desire to interfere he bears a strong resemblance to Stella's uncle by marriage, Cyprian.

Wither has a friend even nastier than himself called Mr Spurrey, a rich old bachelor whose chief pleasure in life is frightening people with alarming pieces of confidential information. 'Had he lived in a savage tribe, Mr Spurrey would have been buried up to the neck in earth and left to die. . . . This is one of the unobtrusive gifts to mankind of civilisation, gentlest of the sciences. It seems small: yet if we started to be logical about the uses of the Mr Spurreys, civilisation would quietly die.' Because the mood of her writing is naturally tolerant and benign, when Stella does unexpectedly let her viciousness off the leash the effect is exhilarating. But Spurrey's role in the book is more than just ornamental: before the end both his malice and his pathetic sadness as a character have a role to play.

The nearest house of major importance to the Withers is 'Grassmere' (separated from the Withers by the Nightingale Wood of the title) and it is occupied by Mrs Spring, her son Victor and her niece Hetty Franklin. Victor, the Prince Charming of the story, with his blond good looks and vulgar lifestyle, is another version of Walter Beck, but this time glamorised and made more ridiculous. As well as being the owner of a fruit canning factory, Victor runs Spring Developments Ltd which was 'gaily destroying the country' and at odds with 'the dreaded secret police of the S.P.R.E. [Society for the Protection of Rural England] and the National Trust gang'.

Stella's revisiting of Walter is carefree, more in satire than in sorrow. Her Prince Charming's attitude to money, when contrasted with old Wither's approach, is almost to be commended. 'Victor treated money, not like a tyrant that must be fawned upon and bullied, but as an old pal; he stood it drinks, so to speak, and it stood him more drinks in return.' The effect is beguiling. She casts a satirical eye on the moneyed late 1930s' luxury of Victor's home:

> If gin was spilled upon a cushion of bright plum-red velvet with a heavy silver fringe, then that cushion disappeared and another one, of black satin embroidered heavily with irises in fourteen natural shades and costing 49s. 11d took its place. Should an ashtray in the shape of a winsomely begging Sealyham fall on the floor and chip an ear, away it went, and another, in the shape of a coquettishly imploring Cairn, appeared in its stead, each having cost 37s. 6d.

She loves to conjure up the sleek Art Moderne atmosphere that wafts from the glossy full-page advertisements for De Reszke cigarettes and Hispano Suiza motor cars in society magazines of the period, and then slyly subvert it:

> The dining-room at the White Rock Hotel was designed to re-

semble the deck of a luxury liner, and the waiters were condemned to dress like stewards. There were stylised waves and seagulls on the walls, narrow waxed blocks of parquet that suggested deckboards on the floor, and a bevy of sea gods, dolphins and contemporary bathing beauties wallowing on the ceiling. The spiritless energy of these frescoes was much admired, and people came from near and far, so to speak, to look at the place.

One of the delights of the book is the character of Falger, an old tramp who used to be a model for artists such as Alma-Tadema and Holman Hunt ('Beautiful, I used to be. A fair treat. Am still, come to that'). A monster of cheerful, self-approving egoism, he is good for nothing but to 'be offered as a mascot to an inferiority complex clinic'. He invites young girls to watch him bathing in the nude, purely, he says, so that they can admire his physique. As he remarks: 'When it ain't Art it's dirt, but if it's Art it's all right, see?' Damien Hirst could not have put it better.

Falger stands as the opposite end of the spectrum to the tight middle-class snobbery of the Essex men and women whom Stella is mostly describing. Though known in the community as 'The Hermit', he is far from being a saintly character. He is dirty, violent and deeply selfish; but he is much happier than the Withers of this world, because he is, as Stella puts it, 'an individual and not a type'. By a type she means someone who conforms unwillingly or unthinkingly to a particular social pattern. As Victor's cousin Hetty observes, Viola in her small way is an individual, whereas Phyllis, her rival for Victor's affections, though infinitely more sophisticated, is a type. Tina becomes an individual by falling in love with the family chauffeur. Hetty finds fulfilment by going to live in London with an alcoholic poet.

The characters of Falger and Hetty show that being an individual is not necessarily a moral activity in the conventional sense; but it has moral implications because real virtue is only possible to the individual. The characters of Tina and Saxon, the chauffeur, find goodness in themselves and each other by breaking out of their respective social ghettos, even though towards the end the unexpected appearance of a large sum of money threatens to divide them. The book has a number of interesting things to say on money and the lack of it, and their respective effects on human character.

Stella is always good on the subject of money and poverty in her novels. Most of her young heroines are impoverished and have to get by on small salaries or allowances. She can make vivid and interesting the exact and crucial difference that the loss of an apparently trifling sum of money each week can make to a person's life. She could also from experience describe the horrors of being thrown out of work and having nothing to stave off destitution but a few dwindling pounds in the Post Office. Male novelists who have not had to handle a domestic budget from day to day tend to be vaguer than women writers on this subject.

In *Nightingale Wood* the distinctive Gibbons authorial voice is never intrusive because it has so many witty and pertinent things to say. It is at one with the narrative, which plays cunning tricks on the reader. Just as the story seems to be hastening towards a straightforward romantic conclusion it is turned aside by an ironic twist in the plot. Some of these twists have a surprisingly modern feel about them and include the suspicion of homosexuality and the use of a four-letter word. The Word, uttered by Falger, is not spelt out, of course, but it is quite obvious what it is and it plays a small but significant part in the plot. What matters is not the word itself but the effect it has on its hearers, which is enjoyably described. (Poor Mrs Wither is the only one who has never actually heard it before: thus the most demure character is the least shocked.)

The publication of *Nightingale Wood* in 1938 attracted the attention of a young contemporary historian and journalist, Dr Fritz Walter Pick, a German patriot disgusted by the racism and barbarity of the Nazi regime. He came from a family with good political connections and as a student in Berlin in 1933 had witnessed the infamous book-burnings. His field of research was Anglo-British relations, and he had written an article in a prominent German newspaper on Kaiser Wilhelm's notorious interview for the *Daily Telegraph* in October 1908. In the article he had emphasised the peace-loving nature of the British and the aggression of the Kaiser. It would not have required much intelligence to see Hitler's rantings prefigured in the unstable arrogance of the Kaiser's outpourings thirty years before, and to take them as an omen of impending disaster now, at the time of the Munich Crisis.

As a member of an academically based circle known as the

Nikolasseekreis, Dr Pick believed in the power of the word to counteract the evil of Nazism. He wanted to disseminate works with a strongly democratic and pro-British bias, and planned to bypass the censor by using the publishing firm of Essener Verlagensanstalt. Although the German press was under the control of Dr Goebbels, Minister for Propaganda and Enlightenment, his great rival Reichsmarschall Hermann Goering retained control over the Essener Verlagensanstalt, which produced fine-quality books.

Pick translated four books in 1938 and published them through this firm. The most important was the autobiography of Sir Austen Chamberlain with a preface which Pick had specially commissioned for this edition from Sir Austen's brother, the then Prime Minister, Neville Chamberlain. To this was added *Ourselves and Germany* by Pick's friend and ally the Marquess of Londonderry, a man who, as Air Minister, would have been of great interest to his German counterpart Goering. Pick also translated the memoirs of Richard Haldane, a British statesman, partly educated in Germany, who had played an important role in events leading up to the First World War. The fourth title was *Nightingale Wood*, which Pick chose partly to disguise his real political intentions, partly to show England to Germany in a warm and sympathetic light.

Though Hitler himself had always professed a love of England – indeed he had confided his anglophilia to Hugh Walpole, who had befriended him at Bayreuth in the early 1920s – a lot of anti-British propaganda was being disseminated in Germany at this time. Pick was therefore looking for a book which would exemplify all that would seem good about England to a German: the charm of the countryside; a fresh and genial romanticism; and gentle wisdom wittily expressed: in short, *Gemütlichkeit*. He found it in the newly published *Nightingale Wood*.

Though Pick worked at high speed, he produced an elegant translation, the only sign of haste being his rendering of 'hansom cab' in German as 'beautiful carriage'. Published as *Das Nachtigallenwäldchen*, it was superbly printed on fine paper and had a cloth binding of floral design, with a different but complementary floral pattern on its slip case. A label on the case and on the binding bore its title in pale green and pink, together with a picture of a straw hat on a rustic bench. It is a thing of beauty, and Stella considered it the most excellently produced of all versions of her works.

In the *Essener Almanach* for 1938 Pick emphasises the theme of class in *Nightingale Wood*, saying that the book touches on the subjects that John Galsworthy wrote about, but in a more humorous and satirical vein. Galsworthy is mentioned because he was a Nobel Prize winner and the kind of serious, slightly stodgy English writer with whom most literate Germans would be familiar. Comparison with him would establish Stella's credentials in their eyes. Pick adds: '. . . but one can also open it [the book] to see England, the country and its inhabitants, and watch them live, laugh and love'. He does not make the same mistake about Stella as the German authorities later did about P. G. Wodehouse when they assumed that lightly mocking a few brainless aristocrats was the same as attacking English society. While Wodehouse played an elegant series of variations on stock musical comedy themes, Stella was engaged in rather more serious social criticism, but this still did not amount to subversion. Rather charmingly, Pick says elsewhere that the book is to be enjoyed 'like a tasty white wine punch'.

The subject of anti-Semitism is touched upon lightly in *Nightingale Wood*. When Tina and Saxon escape to London they take up with a Jewish family, the Baumers, who live in a mews near to theirs. Baumer is an artist and Tina had been at art school with his wife. They are bohemian in the best sense of the word: cultivated and tolerant, givers of parties full of interesting people, encouraging and argumentative. They are the most completely civilised people in the book: that is to say, they care about ideas; and they are thoughtful about themselves, others and the world at large. Needless to say, the other Withers are suspicious when they hear about them; they talk scornfully and fatuously about 'Jews in mews'. In other words they exhibit that mild but stubbornly ubiquitous brand of anti-Semitism which was characteristic of England between the wars. Some German readers must have been prompted to reflect on their nation's own more virulent strain of the disease.

Das Nachtigallenwäldchen was favourably received in Germany and sold well, going through several editions. Dr Goebbels and his censor were enraged by the publication and success of Pick's translations, but there was nothing they could do as Goering's protection made the books unassailable. Moreover, Hitler had been presented with copies of all four works and had put them in his library.

It is curious to think of this witty and charming book as a secret weapon in the fight against fascism, but it is not, on reflection, inappropriate. Everything in Stella's being was opposed to the Nazi ethos, and had been since its earliest manifestations. She hated that bullying, arrogant, humourless posturing which was so much a part of the Gibbons temperament, even down to the love of Wagner. Perhaps this was why she had recognised the threat of Nazi totalitarianism so early. (But her brother Lewis had been, for a brief while, a Mosleyite.)

At the time Stella did not know of her book's part, however small, in the fight against Hitler, and was only told of it by Dr Pick's son in the 1970s. In 1942 Dr Pick had, however, published an account of this venture in his book *The Art of Dr Goebbels*, something which put his family and friends in Germany at great risk.

In an article written for *St Martin's Review* in October 1938, Stella claimed that as a novelist she had no politics and that she wrote to entertain, but that this did not mean she had no principles. She explained:

> I write because to write is to me as natural and as necessary as to breathe, and I write to *express my picture of the world*. That is all, but I am only able to make these simple statements after years of struggle and doubt – not with the writing itself, for that has always been a delight – but with the idea behind the writing, the picture of the world that has been slowly forming in my mind.
>
> I suppose that writers may be gently divided (there is more than enough roughness about nowadays, so let us divide gently if we divide at all) into three types; those who have made their own picture of the world and show it forth in their books, those who have axes to grind, and those who simply reflect the world like mirrors. I believe that the first type is the born or natural novelist and that his whole duty is to present his

picture of the world as vividly and truthfully as is possible; and I quarrel with the propaganda-novelist because he uses his people and his story as Cases to prove his political theories. I quarrel with the mirror-novelist because he pitches his scenes and people onto paper without shape or conclusion. The first writes with too much conclusion behind his writing, the second with no conclusion at all, and while the one appeals to the reader's soft head, the other with his dreary pictures of whining, discontented sub-humans appeals to the reader's soft nerves, for the mirror-novelist prides himself on being unsentimental and does not talk about hearts being touched.

Well, that sounds as if I think my own way of writing is the only right way, and that is just what I do think – after years of doubt – or I should not write as I do. I love my work, I am humble about it, and I dare to hope that I have a religious attitude towards it. . . . If a writer is faithful to his picture of the world, faith will glow like light in his work, however trivial the work may be.

In 1938 Stella also published her third book of verse, *The Lowland Venus*, which is of the same high standard as her previous collections. The longest and most important poem was 'The Marriage of the Machine' which reflects on the evils of industrialisation. It is both forward- and backward-looking. It harks back to the horror felt by the Romantics at the coming of the industrial revolution:

> I saw the Wheel, the only god
> Who eats his massy flesh
> Who ceaselessly weaves energy
> And doth devour the mesh . . .
>
> And where that rolling shadow fell,
> Dying within the shade
> Lay starving mannikins, whose dreams
> That fearful strength had made.

On the other hand it deals with issues of industrial pollution which only became fashionable in the 1960s. The Sea sings:

Oh my tides, my rocks and waving flowers,
What is your sickness?
What hurts you, my dolphins, my seals
In your slipping quickness?
What oil, what poison lulls
Your wings and webs, my cormorants and gulls?

Among other poems in the collection particularly good are the
'Six Songs', of which the last is perhaps the most memorable:

Soft, but clearly, sweethearts,
Tolls the passing bell
Through this haunted heaven
Where we have to dwell.
Therefore, friends and husband,
Love we well.

Where the open flower
Dances by her leaf,
Through the fullest hour
Blows the breath of grief
Warning child and mother
Life is brief.

Child and friend and husband,
Hear the warning sigh.
Beauty ends in sorrow,
One of us must die
And one must watch a coffin
Passing by.

If love could choose, the watcher
Should be I.

In John Gawsworth's anthology of *Neo-Georgian Poetry*
(*1936–1937*) the poem was printed separately as 'The Bell'. It
was one of Stella's finest lyrics; it was also prophetic.

CHAPTER 6

'A Woman's Diary of the War'

The possibility of war had a profound effect on Stella. She had a great attachment to what she called 'the good Germany', and her affair with the German Walter Beck was still a deep if hidden wound. There is some evidence that before the rise of fascism Stella was inclined towards pacifism. Renée's diary for 7 February 1932 records that Stella and her future mother-in-law Jessie had an argument about pacifism, the implication being that Stella stood for the latter.

By 1938, reluctantly, she was beginning to change her views. There is a note at the beginning of *The Lowland Venus*: '*The Marriage of the Machine* is unfinished because the enthusiasm which I felt for the idea of the poem some five years ago has vanished; also, my views on the probable industrialisation of the world have changed.' The wording is ambiguous, but it seems that Stella had come to realise that industrial power in Britain was needed to manufacture the weapons to fight Nazi Germany. The vague Luddism and nature mysticism of the poem would not do in the face of savage facts about tanks and aeroplanes. Nevertheless, by the time the poem appeared again, in 1950 in Stella's *Collected Poems*, the note had gone.

It was becoming apparent that external events were going to mar the hard-won tranquillity of her life with Allan and Laura. She worried about the international situation. In 1938, Stella became pregnant again but lost the child. She told Renée that she had miscarried because of her anxiety over the Munich Crisis.

Further evidence of her state of mind emerges from her correspondence with the German translator of *Nightingale Wood*. On 29 March 1939 she wrote to Dr Pick: 'To be truthful, I have been so *wretched* about the international situation that it's only with difficulty that I can get through my everyday affairs at all.' On 11 June: 'Oh! how I wish England and Germany would kiss and be friends. One hangs on, hoping and praying, until one's teeth seem to ache with the effort. Have you *really* decided to adopt British nationality? I wouldn't presume to advise you, but surely you will think seriously before giving up your own country – Christmas trees and lieder and Beethoven – such lovely things to give to the world!' On 28 August:

> It seems hopeless, but somehow I haven't given up hope – I don't know why. It's true I did cry for a whole hour when the Nazi –Bolshevist Pact was announced, but now I feel better – for some reason strength comes from somewhere at these times. Of course, if the worst happens I may be a hopeless coward – I don't know. It must be dreadful for you – I do sympathise with you so deeply and wish I could think of something comforting to say – do remember that the good things last for ever, no matter if they seem to die, and that it is something to have loved and worked for them.

Soon after war was declared in September 1939 Stella had Laura evacuated with Auntie Ru to Allan's mother, Jessie Webb, at Ditchling in Sussex where she and her husband Charles had bought a cottage. It was not a happy time for Laura who found her ailing grandmother, then approaching seventy, rather dour, and she returned to Oakshott Avenue the following January.

Published on the eve of war in 1939, *My American* has a strong escapist element to it. Apart from a passing reference to an air raid warden there is no mention of the world events about which Stella felt so deeply. It is as if she has sealed herself off and written this 'romance', as she called it, in a kind of trance. One of Stella's books which I inherited after her death is Alister Hardy's *The Biology of God*. In it she has underlined a quotation from William James about the mysterious power which, in times of crisis, 'raises our centre of personal energy, and produces regenerative effects unattainable in other ways'. Against this Stella put an asterisk and wrote this footnote: 'I only once – if then – experienced it at the height of the Munich crisis, 1938.' *My American*, an intensely romantic novel, must have been produced in this heightened mood while she was recovering from the double trauma of Munich and her miscarriage.

If *Nightingale Wood* is a version of *Cinderella*, *My American* is a variant of Hans Andersen's *The Snow Queen*, a quotation from which appears on the dedication page. It was one of her most commercially successful books, though it lacks much of the humour and vivid characterisation of her other work.

It begins in the autumn of 1928 at Kenwood on Hampstead Heath, where a nine-year-old Amy Lee meets an American boy, Robert Vorst. The novel follows their respective fortunes until they are brought together in the final chapters. As in *The Snow Queen* it is the girl who seeks out the boy, but it is Amy who has a splinter of ice in her heart, put there by her ambition and success as a writer. The boy is also wounded, but by guilt at having killed a child in a road accident.

The story of Amy and Robert resembles that of Allan and Stella in that it is about the coming together of two people, both in their different ways wounded by the world. Allan, like Robert, had an easy childhood and a warm, unambitious nature, but suffered from a breakdown in early manhood. Stella, like Amy, had a tough childhood which helped to forge the steely, secretively ambitious side to her character. Imagination, however, has made alterations, and the differences between fiction and reality are as illuminating as the similarities.

Amy is another of Stella's socially dislocated heroines. She is the daughter of a 'gentleman', albeit one who has married beneath him and chosen low company and pursuits. Tim Lee is a gambler and a drinker, and seems to have been modelled on Stella's eldest brother Gerald with a touch of her father. Amy's mother Edie, dead before the story begins, had been loving, serene and humorous, an idealised version of Stella's own mother. After her father's death Amy is brought up in a lower middle-class environment, a baker's family, well and unsentimentally described. Her voice has a 'cockney whine' which, when she begins to work in journalism, is slowly and unselfconsciously dropped. I suspect this was what happened to Stella, for her voice, as I remember it, had the chiselled, slightly over-refined quality of an acquired accent. (Later in life she found the 'off' accents of her two grandchildren one of the very few things about them for which she did not care. Her objections, however, were entirely on aesthetic grounds.) Stella's own sense of having no particular social status – it did not amount to insecurity – is what gave her writing about class its distinctive objectivity and acuity. Equally, the outsiderish attributes of her heroines made them, like her, both vulnerable and tough.

Amy as a writer is Stella, but without her sophistication or intellect; and, to create her character, Stella projected her immature, adolescent self into Amy's adulthood. Amy writes romantic adventure stories of the kind that Stella wrote at the age of twelve, based on Rider Haggard and Ouida. Like Stella, Amy is a 'natural' writer for whom the process of writing was a pleasure and a necessity. Amy as a writer is different from Stella in that she is less interested in reflecting on the quirks and vagaries of human nature than in creating an alternative world, simpler, more dangerous and more exciting than reality. One can see Stella wanting to be that kind of writer – indeed, to a certain extent trying to be in this book; but this was not the kind of writer – or person – she really was.

One of the most curious aspects of Stella's character was that in many ways she wanted to be simpler and more ordinary than she actually was. It could be seen in her hatred of publicity: she much preferred being Mrs Webb to Stella Gibbons. I remember her telling me in the late 1970s how she had found what she considered was a nice greengrocer's and was very cross that someone had told the people in the shop that she was an authoress. She was afraid of going there again in case she was treated as an oddity or, worse still, a celebrity. When I made a remark which implied that I thought her reaction excessive, she seemed mildly offended. But, more than that, she was troubled by the complexity and ambivalence of her own thoughts and feelings. Especially when she became a Christian in her later years, a part of her would have liked to have been *un coeur simple* with a strong untroubled faith, but her mind was too enquiring and subtle for that. All her life she found some solace in writing about people less complex than herself. Because she respected such people and felt no inclination at all to condescend, she wrote well about them.

This craving for simplicity accounts for her violent detestation of Freud and all his works. Suspicion of psycho-analysis is evident as early as 1922 in her *University College Magazine* story 'The Doer, A Story in the Russian Manner'. Freudianism was quite gently satirised in the shape of Dr Müdel, the state psychiatrist, in *Cold Comfort Farm*, but as she grew older her antipathy became excessively vehement. In one of her pencilled marginalia to *The Biology of God* she wrote of Freud: 'That old man has done more harm, in about 6 different directions, than Napoleon, Hitler and Torquemada put together. They, at least, only destroyed the body; they didn't kill all hope and idealism. I hope he knows it now.' She saw him as guilty of encouraging, through analysis, that emotional self-indulgence to which her family had been prone, and of sullying the purity of the most apparently noble of motives. He was to her the archpriest of what she used to call 'poking about', putting a stick into the clear waters of the mind and stirring up the mud of the unconscious at its bottom. For her the woodshed, once escaped from, should remain firmly locked. Current thought, since the unmasking of some of Freud's more questionable methods, has moved in Stella's direction.

My American alternates between the stories of Amy in England and Robert in America. The American sections are vivid and completely convincing, especially the description of New York in a heat wave, but not particularly remarkable unless you know that Stella never visited America in her life. She derived all the detail from assiduous research and a wide knowledge of American literature. She also must have got much from American films, for which she and Allan shared a passion.

Writers occasionally like to test themselves by undertaking to write outside their natural scope. The effects they achieve are often interesting, and with good writers like Stella there is no sense of strain, but the effort often bleaches their style of what makes it distinctive. This is what happens here. There are no sly, sardonic asides or penetrating aperçus in Stella's best manner. The American sections were her tribute to the literature she had loved as a child. Writers such as Susan Coolidge, Louisa May Alcott, Augusta Wilson and Edgar Allan Poe had offered her the experience of a very different perspective on the world expressed in very familiar language. She continued to read Poe's poetry, which she enjoyed in spite of – or perhaps in part because of – its excesses and occasional absurdity. I remember how amused she was by a French translation of Poe's 'The Raven' that she had found. The translator's version of the refrain: 'Quoth the Raven "Nevermore!"', though verbally and metrically an exact rendering, somehow did not achieve at all the same effect as the original. It was: *'Dit le corbeau: "Jamais plus!"'*

Of later American literature, the writers she liked best were Fitzgerald and Hemingway (Faulkner was a little too like Mary Webb for her). But though she very much admired Hemingway's early stories, in particular 'The Snows of Kilimanjaro', she thought his style had a deleterious influence on other writers. She told me that there was a period when even writers of stories in women's magazines were trying to write like Hemingway, with invariably comic results. Needless to say she did not care for his over-masculine attitudes, and once told an interviewer that her idea of hell was to have to go shopping for fishing rods in Harrods with Ernest Hemingway.

The best sections of *My American* deal with the slow development of the gifted but emotionally retarded Amy. Stella vividly evokes from memory the narrow but intense world of an imaginative child, and that passion for solitude which is felt by those who have it as strongly as an alcoholic feels about drink. Amy goes to work on an old-fashioned boys' paper, the *Prize*, and this is one of the few occasions when Stella used her journalistic experience in a novel. She never worked on a publication like the *Prize*, but in the office scenes she evokes something of the atmosphere of the *Lady* which, like the *Prize*, was, at the time when she worked on it, in gentle decline. She situated the offices of the *Prize* near St Paul's, not far from Fleet Street and the *Evening Standard*.

Amy becomes a best-selling writer of adventure stories, but, though rich, she finds herself unfulfilled; while in America Robert, set for a good though unexciting career as a doctor, accidentally kills a child in a car crash. A gangster friend of his fixes the jury and Robert leaves the district and medical school consumed with guilt. Amy visits America on a lecture tour, partly because of her childish memory of 'her American'. She and Robert are reunited, and the story reaches a not entirely convincing climax involving a kidnapped child and a gangster high on marijuana. Robert becomes a doctor and marries Amy.

Quite a few of Stella's heroines marry doctors. This fact lends itself to Freudian speculation which, in deference to Stella's views on the subject, should be avoided.

After the exciting episode of the pot-crazed gangster readers are asked to believe that Amy is cured of writing adventure stories and embarks on her 'second manner' of conventionally feminine domestic novels. 'Her stories of family life communicated (because she herself felt it) to the passing of an examination or the breaking of a betrothal the excitement she had once given to escapes from death and last-minute rescues, and she charmed her readers by showing them the variety and interest of every day.' There is a sense of wish-fulfilment here, as well as an apologia for not repeating the satirical brilliance of *Cold Comfort Farm*.

The final happy-ending chapter takes its time, as if Stella is loath to let go of the dreamlike contentment of her hero and heroine. It is an incantation to domestic happiness and goes on well past the time when one feels, like Mr Bennett, that we have been delighted long enough. Nevertheless, even into this over-ecstatic close Stella injects a realistic note of fear and the recognition that all happiness is transient. Her daughter Laura pointed out to me that the description of Amy's fears offers an insight into Stella's sometimes over-protective nature, particularly as a mother. Still, the over-riding intention is to reaffirm the belief that 'It Does Sometimes Happen'.

When it came out the book entranced a young woman called Suzanne Ebel, who wrote a fan letter. Stella wrote back and a friendship began which was deep, sustaining and lifelong. In a letter to her in the 1970s Stella wrote: 'I really feel I *had* you as a daughter when I was about 18!' Suzanne understood Stella both as a woman and as a writer. She had been particularly attracted by the descriptions of Amy writing in *My American*, and how Amy enjoyed it when the book 'was beginning to run' (a phrase Stella used when talking about her own writing). The idea of literary work as a pleasurable activity in itself struck Suzanne as unusual and exciting, and this, she told me, inspired her eventually to become a writer herself. She had her first novel published in 1964 and has written many successful books, more recently under her married name Suzanne Goodwin.

Writers are inclined to emphasise the agonies of literary endeavour. The puritan in us tends to attach most importance to what we least enjoy, with the result that for some genius is the art of being infinitely pained. Stella found this attitude affected: she enjoyed writing and was quite prepared to admit as much.

In November 1939 Stella began to write a series of monthly articles for *St Martin's Review* entitled 'A Woman's Diary of the War'. The journal of the famous London church of St Martin's-in-the-Fields was, at the time, considerably more than a parish magazine and boasted some distinguished contributors, among them Dorothy Sayers, Cecil Day-Lewis, Siegfried Sassoon and Walter de la Mare. The novelist Howard Spring, like Stella, became a monthly contributor. The connection had begun in October 1938 when Stella was invited to contribute an article to the *Review*'s Literary Supplement on 'The Whole Duty of a Novelist'. The following month a short story of hers was published.

The diary chronicles some of the events of Stella's life during the war, but more significantly it records the change in her attitudes and the deepening of her character that war produced. These changes resulted in two of Stella's most mature and accomplished novels *The Bachelor* (1944) and *Westwood, or The Gentle Powers* (1946).

The 'Diary' enabled her to debate with herself how precisely she should think about the war, because initially it simply filled her with despair. In writing about it for the public, she set herself the task of trying to find the positive aspects without ignoring the horrors. In her first article, in November 1939, she wrote:

> Oh, how I wish I could get the ordinary people of nowadays into a book! Every shop I go into has a gentle, brave democrat behind its counter. The friendly little woman who keeps the shop where I buy my small daughter's socks observed meditatively, at the end of a conversation about two of the important foreign gentlemen who are too much with us: 'Yes. The trouble with those two is, they're old fashioned. *The rest of us have grown out of it.*'

Her own attitudes to the war, as she wrote in February 1940, were subjected to critical scrutiny:

As soon as I give way to a satisfying fit of fury against aggressors, German or Russian, Italian or Japanese, I read or hear of some small incident that shows the humanity behind the monster; and my fury fades and I go back to my usual state of utter misery about the whole business. No emotion is so sustaining, so warming and satisfying as righteous indignation. That is why it has to be rooted out of my nature as if it were a disease.

In the face of these strong feelings she was striving, not always successfully, for a certain detachment. In June 1940 she explained, 'A[llan] advised me to cultivate the Historical Eye in reading the war news. I tried and found it soothing (the Eye, not the news).'

The consolations that she sought in wartime were not commonplace pieties but peculiar to her nature so that, taken out of context, they almost seem callous. Her December 1939 piece includes this passage:

The black-out has given millions of Londoners their first sight of real starlight. (I don't expect this is much consolation to them but starlight happens to be my favourite light so I like to put in a word for it.) The bigger stars now have a pool of light round them. Byron's line –

Isles of Light,
So wildly, spiritually bright

is seen to be true, as well as lovely. He must have seen the stars looking like that over eighteenth-century towns.

She also told her readers that she was giving up trying to read ultra-modern poetry because the advertisements had told her to keep calm and cheerful, and such verse was not conducive to cheerfulness. The remark was only half meant as a joke. There was a puritanical streak in Stella which made her read things she knew she would not enjoy so as to widen her horizons and improve her mind. And now external hardships were releasing her from these self-imposed penances. It was another tiny blessing.

The fall of France in June 1940 cast Stella into deeper gloom. She had a particular love for the country, its culture and, especially, its literature. In August she wrote in the 'Diary': 'I cannot write about the fate of France, because I know what the English Queen meant when she said that Calais would be written on her heart when she was dead. "France" will be written on mine.'

Her spirits were raised, however, when she heard the defiant tones of General de Gaulle on the wireless. The speech began, as she recalled, '*Moi! Général de Gaulle . . . !*' She was so inspired by his words that she wrote to thank him, and received in return a signed letter dated 27 June 1940. Formal as it is, the letter has a touching dignity which is a faithful echo of an aspect of the General's nature. Translated, it reads:

Madame,

The sentiments expressed in your letter are a precious encouragement to me. I thank you most warmly.

In these tragic hours for the history of the world, all those who still possess liberty should resolutely unite to resist and to conquer.

Please be assured, Madame, of my devoted respect.

C. de Gaulle.

One of the problems that preoccupied her in 1940 was how much she should tell five-year-old Laura about the war. In July she wrote:

I collect impressions from other mothers about how they 'adjust' their children to the fact of war. Some have kept them in complete ignorance; others have carefully explained as much as a five-year-old mind can take in. It has not been much use trying to keep the war from Laura; she has taken a lively interest in the leading personalities and has turned all her dolls into refugees. The other day at a children's tea party my hostess was rather disturbed in the midst of a grave discussion about Keeping Their Little Minds Away From It As Far As Possible, to hear a voice exclaiming joyfully: 'I'm Hitler, coming down in a parachute!' and there was Laura, hopping about with a large garden umbrella. We have told her that we must take shelter during a raid because our guns will be firing at the aeroplanes and trying to hit their wings and bring them down, and therefore there may be little splinters of shell which might sting. I am strictly careful that she shall hear no horrors, of course. It took me some time to realise that the child's mind does not work like an adult's and that they cannot foresee the future (half the horrors of fear are caused by this foreseeing) because they are so busy with the present.

By the time Allan had finished the run of *Moonshine*, a revue at the Vaudeville Theatre, he had decided to enlist, in spite of the fact that at the age of thirty-three he could quite easily have avoided the services and pursued a successful stage career. On 18 July he joined the Middlesex Regiment, and was stationed at Mill Hill quite close to home. Stella's feelings about his enlistment were mixed, but on the whole she was proud of him. She retained to the last a romantic, Ouida-like devotion to the armed services, and in particular the British Army.

In August, Stella wrote that

there are plenty of things to do at home, because we are now a large family party. My father and mother-in-law and my lovely young sister-in-law Renée (named after a Huguenot refugee ancestor) have come to stay with us before moving into a house almost opposite our own in this road, and we 'sit down' eight to meals every day. [Stella, Laura, Allan, Aunt Ru, Renée, Charles, Jessie, and Stella's other sister-in-law Enid, Lewis's wife.]

Renée comes into the High Street where the cheap shops are, and helps me carry up enormous shopping baskets crammed with food. She goes down very well with people who keep the stalls, as she is gay and friendly as well as lovely. One man in the fish shop darted at her in the intervals of slapping bloaters down on the board, and cried 'Ain't it a lovely war, duck?' to her great amusement.

Renée, temporarily out of acting work, became a shelter marshal in Parliament Hill Fields. An Anderson shelter was built in the garden at Oakshott Avenue, to which much of this extended family repaired every night. Some of Laura's first memories were of Stella reading aloud to them in the shelter what she had been writing during the day.

The shelter held no terrors for Laura and she slept well. On one occasion Stella observed that

> she had slept soundly all through the heavy sounds and had only once murmured, when half aroused by a louder salvo than usual: '*Is that our guns? They have a noble sound.*' When I remembered this in the morning, I thought: 'That cannot have been said by Laura; it has the authentic ring of Nelson at the Battle of the Nile or Hardy at the Cape Verde action' or anyone famous at any historic battle. Nevertheless, she did say it, for I remember sitting upright with a jerk, in the dimness of the shelter, and staring with astonished, sleepy-laden eyes at my surprising daughter.

In 1940 Stella brought out a volume of short stories, *Christmas at Cold Comfort Farm*. The title story had been written for the 1938 Christmas number of the *Bystander*. An amusing enough mining of an old but rich seam, it describes a typical Christmas at the farm before the coming of Flora Poste. It is a parody of the worst sort of family Christmas: everybody is following its rituals without even attempting to invoke its spirit. Adam Lambsbreath dresses up as Father Christmas in two of Judith's red shawls. There are unsuitable presents, unpleasant insertions into the pudding and some good Starkadder table talk over Christmas dinner. Aunt Ada Doom orders Amos to carve the turkey, adding: 'Ay, would it were a vulture, 'twere more fitting!' and there is poignancy in Judith's: 'Amos, will you pull a cracker wi' me? We were lovers . . . once.' To which Amos naturally replies: 'Hush, woman. . . . Tempt me not wi' motters and paper caps. Hell is paved wi' such.'

When it was originally published in the *Bystander* the story had illustrations to which Stella objected. Her complaints had to be dealt with by the art editor, John Oliver, who was to meet and marry Renée in 1946. Somehow he managed to placate Stella. Like many authors she was rarely satisfied by illustrations to her work, and could sometimes take this dissatisfaction to extremes. At some time in the 1950s Allan commissioned the artist Mervyn Peake to do some sketches for a de-luxe edition of *Cold Comfort*

Farm. Stella was so appalled by what she saw that she not only forbade the new edition but destroyed the original drawings.

She would frequently object to the designs of her dust jackets. The response of her publishers, who must have had a thorough knowledge of her character, would invariably be that the artist in question was an impoverished young man with a wife and several children to support. Stella would immediately relent and waive all objections. She once said to me that, though she did not mind that these designers were chosen from the ranks of struggling young artists, she did wish that the reason for their having to struggle was not always so painfully apparent.

Christmas at Cold Comfort Farm as a collection is an improvement on *Roaring Tower*, but it is still not Stella on top form. It does, however, contain a few pieces which rise above the superior magazine story level of the rest. In the 1943 edition of the *Writers' Directory* Stella wrote that she considered that 'Sisters', included in this collection, was her best short story. A do-gooding spinster called Elaine Garfield out of charity takes on Iveen, a single mother, as a helper in her house. The villagers regard Miss Garfield as kind but foolish. When Iveen is insulted in the village, Miss Garfield, to make her feel better, reveals to Iveen that she too 'fell' with a young officer in the Great War, so she and Iveen are 'sisters'. On hearing this, Iveen's mother will not let her daughter go back to Miss Garfield, whose attitude and conduct she now deplores. 'In the end, it was not the contempt of the village but its incredulous, half-amused sympathy that broke Elaine's courage.' Miss Garfield leaves the district. This gently ironic little tragedy, reminiscent of Maupassant, is indeed an excellent story. It is a pity that Stella did not write more in this vein.

'The Murder Mark' is an elegantly sinister little thriller inspired by Stella's fascination with hands and palmistry, of which she was an amateur practitioner. Curiously, its manner and matter are not unlike Hugh Walpole in his gothic mood. 'Cake', in which an emancipated young female journalist goes to interview an old suffragette, is a nice study in contrasting generations of women. Maudie Allworton, the suffragette, is puzzled by the new woman that she helped to create: '"Thirty-five years ago there simply weren't women like you, Miss Roscoe, anywhere in the world. ... Women were either fools or feminists. But you don't seem to be either."' Maudie's Hampstead flat is minutely and tellingly described. It is all excellent until the trite ending in which Jenny Roscoe, the journalist, decides to go back to her dull husband and have babies.

Often the least good stories are the most personally revealing. Such is the case with 'The Walled Garden'. Susie, the wife of a country doctor, invites some friends from her raffish past life as a fashion artist to stay. They arrive with Helga, a disgruntled, vampish character. Helga appears to be good with the children, and when the Nanny decides to leave, one of Susie's friends proposes that Helga should take her place, especially as there is something going on between her and Susie's brother-in-law, Ted. Susie rejects this proposal on the rather suspect grounds that the local community would not approve and that she has a 'position to keep up'. Nanny overhears this, decides to stay after all, and peace is restored. Her doctor husband says in conclusion:

> 'A marriage has got to have a wall round it, like the garden. Inside the wall everything's safe. It's got to be, so that the fruit can grow.'
> 'But surely *all* marriages aren't like a walled garden?'
> 'All proper marriages are,' answered her husband.

This was undoubtedly Stella's point of view. What causes unease is not so much its expression, but the finality with which it is expressed. The pressures and ironies of the story up till that point make it clear that Stella was perfectly capable of suggesting other ways of looking at the situation. It is as if she has deliberately willed this rather suffocating attitude, locked herself in her walled garden and thrown the key over the wall.

Stella's output in this period was remarkably prolific considering how heavily occupied she was on the domestic front. To augment the egg ration, she began to keep some rather bedraggled hens at the end of her garden, and the woman living next door to her complained about the noise they made. Her name was March Cost, then quite a celebrated novelist, and a rather more fashionable one than Stella. When she said that the chickens disturbed her writing Stella, whose powers of concentration were more robust, was unsympathetic.

Allan was posted to an officers' training unit in March 1941. 'Before he went,' Stella wrote, 'he had a few days' leave which we spent madly going to all the best films in London.' In July Allan received an emergency commission in the King's Royal Rifle Corps, and in October he was made a Motor Platoon Commander. He took pride in his work and received very favourable reports from his commanding officers which, like his theatrical press clippings, he meticulously preserved.

In 1941 Stella's novel *The Rich House* was published. Its setting is Seagate, an East Coast resort based on Clacton where she went on holiday as a child. Some of the place names are those she devised for the imaginary Essex of *Nightingale Wood* (Chesterbourne, Dovewood, Bracing Bay and so on); there is also a roadhouse called the Red Barn, whose fashionable horrors are amusingly described, which has been built by Victor Spring's company, Spring Developments Ltd. Stella had a habit of introducing references to characters and places from previous works into her novels, though, with the exception of *Conference at Cold Comfort Farm*, she never wrote a sequel.

The action of *The Rich House* takes place on the eve of the Second World War, and Stella shows just how little the coming conflict meant to most people in a quiet English seaside town. The tone of the book is set by its epigraph from Tolstoy's *War and Peace*: 'Everyday life – the practical life of each individual, with its home questions of health and sickness, of toil and rest, with its intellectual aspirations and tastes for science, poetry, music, what not, with its passions, loves and friendships – ran its regular course, without troubling itself to any serious extent about an alliance or breach with Napoleon.' Mussolini is listened to briefly on the radio and then switched off; jokes are made about Hitler; the more serious citizens of Seagate borrow books from the library called *Europe – Whither?* or *Can America Stay Out?* Towards the end of the novel some actors in a café discuss the coming war, but only in terms of how it will affect acting styles:

'That throw away your lines stuff will go right out.'
   'In the last one they wanted the lightest stuff they could get.'
   'Light, Sylvia, but not sophisticated. There's a big difference.'

'*Need* you babble about the bloody war, darling? Every time
I see a tank on the movies little Joanie nearly fwows up.'

Otherwise everything goes on as normal, but the sense of
impending doom is ever present. It is an integral part of the
book's principal theme. That theme, a recurrent one in Stella's
books, particularly in this middle period, is the possibility, but,
at the same time the immense fragility, of earthly happiness.

This is exemplified by one of the plot motifs. A series of
anonymous letters puncture the calm of Seagate. They are not
overtly malicious – they even praise their recipients, in a rather
condescending manner – but they are subtly intrusive and invariably tell the recipient how lucky they are. Nobody feels they can
go to the police with them, but one of the protagonists, Pauline
Williams, takes a sample letter to show to an old man, Archibald
Early, the owner of the Rich House of the title. It is old Early who
identifies their menace:

> Happiness and comfort and contentment are very rare. When
> we have them we are like savages; we are afraid to bring them to
> the notice of the gods in case they become jealous and take them
> away. This letter brings your friend's happiness to the notice of
> the gods and therefore she fears that it may be taken away. I
> should say that it was written by a person who is envious and
> spiteful but not wicked; someone who has not the courage to
> write an abusive letter, and who may even hardly realise the
> pain they are inflicting.

Stella herself disliked being thought fortunate. On several
occasions she repeated to me something that her old friend the
poet Anthony Rye had once said to her, to the effect that she
was 'the darling of the gods'. It had irked her. Perhaps she felt
a tinge of Mr Early's superstition, but mainly she resented the
remark because it seemed to her unjust. Her literary success was
hard won and by no means unqualified; and she had had her share
of sorrow and hardship. The lives of others often look easier and
pleasanter than our own, a fact of which Stella was aware. Rye
was a good minor poet, his life had been an agreeable one in many
ways, but his writing had never been very highly acclaimed.

Though old Mr Early's words echoed some of Stella's thoughts, he is far from being a paragon of ancient wisdom. Archibald Early is one of the triumphs of this book. He is a once famous and gifted Edwardian actor, now long retired, and Stella manages to capture the elusive, fading glamour of the man. Great artists in fiction are hard to bring off, but Early is made believable by his very inconsistencies. He is both intuitively wise and intellectually vapid, vain but not egotistical, sensual and yet unworldly. He is a man no longer entirely living in the present, which accounts for both his charm and his exasperating absurdity. Old Mr Early not only defines the nastiness of the anonymous letters, he also identifies and catches their sender in a scene of exquisite comic ambiguity.

The Rich House, like so many of Stella's books, has central weaknesses but many peripheral strengths. The two main characters, both young women, are well realised and convincing as people, but frankly not very interesting. They are, like so many of Stella's heroines, women whose true fulfilment in life lies in marriage and children. There are some over-long passages of description, and the plot at times drifts rather than drives along. Once or twice a moral is pointed in an unnecessarily bald way, a bad habit which Stella shared with greater writers such as George Eliot.

On the other hand the atmosphere of Seagate is sensitively evoked, and the characterisation is always shrewd and often profound. As usual in Stella's books a wide social spectrum is covered with assurance. Some of the action takes place in the world of the theatre. Fictional treatments of theatrical life rarely convince, but Stella has managed to bring to life the sights, smells and moods of a very ordinary seaside repertory theate. In particular she conveys perfectly, in Mr Early and his grandson Ted, a certain quintessential type of actor for whom the fantasy of the stage is more real than the reality of everyday life. Consequently they are only truly themselves when inhabiting a part; off stage they give much less convincing performances.

Stella understood the theatre very well. She was a former theatre critic whose uncle, brother and husband had been or were on the stage; but it was her sister-in-law Renée who gave her most help with the theatrical episodes since it was she who had had most experience in provincial repertory. Renée also gave her the idea for one of the crucial scenes in the book where young Ted Early in his first job proves that, as an actor, he has what his grandfather calls The Spark. Stella had envisaged a new play being tried out at the Seagate repertory theatre. It was to have a medical setting, and she wanted a scene in which a young actor with a small part could make his mark. Renée suggested that Ted could play a patient who suddenly and miraculously found he could walk again.

The first night of this play is vividly described in the manner of a Tolstoyan battle scene through a multiplicity of vignettes, snatches of conversation and thoughts of those present. It is the one occasion when most of her large cast of Seagate characters are under one roof at the same time. She has even introduced herself in the very minor role of the author of the new play, Elizabeth Bayne – 'She wrote that frightfully funny book. I forget what it was called, a sort of skit' – and through the dialogue of members of the audience she comments wryly on the way some people reacted to the author of *Cold Comfort Farm:*

> 'Looks quite ordinary,' observed Estelle's fiancé. . . .
> 'Yes, doesn't she. I was so disappointed when I saw her photo after I'd read the book. I thought she'd look very sophisticated and witty. Did you read it?'
> He shook his head.
> 'Oh, you must, Jack. It's a yell. I'll lend it to you. Don't let me forget.'

The play itself, *White Glory*, is represented as well-intentioned but mediocre. 'Poor dear woman, why couldn't she stick to comedy?' thinks the critic down from London.

In October 1941 Stella wrote in the 'Diary' for *St Martin's Review* that

> the war has done me good. I have lost a stone in weight and I am not frightened any more. I don't mean not frightened of air raids: I am; but I have stopped having nervous fears about awful things happening over which I have no control. I get a dour satisfaction out of managing the rations, salvaging, fire watching, and feeling I am trying to work for a better world with millions of other people. I am quite sure what I like, and

what I believe, and what I want. I have developed patience and take the longer view. I am not so silly and solemn. I am less, and yet somehow more, tolerant. In short, I am happier.

In November:

a colony of our Russian Allies has come to live in this road. . . . Fired by my enthusiasm for foreigners, no matter what sort, I began by smiling and saying 'Good Morning.' No effect. Every morning a convoy of delicious fat children with green eyes, sallow skins and pale brown hair was brought safely into port from the Heath by a guard of plump Mammas with the same colouring, and every day I smiled and said 'Good Morning,' with absolutely no effect. However, Laura and I, after careful practice, did a Communist clenched fist at them one morning with instantaneous results. Beaming smiles, bows that would have graced Old St Petersburg, and hand-kissings from one Russian about the size of a small biscuit-box who can't walk yet, but is pushed about by his large calm Mamma in a pram.

This was the beginning of a lifelong relationship with Hampstead Russians. By the end of the 1960s there were Russians from the Trade Delegation living to right and left of her, as well as in the house at the end of the garden. ('I'm like the Light Brigade,' Stella said.) Cordial relations were maintained, despite several of them at various times being despatched home as suspected spies, and every Christmas a welcome bottle of Stolichnaya vodka would appear on Stella's doorstep. Laura developed a passion for Russian literature. Her son Daniel, a fluent Russian speaker, has written guides to Moscow and St Petersburg and married a Russian girl.

In June 1942 Stella's Aunt Louise died. Stella wrote in the 'Diary' for July:

The last of my older relations has died; last, that is, except an uncle [Fred] who has been in America for fifty years and whom I have never seen. There is no one to resent my writing down that Aunt L[ouise] was a 'typical Victorian'; as passionate as any heroine of Rhoda Broughton or Ouida, and afraid of life, and, up to the very last, self-deceived. Her beauty lasted until she was old, but it was wasted and she died widowed and childless. In these circumstances the task of sorting her papers and small possessions was unspeakably pathetic. Every packet of old postcards of Rome, every receipt for the past twenty years, every Christmas card and letter, was carefully labelled, and there were boxes filled with ribbons and old broken jewellery and little doilies that had been hoarded from long before Laura was born. And there has been the usual slight confusion about the Will, and some people were left out, and others put in, and, in short, we all felt slightly indignant, and that we had done a great deal of work and none of us were really satisfied. . . .

At the beginning of June 1942 Allan had embarkation leave. Stella wrote the following month: 'We have been very lucky so far, and now there is nothing to do but try to be as cheerful as the millions of other women all over the world who are bearing the same unhappiness.' She had the good fortune to know that Allan was not likely at his age to be a combatant. On 17 July he left for the Middle East, as Assistant Adjutant 2IDT Middle East Force. He had a desk job and spent most of his time in Cairo.

Stella's life in this period was active to the point of being strenuous. She attended keep fit classes, did fire watching and, at one point, even decided that she wanted to go and work in a factory. This idea was immediately, and sensibly, squashed by the rest of the family. But maintaining the household was work enough for her, and her heart suffered. In January 1943 she wrote:

I have got an enlarged heart through carrying parcels up these hills and generally overdoing things, and have had to lie in bed for a month, receiving the commiseration of my friends and acquaintances and feeling the Happy Hypocrite when they said how bored I must have been. Bored . . . I, who have not for years had more than ten minutes at a time to gaze out of the window, who have never been able to read for longer than an hour and very seldom that! I read and read and read. I read Lecky's *History of European Morals* and *The Tale of Genji* [the early Japanese novel by Lady Murasaki, translated by Arthur Waley] and *The Last of the Barons* and *Rienzi* [both by Lord Lytton] and *The Times* every morning from the Personal Column to Old and True, and Ouida's *Ariadne* and Tolstoy's *Resurrection*, and I finished *Dombey and Son* too. I got drunk with print, and I arose at the end of the month feeling more grateful than ever to the great writers, and humbly glad to be a writer myself.

If, as Stella claimed, *Cold Comfort Farm* came at the right moment, *Ticky* (1943) almost certainly came at the wrong one. This most engaging novel was her personal favourite, and it is – always excepting *Cold Comfort Farm* – by far her most original one.

Interviewed for *Leader* magazine in 1945, she said:

> Hardly anyone liked *Ticky* and I like it perhaps best of all my works. It was originally a saga I used to tell my brothers when I was eleven and they were respectively seven and three. It began with my imitating the alleged voice, fruity and haughty and affected, of Major Pillichody, a character I had found in Harrison Ainsworth's *Old St Paul's*. His name greatly attracted me and I used to relate his imaginary exploits to my audience, sitting on a bed in one of the attics. Round Major Pillichody a whole circle grew up: Major Milde, his friend who hardly dared open his mouth, two reckless Ensigns Cussit and Dammit – (I only had the vaguest idea what an Ensign was, but I had the word firmly enough.) – and the austere and domestically terrifying figure of Queen Victoria who was always descending on The Club where the Bucks lived and demanding to see the mess bills which were huge.

Set vaguely in the mid-nineteenth century, *Ticky* revolves around a crack regiment called the First Bloods who live in the centre of London in a fantastic building called the Club which also houses the Regimental Academy (run by a Dr Pressure) and the quarters of the regimental servants, called the Waiters. Major Pillichody, who became Major Pillichoddie in *Ticky*, is, like Ainsworth's character, a hard-drinking, moustachioed *miles gloriosus*.

The book is dedicated to '198380 [Allan's serial number] and The Rest of the British Army'. It was perhaps intended to be taken as a light-hearted tribute to the virtues of the British fighting man, as can be inferred from the quotation from Ouida's *Under Two Flags* on the dedication page: '"There aren't better stuff to make soldiers out of nowhere than Englishmen, God Bless 'em! but they're badgered, they're horribly badgered."'

It is hard to describe the style of the book except to say that it appears to be by Daisy Ashford out of Ouida, but more knowing than either. This is hardly surprising given the origins of the story, and Stella's lifelong passion for Ouida. The Club, which is the home of the First Bloods, is the fantastic construct of a childish imagination, not dissimilar to the Crystal Palace in Daisy Ashford's *The Young Visiters:* 'The mighty building with its twin glass towers glittered darkly against the heavens, which were still partly obscured by flying clouds. The North Tower, indeed, was temporarily concealed in mists from which its pointed summit emerged, remote and awesome as a mountain peak.'

The building is so vast, in fact, that officers travel about inside it by horse-drawn tram. It is an all-male society, and even the Waiters keep their wives and families outside the confines of the Club ('on pain of shootin'') and are only allowed to look at photographs of them for three and a half minutes every day. The docking of their 'Daguerreotype Time' is one of the milder punishments that the officers can inflict on them, for a Waiter can be shot in the leg for breaking a plate from the regimental dinner service. (One of the Waiters, incidentally, is Fig Starkadder 'a gloomy man, reputed to come from Sussex.') The 'men' of the regiment are another class and generally support the Waiters. They are also bound by their own set of senseless rituals and regulations, such as 'pipeclaying scran-bags' and polishing a coal-bucket which is never used to carry coal.

A perpetual war is going on between the Colonel of the regiment and the Waiters over a piece of land in the Club grounds which the waiters have as a recreation area and which the Colonel (who wears a perfume 'named *Blood and Iron* which had been especially created in Paris for a lady friend of Bismarck's') wants to add to the Regimental Estates. The Waiters know that the previous colonel gave it to them and that the gift was recorded in a Charter which now cannot be found. The vital document is eventually discovered in the nick of time wrapped round the handle of a shrimp kettle, and peace is restored.

There is something odd, inconsequential, even mad about *Ticky*.

Some readers may simply be baffled by Major Pillichoddie, who
keeps Queen Victoria from inspecting the regimental accounts too
rigorously by supplying her with household hints such as putting
vegetables in salt water to drive the insects out of them, or cleaning
picture frames with potato peelings; or by Lieutenant Toloreaux,
who is seized one morning by an impulse to jump over the pews
of the Regimental Chapel, wrapped in the Union Jack and reciting
'My mother said . . .'; or by an aristocrat whose aunts were 'unable
to eat the bread and butter for tea unless it was cut so thin that it
floated away on the breeze as the butler carried it along the picture
gallery'. Those who are entertained by these and numberless other
absurdities, many of which – like the flying bread and butter – were
invented by Stella as a child, will enjoy the book.

For underneath all this airy fantasy lurks an unmistakable
strain of serious mockery at all-male societies and their divisive,
competitive aspects, and this is what gives *Ticky* its backbone. It
is the women in the book who are instrumental in crossing the
social boundaries and making peace between the officers and the
Waiters. The absurd customs continue, and no doubt Waiters will
still be shot in the leg for breaking dinner plates, but hearts and
minds have been softened.

The middle of the Second World War was perhaps the wrong
time to satirise, however obliquely, the ridiculous and dangerous
rituals that surround the male aggressive instinct. Stella comes
nearest to showing her hand when Dr Harrovius Pressure, the
archetypal Victorian pedant, is confronted by his former mistress,
the delightful Mrs Lovecome, by whom he had an illegitimate
daughter. Dr Pressure has been pretending to the world that
he is a widower and to his daughter Beatrice that a portrait of
the hideous Miss Ida Mould – 'a good pure devoted Christian
worker' – is the likeness of her late mother. (Did the name of
her former friend Ida Graves flit through Stella's head when
she invented that?) Mrs Lovecome enters Dr Pressure's study and
finds him working on his interminable *History of Weapons Both
Civilised and Uncivilised from the Earliest Times to the Present
Day*. She briskly dismisses his efforts as 'unpleasant . . . dull,
alarming and unnecessary'. Pressure is outraged and hits back
with a biting comment about 'the female mind', to which Mrs
Lovecome rejoins that Toppendorf of Leipzig has already written

such a history anyway. 'If I made half the fuss you do about things I'd have been dead by now,' she concludes.

The book ends, like most of Stella's, with several ecstatic marriages. The hero, Ticky, marries one of the Waiters' daughters and Mrs Lovecome makes an honest man of Pressure. As Mrs Lovecome says, it is all 'quite like one of dear Miss Braddon's stories – although personally I prefer Ouida'. Stella specifically repudiated the suggestion of one of the critics that it was a straightforward parody of Ouida, 'my dear, my underrated, my nearly great Ouida,' as she called her in *Leader* magazine in April 1945. The book is really a kind of tribute to her.

In that interview she says:

> Ouida's books need some defence nowadays, I suppose, for they are often absurd. However it is an absurdity I prefer to contemporary absurdities in literature. I love her presentation of romantic love (this method of presentation has literally gone out of the world and is as extinct as heraldry or hawking); I love her beautiful, single-minded people, and her innocent snobbery, and her passionate love of the poor and helpless. My favourite literary mixture is beauty and absurdity, such as there is in my favourite play *A Midsummer Night's Dream*.

This mixture is present in *Ticky*. In that respect, the closest parallel to the book's style and approach is perhaps Max Beerbohm's *Zuleika Dobson*.

The other influence, or source, is that of the once popular nineteenth-century Irish writer Charles Lever who wrote many novels, some dealing with military life in the mid-Victorian period. From him Stella borrowed the period setting (rather earlier than Ouida, even though she is anachronistically referred to) and one of the chief characters, the lively Irish officer Barry Molloy. A quotation from Lever's *Tom Burke of 'Ours'* accompanies the one from Ouida on the dedication page.

In the mid- to late thirties there was a vogue for Victoriana, which was just beginning to be seen as picturesque and amusing rather than old-fashioned. Those in the know began to buy up stuffed birds under glass domes as modish, if camp, accessories. Novels, and particularly plays, set in the Victorian era became popular, culminating in the 1937 production of Laurence Housman's *Victoria Regina* in which

Allan had played a footman. Had *Ticky* been published then it might have been appreciated as an amusing fantasia on Victorian themes, and a nice counterblast to rather stodgy period pieces such as Housman's play and *The Barretts of Wimpole Street*.

As it was, wartime England had rather lost the taste for this kind of playfulness, and though *Ticky* did not do badly it never had the kind of success or acclaim that Stella felt it deserved. The *Times Literary Supplement* reported that 'although not so cruelly near the edge of reality as *Cold Comfort Farm* . . . Miss Gibbons yet proves herself in *Ticky* to possess a natural and effortless talent for the burlesque'. It went through several editions and Stella was delighted to hear of at least one officer, Captain Tickner (the journalist Charles Tickner), reading *Ticky* to his men on campaign in the depths of the Burma jungle.

Towards the end of 1943, Stella began to feel that the war was nearly over. She finished her 'Woman's Diary of the War' for *St Martin's Review* in November, and in her penultimate article, in September, speculated on what she recalled most vividly from the last four years:

> I remember the taxi driver who drove me home on a sunny day in the height of the Battle of London, and who gazed out dreamily for a moment across the view of the city from Highgate Hill muttering to himself, 'The things I've seen! The things I've seen!' I shall remember for ever the long splendid note of the 'Raider's Passed' [i.e. the All Clear] ('it's like the sun coming out after rain,' Laura said). I shall remember for ever, too, the steady sound of A[llan]'s footsteps walking away into the blackout, night after night, during the dark months of 1940 and '41, at the end of his evening's leave when he was stationed near home.

CHAPTER 7

Yelping at Saints

Early in 1944 a bomb hit the Longmans warehouse in London, destroying most of its contents. Many of Stella's novels became unavailable as a result, and only *Cold Comfort Farm* was reprinted.

While Auntie Ru stayed at Oakshott Avenue Stella decided to take her daughter away from the doodlebugs for a while. She and Laura went to stay at Elm Tree Farm, Wortley, near Wotton-under-Edge in Gloucestershire, where they had gone for a brief holiday two years before. It was an ancient Cotswold stone farmhouse and belonged to a family called Daw. The daughter of the house, Beth, has vivid recollections of their visitors.

They stayed there from June until harvest time 1944 and enjoyed themselves greatly in spite of an acute water shortage. Stella was given a small sitting room where she could write. It was above the kitchen and she could hear the ash being raked out of the kitchen stove every morning. This process was referred to as 'riddling the Esse', Esse being the brand name of the stove. The phrase had a mysterious poetic ring about it for Stella, and she put it into the novel on which she was then working, *Westwood*, which is set in Hampstead. But she also had time to observe the practicalities of farm life in wartime, with its land girls and its Italian prisoner of war farm hands. All of this was stored for future use in her 1949 novel *The Matchmaker*.

Stella's first impressions of Elm Tree Farm, as recorded in *St Martin's Review* in November 1942, had been intensely romantic:

> The farm was five hundred years old, and the domestic pattern there was, as it happened, as beautiful as the house, with that mingling of young and old life (only the young son was away

at the wars) that makes a harmonious whole. I had the curious feeling the whole time that the poet Horace (whose poems praising country life I have never read by the way) would have appreciated these dark shining oaken floors, the great blue-grey bull with his moist lip and majestic eyes, the old farmer with his stories of the bad old days fifty years ago, and the two Hebe-like daughters with wheat-fair hair, who drove the tractor because their brother was away. It is very old, wild country all about there. There are ancient caves in the depths of a wood, and wild slopes threaded with badger-runs among tangled plants and tiny wild flowers with pungent scents, and shallow marshes overgrown with wild watercress, more biting to the taste than the cultivated kind, and scattered with ankle-twisting stones. I got soaked through with fresh air and got into that state (always easy for me to get into) when I never wanted to come back into the house at all. One day when I am old I shall go out on one of those wild walks and not come back; a very good way to die.

This was the countryside as the author of *Cold Comfort Farm* liked to see it – more a Virgilian than a Horatian vision, as it happens. One of the reasons why she had objected to the Mary Webb school so violently was that it had not subscribed to this tranquil pastoral idyll. However, in the same article Stella did add that Laura was not so struck with all this rural splendour and that she 'pined for Spam and Woolworths'.

The Daw family, and Beth in particular, observed with amusement mingled with occasional exasperation the dreamy side to Stella's character. Beth recalled that Stella was missing one day at lunchtime. Mr Daw, who insisted on punctuality at meals – particularly lunch, the main meal of the day – sent out search parties with cowbells to summon her. She eventually arrived late and apologetic, having been sitting on a stile and planning her next novel. On another occasion she volunteered to stir the jam which was gently bubbling on the stove. A thought distracted her and she ceased to stir, with the result that the jam with its precious load of rationed sugar was burned and entirely spoilt. She was deeply apologetic once more, and was forgiven.

The countryside in wartime had a special attraction for Stella, as she recalls in *The Matchmaker*:

The spirit of place is changed if many people go to it; it can no longer be itself. Since the solitude enforced by the war had come over these tracts of land, they had been able to be themselves once more. Their flowers had budded, blossomed and faded unpicked, their blackberries had slowly ripened and then rotted richly on the bushes, weeds grew with furious speed and strength over the footpaths and against the hedges and stiles. Only the aeroplanes passed over these woods and fields, and left no trace of their ominous shadows. Loneliness could do what it would with such places, and fortunate were the few people who saw what it made of them.

Beth taught Stella to ride the farm pony so that she could go over to the nearest village, Alderley, to see if there was a letter from Allan. She was missing him badly. When Beth visited her in London later on, Stella, Flora-like, took her to the theatre and helped her buy smart clothes.

When, out of the blue in 1980, the writer John Braine wrote Stella a letter of appreciation and admiration, he mentioned that he had been rereading her 1944 novel *The Bachelor*. It was, indeed, a favourite among her fan letter writers and offers conclusive evidence that Stella's literary output after *Cold Comfort Farm* was not a decline but a development. Braine wrote in that letter: '. . . from your first book onwards you've extended yourself, you've kept on growing. You have a marvellous eye for the social scene – no-one is more accurate. And you've created a diversity of characters – your range is very wide. Above all you're superbly readable.' All this applies to *The Bachelor* – which is not to say that it is as delightful and brilliant a work of art as *Cold Comfort Farm*, simply that the rewards it offers the reader are deeper.

One reviewer even detected the influence of Proust, and said that it was less parochial in attitude than some of Stella's books. There is, in fact, nothing Proustian about *The Bachelor* although there are references to Proust in the text. Parochialism, however, is an accusation Stella could easily have rebutted. 'Not that I despise the Parish Pump,' she said in an interview for *Leader* magazine in April 1945, 'indeed in some ways I prefer it to the flashing stream.' This was a passing poke at Charles Morgan, author of *The Flashing*

Stream. On the subject of Proust she said that 'after reading Proust with pleasure for days I will suddenly get very impatient with him, and then I turn to Dickens whom I love; Charlotte M. Yonge, Jane Austen, Charlotte Brontë, Louisa M. Alcott, Kipling, or Ouida.'

The Bachelor is one of two novels by Stella which deal specifically with Britain in wartime. No heroics are offered, but there are some unforgettable images and vignettes of the Home Front: a middle-aged Englishman in his walled garden at dusk, dampening the bonfire for the blackout and hearing the drone of a bomber squadron overhead; a young Balkan exile screaming abuse at two bemused Italian POWs in a quiet meadow; two lovers listening to a record of the Warsaw Concerto while outside the distant anti-aircraft guns boom and thump, or walking past the bombed ruins of the Café de Paris in the rain.

The main setting of the novel is Sunglades, a large house in Hertfordshire lived in by an unmarried brother and sister together with a floating population of dependants, relations and refugees. The brother, Kenneth Fielding, the 'bachelor' of the title, is an unimaginative, emotionally repressed but fundamentally decent man kept in check by his domineering sister Constance, who believes that he would 'make a fool of himself over a pretty face'. He is a sympathetic and completely realised character, a good example of how well Stella understood the masculine mind. Constance is the stronger personality, full of 'unpleasant virtues', more intellectual than her brother, but also more foolish and self-deceiving. She is a pacifist who believes that the war has come about through 'misunderstanding'. Most of her philanthropy, like Mrs Jellyby's in *Bleak House*, is telescopic and she prefers to bestow it on interesting refugees than on dirty children evacuated from the London slums. As Stella remarks: 'Charity begins at home but it is often more convenient to exercise it upon foreigners.'

Into this household, at Constance's invitation, comes Vartouhi, an exile from an occupied Balkan nation called Bairamia. She is from a rich peasant family and has the fierce barbaric virtues (and vices) of her caste. Though valued at first for her hard work and loyalty, she causes havoc in the well-ordered ménage of Sunglades. Her clash with Constance is that between the civilised and uncivilised approach to ethics, the one 'spiritual', the other materialistic; it is the contrast which C. S. Lewis drew between moral earnestness and moral action. Constance's attitude to the Axis Powers is conciliatory and ineffectual; Vartouhi's is fiercely vindictive, but more in touch with reality. Some excellent comedy is derived from Constance's attempts to produce a moralistic message play called *Little Frimdl and the Peace Reindeer*, whose purpose, vaguely, is to foster worldwide harmony and understanding. Stella's parody of this peculiarly deadly form of drama, of which I have had some experience, is unerringly accurate. She may have drawn on a play she saw at the beginning of the war in which her father-in-law, a tireless amateur actor, took part at the Questor's Theatre, Ealing. Set in the Dark Ages with dialogue to match, its stated intention was to 'end the war', failure to achieve which can have surprised nobody but its author.

Stella is not, however, pouring crude scorn on intellectual idealism. In the character of the young economist Richard Marten she portrays an intellectual whose idealism is genuinely heroic, and she manages to make him real by giving him some of her own characteristics. As well as liking ideas he is an observer of human nature and 'found the spectacle of a person without imagination curiously restful'. He actually likes the human race, unlike many of his friends who 'had that dislike of their fellow creatures which accompanies the reformer's temperament . . .'. His more private emotional inclinations are also similar to his creator's. On more than one occasion, and in almost identical words, Stella told me that she, like Richard, 'strongly disliked talking about [her] troubles to anyone and was inclined to despise people who could not keep their woes to themselves but unloaded them on their friends'.

It is as if, through the character of Richard, Stella was trying to work out her own moral and political position. At one point Richard says, reflecting Stella's own tentative, undogmatic approach: 'I am not a member of the Party, but what political views I have approach nearest to Communism, I suppose.' Though she liked people to be individuals, she disliked and distrusted the cult of the individual. Through the character of Richard she meditates on her very personal dislikes (derived from her Gibbons experience) and applies them, as she had not done before, to the macrocosm of international affairs. The curious subtlety of her approach is that she expresses her thoughts through an ideology, Marxism, which was in many ways alien to her:

This preoccupation with personalities. . . . is a *bourgeois* disease that will disappear with capitalism. People like this old man, whose personalities are swollen beyond normal size, exhaust ordinary people and waste their time by provoking endless discussion and argument and marvellings at their behaviour, and the principle even extends to nations; we have the swollen state which draws unnatural attention to itself by roaring about its misfortunes and rights. The beauty of a team of actors such as the Russians and the French produce, or a field of buttercups or a swarm of fish, the beauty and fitness of the norm, is lost on these personality drunkards. . . . I like to lose myself in a crowd. Then I'm most myself.

The 'old man' referred to by Richard is Constance and Kenneth's raffish father, a delightful character who earns a precarious living setting up night clubs. He comes down to borrow money from Kenneth in order to set up an establishment called The Last Banana. Despite being thoroughly egocentric, he is a life-enhancer and not quite the monstrous personality that Richard has adumbrated. Nevertheless Richard's point still stands, today perhaps even more than in 1944; for it is the obsessive preoccupation with such personalities to which he objects.

The book ends with the usual fanfare of happy marriages, but they have all been convincingly and entertainingly achieved. Even Constance gets her man – the appalling Dr Stocke, author of *Little Frimdl and the Peace Reindeer*.

In her interview for *Leader* magazine in April 1945 Stella assessed her abilities as a writer:

I have always been handicapped by a moral attitude towards my work. I cannot take a detached interest in the cruel, the neurotic and the perverse, and the kind, the normal and the good. Hence I don't feel I shall ever be an artist in fiction. I also suffer from having too many themes in a book, unsupported by strength of plot, clash of interests, or passion. I am wrestling with these difficulties (not very hard as I do not mind them much) and hope one day to do away with some of them.

It is a self-analysis remarkable both for its harshness and for the accuracy with which it anatomises her faults. Nevertheless this was the period in which Stella was producing her best mature work.

Her working methods are described in the same piece:

> A story sometimes stays in Miss Gibbons's head for years rolling idly about. . . . Meanwhile she makes notes. Usually the plot comes first, then the people. She writes with a pen and can work without getting tired for about four hours. She likes a glass of water on the table to sip and prefers to work in the morning every day, but she seldom gets the chance because of family interruptions.

By the end of April 1945 Stella had completed what is probably the finest and most elegantly constructed of her mature novels, *Westwood, or The Gentle Powers*, published in the United States simply as *The Gentle Powers*. The *Leader* article commented: 'Dislike of violence and solemnity in fiction, music and personal relationships suggested the theme of her new book *Westwood, or The Gentle Powers*, just finished. It tells of the effect upon a young schoolmistress of the gentle powers, [Pity, Affection, Time, Beauty, Laughter] and how her nature was greatly changed.' The *Times Literary Supplement* called it 'an excellent study in growth'.

The action takes place in 1943–4 and begins with a haunting evocation of London towards the end of the war:

> Weeds grew in the City itself; a hawk was seen hovering over the ruins of the Temple, and foxes raided the chicken roosts in the gardens of houses near Hampstead Heath. The shabby quietness of an old decaying village hung in the streets, and it was a wonderful, awe-inspiring thing to see and feel. While the summer lasted, the beauty was stronger than the sadness, because the sun blessed everything – the ruins, the tired faces of the people, the tall wild flowers and the dark stagnant water – and during those months of calm, London in ruin was as beautiful as a city in a dream.

The book's heroine, Margaret Steggles, is a schoolteacher who comes to London to take up a new post at a girls' school. She has a nagging, miserable mother and a casually unfaithful father, and believes herself to be constitutionally unhappy. Nevertheless she imagines that she has not suffered enough and that, in the words of her favourite writer, Gerard Challis: 'Suffering is the anvil upon which the crystal sword of integrity is hammered.' But Margaret's need is not for more suffering – not, at least, in the romantic, egotistical way that Challis conceives it – but for the Gentle Powers.

Through a dropped ration book Margaret gets to know the Nilands: Alexander, a well-known painter, his wife Hebe and her parents the Challises who live at Westwood, an elegant house in Highgate. Hebe Niland's father is the playwright Gerard Challis whom Margaret idolises. Both the Nilands and the Challises have great charm, and, with the casual selfishness of the privileged, they take advantage of Margaret's slavish admiration.

Margaret believes she has found happiness through her association with these exciting people, but slowly she becomes disillusioned with them, and, in that process, finds her own particular path to fulfilment. That path is not marriage, which is the ending of so many of Stella's novels, but something more complex and problematic, and the book is all the better for that. It reflects Stella's own gropings at this time towards a religious faith. Margaret represents that side of her which found more happiness from wanting than from having, the poetic side which was 'amorous of the far'. For such people, as one character observes towards the end of the book, 'the only "thing" that a human being can go on wanting all their life, *and* be satisfied with just wanting, is God'.

Despite the seriousness of its themes the book contains some of Stella's very best comedy, which reaches a perfect climax in Kew Gardens where Gerard Challis is exposed both to his admirer, Margaret, and to Hilda, the young woman he professes to love, as a fraud. The moment is saved from farce by the fact that it is delicately handled and that it is character rather than crude coincidence which has brought three people to a moment of revelation which is almost equally uncomfortable to them all.

The article in *Leader* magazine written before publication, states that: 'The book is also an attack on a type of solemn person who goes round saying that people ought to suffer, and that only suffering and tragedy call out really worthwhile characteristics. [Stella observed:] "So far as I am concerned, cheerfulness will keep breaking in and though *Westwood* is not another *Cold Comfort Farm*, it preaches the same moral. I do *dislike* solemnity."'

The chief object of *Westwood*'s satire is Gerard Challis, a character who, Stella later admitted, was firmly based on Charles Morgan. Then a highly esteemed novelist, playwright and critic, Morgan was nothing if not solemn. He was a suitable target for Stella since he was something of a cult, just as Mary Webb had been when Stella was writing *Cold Comfort Farm*. It was fashionable to say you admired Charles Morgan; it established your spiritual and intellectual credentials.

In 1938 London audiences had been treated to his play called *The Flashing Stream*, on which Stella based the parodic scenarios of Challis's plays. It is shocking to think that this ludicrous, pseudo-profound melodrama was not only taken seriously but could actually have been praised highly by reputable critics such as James Agate. Others, however, had found Morgan hard to take and had ventured to say that he was lacking in humour. In the essay 'On Singleness of Mind', which he appended to the published version of *The Flashing Stream* that same year, Morgan hit back at his detractors with an astonishing tirade. After making the breathtaking and possibly blasphemous assertion that neither Shakespeare nor Jesus had a sense of humour, Morgan went on:

> Milton had none; Wordsworth none; Shelley none; Nelson none. . . . The sense of humour by which we are ruled avoids emotion and vision and grandeur of spirit as a weevil avoids the sun. It has banished tragedy from our theatre, eloquence from our debates, glory from our years of peace, splendour from our wars. . . . It is talent's sneer at genius, in whatever form genius appears. It is mediocrity's hatred of the Spirit of Man, a blanket on vision, a yelp at saints.

This is grandiloquent, self-serving twaddle, and Grandfather Gibbons himself could not have put it better. In *Westwood* Stella wrote that 'Mr Challis had no use for humour; he had more than once publicly and severely put it in its place (where, with Shakespeare and Jane Austen, it stayed).'

Charles Morgan is occasionally cited today as an example of a once fashionable and venerated writer who is now completely disregarded. He stands as a warning to current idols of the literary scene that posterity may find them less palatable than Dick Francis. Like most writers who once had a reputation, a case can be made for Morgan: in novels such as *The Fountain* and plays such as *The River Line* and *The Flashing Stream* he attempted to explore the serious concerns which were exercising the minds of serious intelligent people at that time. His prose is graceful, if a little too stately for modern tastes, but his characters and situations have very little vitality, and humour – unless you count a sort of desiccated wit – is nowhere to be found. You never feel Morgan is describing life at first hand. There is a fundamental inability to grasp what the world is really like; as if Morgan has reconstructed it in his head, according to subtle, intellectual principles of his own. His work, with its metaphysical preoccupations and schematic characterisation, is not without its parallels in critically acclaimed fiction today. Had the Booker Prize existed in the thirties he would probably have won it in preference to seemingly less durable and elevated types such as Evelyn Waugh, P. G. Wodehouse, or even Stella Gibbons, because there is a recurrent if not invariable critical prejudice in favour of a little dullness.

Stella's dislike – hatred even – of Morgan and all his works can be traced back at least as far as an article of hers in the *Lady* on 25 February 1932 entitled 'When Men Write about Women'. There is some initial confusion because she names the book she is reviewing as *Portrait in a Mirror*, whereas the book she actually discusses is his latest work, *The Fountain*. Perhaps rage blinded her to the error, but there is a certain irony about it in view of the fact that *Portrait in a Mirror* had won the *Fémina-Vie Heureuse* prize in 1930, three years before Stella herself won it with *Cold Comfort Farm*. *The Fountain*, despite her strictures, was to become Morgan's most highly praised novel and was to win the Hawthornden Prize.

The article begins by attacking the arrogance of those male writers who claim to 'understand women' while in fact treating them as objects – objects of devotion perhaps, but still objects. This particularly applies to the character of Julie Narwitz in *The Fountain*. Stella wrote:

Two men of outstanding spiritual force are in love with her. And what is she? She is our old fashioned friend the *femme incomprise*, the mysterious yet childish creature, who never knows her own mind for two minutes together, and has no sense of humour. We can quite see that two unusually intelligent men might love such a creature from sheer force of contrast. Our complaint is that she never comes to life, never for one instant.

Mr Morgan even seems afraid to let us know what she looked like:

'The curve of her shoulders, the uplifted pallor of her face, her throat's gleam, her body's suppleness, her eyes like the challenge of a bayonet in a quiet path – he could not tell her what he saw. . . .'

In *Westwood* Stella writes of Challis: 'He always wrote obliquely of people's charms, making a man say to a woman, *"Your throat is a taut chord,"* or *"Your ankle bone is softly modelled."'* The *Lady* article continues:

Then she talks (as the children say) like a book:

'Do you think that I am a woman who takes a delight in confusing men's lives? There is a part of me that would be freer, more gay, lighter, harder, more brilliant – if you were gone. But it is the worst in me that would profit, and perhaps the best in you.' That is the language of attempted literature, not of life and feeling.

Mr Morgan's generalisations on women are equally amusing. Ballater [Stella meant Herriot], the nice cheerful young officer, says to Lewis [the hero and a flattering self-portrait of the author]:

'And women too . . . you could play hell with them if it amused you. You'd look as if you'd burn them with your austerity – and that's a candle they always die in. Not all women perhaps – the silly ones like a smoother passage – but the women worth having. . . .'

The silly women, gentle reader, are you and me and Miss Smith next door. We like a smoother passage. Life has made you and me and Mrs Smith into human beings, as well as Women with a capital W. If only men novelists would occasionally realise this, we should not be alternately amused and irritated by solemn, over-masculine novels like *The Fountain.*

Condescension masquerading as respect is the besetting sin of the

Western liberal, and Stella would have none of it. Stella had a good eye for the currently fashionable bore. I can remember her at a dinner party in the 1960s neatly dismembering C. P. Snow, who was then highly thought of.

Gerard Challis in *Westwood* is one of the most enjoyable and vicious of Stella's satirical portraits, but he is also a rounded and tragic character. I once asked Stella what it was she had against Morgan, other than the fact that his literary output had been pretentious and over-rated. She said she had found him a sanctimonious character – 'Charly-Morgan-Play-the-Organ', she called him – and she had once heard him expatiating in public on the varied and unusual sex life which he was enjoying, or had enjoyed, with his wife ('Heinz 57 Varieties' was her dismissive phrase for it). A combination of pomposity and sexual exhibitionism – characteristics of Mr Mybug – always excited her contempt.

Stella remembered seeing Morgan, who was drama critic of the *Times* for many years, at first nights wearing full evening dress and a voluminous evening cloak. This tall, spare man with his ascetic good looks must have cut an impressive figure, and known it. Stella's attitude towards ostentation was not indulgent. She told me that she had once seen the occultist Aleister Crowley standing outside the Café Royal. Her impression of him was unfavourable. Was it his air of supernatural malignancy? I asked hopefully. No. She said that what repelled her was that he had the look of a man who was desperately trying to attract attention.

Several readers writing to her in the 1980s asked Stella if Gerard Challis was meant to be Morgan, so the portrait must have been recognisable. When I first read *Westwood* I noted that Morgan himself was mentioned in the text and asked Stella about this. She beamed with delight: 'Ah, that was deliberate, you see,' she said, 'to throw people off the scent!' If that was really her intention, it was a curiously ineffective ploy. Of course, even a cursory look at his life shows that Morgan had his admirable side, but the great advantage that fiction has over biography is that one does not have to be fair.

Challis, like Constance Fielding in *The Bachelor*, is a study in spiritual pride, in what happens when a preoccupation with transcendence shuts eyes and ears to the coarser demands of mundane morality. Constance and Challis are, essentially, devotees of the old Gnostic heresy of dualism – a corruption of Christianity, whose doctrines by contrast have always stressed the integration of body and spirit in the Incarnation. Both characters believe that true freedom is freedom of the Spirit, and that in Challis's words 'freedom of the body is nothing', which is why the war is little more than a troublesome enigma to them.

Challis, however, is a subtler character altogether than Constance, far more intelligent and genuinely gifted, but for that very reason possessed of an even greater capacity for self-deception. He has a passion for intense but Platonic affairs with young women; and he fondly imagines that, because these relationships do not involve physical sex, they are harmless. In fact he thinks that his victims benefit immeasurably in mind and spirit from them. He suffers from a kind of refined male chauvinism.

Challis's function is not simply to divert the reader with an amusing satirical portrait, but also to stand for a specific kind of decadence in Western values. This decadence was becoming apparent towards the end of the war and was one of the causes of the Labour landslide in 1945. Challis's values are both over-spiritualised and coldly patrician. When Granty, the family's faithful old servant, is dying, he remarks: 'She has enjoyed giving her life to us, you know. She is a slave by temperament and has passed her life in slavery; therefore she is fulfilled.'

The Challises of this world are likely to put a higher value on great human achievements and works of art than on individual human beings. This, paradoxically, accounts for the fact that they cannot produce great works of art themselves. In his essay 'On Singleness of Mind' Morgan wrote:

> The terror is not that men will die or that they will die uselessly and in misery, for men are replaceable; we attach overmuch importance to the preservation of our lives, which, in the reckoning of nature, are of small account. The terror is that a sonnet of Shakespeare may be lost as the poems of Sappho have been; or the cathedral of Chartres be destroyed; or the science of mathematics, the art of mathematics, be driven back to a cutting of notches on sticks.

This, published at the time of Munich, was not just nonsense; it was dangerous nonsense. It would have appalled the author of the

Sonnets as much as the statement that he had no sense of humour would have amused him.

The main source of decadence in the book may be Challis, but it pervades the whole household of Westwood. Two American servicemen are invited to dinner and, as they walk back, one of them expresses unqualified admiration at the household's old-world charm; but the other, Levinsky, Jewish and more thoughtful, responds: 'It's got class, anyone can see that, but it's dead on its feet too.' The house itself impresses Margaret in much the same way. She is at first dazzled by its elegance, then, when shown its less public quarters, she experiences a feeling of revulsion: 'There is a point at which age, in a house that is still occupied, ceases to exert a spell and becomes faintly disgusting. This phenomenon is usually accompanied by dirt, which may serve to explain it, but it sometimes occurs when an ancient house is clean, and there is no rational explanation.'

These more generalised intimations are there in the book, running under the comedy and giving it moral substance. Never forced on the reader, they testify to an unusual sensitivity to the winds of change that were beginning to blow. Stella even predicted the death of Morgan's reputation. The first night of Challis's new play *Kattë* has every appearance of a triumph, but for the first time the critics are dissatisfied with his work. His days as a literary idol are numbered. Reverence for Morgan in Britain barely survived the war. In 1953 Dylan Thomas in his talk 'A Visit to America' would refer to a list of engagements as being 'as long as a New York Menu, or half an hour with a book by Charles Morgan'.

In October 1945 Allan was released from military service, having achieved the substantive rank of captain. He returned from the Middle East, and by March the following year was playing Almaviva in *The Marriage of Figaro* at Sadlers Wells. He had been away for over three years, and he never went abroad again. When Stella travelled she either went by herself or with Laura. She once remarked rather coyly to her friend Suzanne Goodwin how odd it was that Allan should let two defenceless and not unattractive females travel alone together. Laura told me that his prolonged separation from England in the war, during which his mother had died, had given her father a strong disinclination to travel. It was also inevitable that Allan and Stella's three years apart should have put a strain on their marriage.

In 1947 Stella was baptised into the Church of England with twelve-year-old Laura standing as godmother. Ten years later, in April 1957, using the third person and calling herself 'Mrs W———', Stella described the final stages of her conversion in *St Martin's Review*:

> At the age of forty she had been reduced to admitting the existence of God, but this magnanimity was modified by the denial of the divinity of Christ: to set on the attacking, or rather, the steering side, was the fact that she had married a Christian, and that within herself there had always existed a feeling, rather than any faith, that a Power of immense beauty, goodness and force did exist.
>
> Finally the struggle became very strong and imperious. So she decided to pray that God would 'reveal to her the nature of Himself.' Somewhere we are told, are we not, to assault Heaven with prayers, and if that prayer is not arrogant enough to be called an assault, Mrs W——— does not know what is. Gradually she began to be drawn irresistibly towards the Idea, and the power, of Christ.
>
> At the age of forty-three the struggle was over: with a last dextrous and loving turn of the guiding switch, the silly sheep that was Mrs W——— went meekly into the fold, and the Shepherd shut the gate.

The language that Stella uses is slightly stilted and suggests the influence of C. S. Lewis, whose novels and popular works of Christian apologetics she had read. Lewis's account of his own spiritual journey in *Surprised by Joy* (1955), though naturally more ample than Stella's, is remarkably similar in tone and substance. Both began their writing careers as poets – Stella being by far the better practitioner – and their apprehension of God had its origins in an awareness of beauty. This awareness was so strong that they were finally forced to the conclusion that its source was some kind of absolute beauty. Both had acknowledged God as a supreme, beautiful but not necessarily loving being before they embraced Christ and the doctrines of the Church.

In Stella's copy of Will Durant's *The Story of Philosophy* there is evidence from the numerous annotations in her hand of more than one serious reading. Against a passage recommending a fearless agnosticism in the face of an uncomprehended universe, Stella wrote: 'This is what I believe, but I hold my belief under the eyes of an inscrutable God who does not love Man but whom Man rightly reveres and worships. Jan. 27 1937.' Against this she later wrote: 'Dear me. 8.11.1973.' It might be tempting to condemn the last comment as too facile except for the fact that what separates these two remarks is Allan's death from cancer.

In the *St Martin's Review* article Stella may have given an impression of finality about her conversion, which was not quite accurate. No doubt she did this for the edification of her readers and the best of motives. In fact, while adhering to the Church of England she remained what she called in *Westwood* a 'God-Struggler', a position summarised by the man in the Gospels who said: 'Lord, I believe. Help thou my unbelief.' She frequently reread William James's *The Varieties of Religious Experience* and works such as Alister Hardy's *The Biology of God*, which attempt to establish some kind of objective scientific basis for the revealed truths of religion. Stella's marginal notes in these works testify to a longing for certainty rather than its attainment. But this element of doubt was not something with which, ultimately, she felt uncomfortable. In *St Martin's Review* in February 1940 she wrote:

When I was younger I used to be disturbed because my mind was so painfully susceptible to ideas. Ideas had more influence upon me than people had. Now that I am older, I am proud of this susceptibility. It is still painful, but I know that it keeps my mind youthful. When I talk with people in their early twenties I feel at ease with them because they too have not 'made up' their minds about everything in Earth and Heaven. (Make up your mind . . . yes, as if it were a bed, and then lie on it and go sound asleep and never worry about anything again until your sleep passes over into death.)

Faith, after all, is not the same as certainty.

For her next novel, *The Matchmaker* (1949), Stella returned to Sussex, the setting for *Cold Comfort Farm* (in an uncharacteristic moment of self-indulgence she even allows one of her characters to quote: 'Something nasty in the woodshed'). This time, however, she consulted reality rather than her own imagination and made use of her experience of wartime exile from London with Laura in Sussex and Gloucestershire. Stella's heroine Alda Lucie-Browne, the matchmaker of the title, is, unlike Flora, an unsuccessful fixer. There is more than a touch of Jane Austen's Emma in her desire to manipulate the lives of others for their own benefit (as she sees it) and for her own personal satisfaction.

Alda, evacuated with her three daughters, has taken a dark, unsuitable cottage in the country. It is 1945, her house in a Northern provincial town has been bombed and her husband is in Germany, helping to resettle the displaced populations of Europe. His official and masculine efforts are ironically contrasted with Alda's private efforts to resettle the four displaced people in her immediate environment. They are Fabrio, an Italian prisoner of war; Sylvia, a stage-struck communist landgirl; Phil Waite, a morose chicken farmer; and Jean, a smart friend of hers. Her plans to attach Fabrio to Sylvia and Jean to Waite go awry. All four are entertaining characters, drawn with considerable depth and insight.

Perhaps the best of them is Mr Waite, the misanthropic bachelor chicken farmer and would-be mystic (possibly named after the occultist and Arthurian scholar A. E. Waite, author of some of the least readable prose in the English language outside feminist critiques of Marxism). He is priggish and fussy – two characteristics usually associated with spinsters – but in an intensely masculine way. There is a touch of Mr Woodhouse in *Emma* about the way he is always worrying unnecessarily over the health and safety of his female acquaintances. He also frets over his own moral wellbeing as a chicken farmer: 'The pamphlets explaining the battery system emphasised that it was not cruel. Mr Waite always wondered what Buddha would have said about it.' His attitude to women is very true to a certain kind of inhibited male: he is never quite at ease in the presence of individual women unless he can condescend to them, but at the same time he has a generalised reverence for Womanhood. He is compared to *Pride and Prejudice*'s Mr Darcy at one point, and his proposal to Jean is almost as awkward and arrogant as Darcy's first efforts.

There is an amusing scene in which he congratulates himself to

Jean on having had the good sense not to marry. He expatiates pompously on the troubles of his married friends. Jean heartily agrees with him and says that she is not going to get married either, but this does not please Mr Waite:

> . . . he shook his head; he turned to look at the face smiling up into his own, and he said:
> 'I don't like to hear a lady say that, Miss Hardcastle. You're doing some poor chap out of a happy home.'

When Jean recounts his views on marriage to Alda, her friend is not dismayed and assures Jean that 'men always talked like this when they were attracted by that particular subject, adding firmly, "It's like moths."'

Jean rather reluctantly accepts Waite's first proposal, but calls the marriage off when Oliver Potter, an old flame, turns up. Jean's choice between the two of them is unromantically real: she loves Potter, but Waite is better-looking. Waite is stolid and humourless; Potter is more entertaining and congenial to Jean. Alda, who had originally promoted the attachment to Waite, changes her mind and urges her to go for Potter. After becoming disillusioned with Potter, Jean, unknown to Alda, returns to Waite who has the unexciting kindness and stability that she needs. And Sylvia, the communist landgirl, decisively rejects Fabrio.

The pace of the book is leisurely, sometimes too leisurely for its own good, but the picture it creates of the countryside during the post-war period of austerity is convincing. There are some fine lyrical descriptions of the seasons in the country, informed at times by Stella's newly found faith in orthodox Christianity, such as this account of a walk back from church on Christmas Eve:

> Faint unearthly light and a deep hush lay over the fields; when a star glided out now and then from behind the scudding brown clouds its bright eye entered the scene as if alive and watching them, and the snow sparkling and crinching underfoot in the torchrays seemed protesting as if aroused from a cold, light sleep. Suddenly bells began to peel, faintly and far away; another tower in the night took up the sound; then St Wilfred's three miles off,

and soon the air was filled with it. Strange, wild, rejoicing sound! untamed yet familiar, having nothing to do with any peace except that peace which comes after unimaginable struggle and *passeth understanding*, clanging and ringing out over the darkened earth to remind it of the unbelievable truth.

The description is immediately undercut when Alda's family find an unwelcome visitor in the cottage on their return.

The final chapter describes the return home of Fabrio, the Italian prisoner of war. A Ligurian peasant, he lives near Santa Margherita where Stella stayed in 1927 and almost met Max Beerbohm. Laura told me that Allan, who read all Stella's manuscripts in proof and offered suggestions, considered this last chapter of *The Matchmaker* to be the finest thing that Stella ever wrote. Certainly it is Stella's later manner at its best. Small incidents and descriptive details, trivial in themselves, are put together to form a convincing picture of homecoming, unromanticised but glowing with ecstatic joy. The girl who has been waiting for Fabrio is not the comely creature that his mind had conjured up in exile. He experiences initial disappointment, but soon his not very powerful imagination evaporates before an acceptance of the more vivid reality.

The book was well received, and many critics remarked on her capacity to make ordinary lives interesting and significant. It came out in April 1949, and in the autumn of that year another novel of hers was published, shorter and slighter than *The Matchmaker*. This was *Conference at Cold Comfort Farm*.

By 1949 *Cold Comfort Farm* had sold 28,000 in the hardback edition and 315,000 in a Penguin paperback. That September, according to a newspaper report, a further 40,000 were due to be printed. It seemed an opportune moment to bring out a sequel, but the critics were almost bound to be disappointed. Some were, while others, like L. A. G. Strong in the *Spectator*, believed that 'Miss Gibbons has done it again.' *Conference at Cold Comfort Farm* naturally cannot compare with the original, but it has its moments.

The book's epigraph is a quotation from Thomas Love Peacock, 'I think it necessary to make a stand against the encroachments of Black Bile', which suggests not only the theme of the novel but also its form. Stella adopts the Peacock formula (to be found in *Headlong Hall, Nightmare Abbey* and other novels of his), which consists in assembling a number of eccentric types in a country house, setting them off against one another, and describing the farcical consequences.

Flora is asked by Mr Mybug to help run a conference of the International Thinkers' Group at Cold Comfort Farm. Most of the male Starkadders – except Urk and Reuben – have gone to South Africa (or 'South Afriky' as it is inevitably called), leaving the female Starkadders bereft. The farm buildings have been sold to a trust which lets the place out for conferences. They have been whitewashed, 'cockered up like a lost woman on Worthing Front', and made into the equivalent of a modern theme park with signs over the doors reading 'The Greate Scullerie' and the like. Reuben's efforts to farm the land have been interfered with by a man from the Ministry of Agriculture – 'brast 'un fer a bowler-hatten skowkerd!' – and, final humiliation, Big Business the bull has lent himself to artificial insemination. Flora is called upon by Reuben to restore the situation.

The chief object of Stella's satire, though, is, naturally enough, the International Thinkers' Group, a diffuse collection of contemporary types ranging from existentialists through various kinds of avant garde artists to an Indian guru. But her approach is on the whole too wide-ranging and perfunctory to strike home. She had forgotten that effective mockery requires a measure of understanding, even sympathy.

However, Stella was attacking the dehumanising aspects of modern high culture, and these deserved to be attacked. Like its ancestor, *Conference at Cold Comfort Farm* is set in the future and is at times amusingly prescient: New York has become the art centre of the world (it was not to become so until well into the fifties); students at RADA are taught how to get rid of upper-class accents; there are euthanasia societies. There is Transistorist Sculpture, which uses perishable goods such as pastry and sausage meat, and Peccavi's painting *The Excreta* is on display. (While I was writing this book the notorious *Sensation* exhibition at the Royal Academy in London was showing works of art in which pastry, sausage meat and, indeed, excreta all featured prominently.)

Stella's introduction of the Sage, an Indian guru, seems to anticipate the sixties, especially in the way he both despises the creature comforts of the West and yet takes advantage of them. His catchphrase 'Everything is Monkey' – Monkey standing for modern technology and 'the restless, inventive spirit in man' – deserves to be better known.

The male Starkadders return from South Africa – 'Whoam, Whoam, like a wounded maggit' reads one of their telegrams – and they shatter the English Heritage decorum of the farm. Fights break out; furniture is burnt; women weep; and Cold Comfort returns to its primal state of chaos. At this point, fittingly, Flora and Stella take their leave of the Starkadders for the last time.

Following her excellent BBC radio version of *Cold Comfort Farm* in 1981 Elizabeth Proud produced a very entertaining adaptation of *Conference at Cold Comfort Farm*. With Stella's full permission, she garnished it with several improvements of her own.

Allan's theatrical career was at this time outwardly flourishing. After playing Almaviva in 1946 he was offered leading baritone roles in the next Sadlers Wells season but turned them down. The nervous strain had been too much. Instead he accepted a small part in *Bless the Bride*, one of the most successful of post-war British musicals. But he was not happy and his discontent took the form of minor – almost involuntary – flirtations. Lacking confidence as he did, he was always surprised and flattered when women found him attractive, as often happened, and his naturally depressive temperament found relief in taking risks.

When Renée had visited Cairo in 1944 with Donald Wolfit's Shakespearean touring company she was able to see something of her brother. At the time he was conducting an affair with an Egyptian girl who was also being pursued by a burly American officer. As they were walking through the streets one day Allan pointed out the officer to his sister, who observed that the possibility of danger which this liaison involved seemed to excite him.

There had always been flirtations and Renée told me that Stella would tease Allan about them, saying that one day he would get his fingers burnt. This happened once with an actress called Sydney Malcolm, the only one of Allan's girlfriends who seriously tried to take him away from Stella.

Sydney was more than ten years younger than Allan and had known him as early as 1938, when she appeared in the chorus of a production of *Così Fan Tutte* at the Open Air Theatre in Regent's Park in which Allan was playing Don Alfonso. Her affair with Allan reached its climax in 1949 when he appeared in a play of hers for which she had written starring roles for them both. Only too appropriately the play was called *The Choice*.

Set in the eighteenth century, it concerned the tribulations of Hester, Lady Rillbourne (played by Sydney) at the hands of her husband Lord Rillbourne (played by Allan), a gambler and a rake. Rillbourne is reconciled to his wife at the end, realising that she truly loves him, and dies a hero's death in the Gordon Riots. With hindsight the plot appears steeped in prophetic ironies. It was put on as a try-out for a week at the Chantecleer Theatre in Clareville Street, Kensington, but failed to please either critics or public. Renée, who was in the cast, had no idea that anything was going on between Sydney and Allan, but her husband John had his suspicions.

When the run of the play was over Stella went to consult Renée and asked whether she should give Allan his freedom. She had no wish to do so, but she wanted Allan to be happy. Both Renée and John told her emphatically that Allan would not be happier if he were free to pursue the relationship with Sydney. A Catholic priest, who had been a prisoner of war with John, was also called upon for independent counsel and the situation was somehow resolved. Allan did not leave Stella; and, more importantly, Stella did not leave Allan. 'She behaved very well over the whole business,' said Renée.

Allan made only one more major appearance in the theatre. In the same year, 1949, he played Luke Marks in the successful revival of *Lady Audley's Secret*, the melodrama based on Miss Braddon's popular Victorian novel. According to one review he was 'formidably robust and callous as the drunken gamekeeper who knows too much for Lady Audley's peace of mind'. His theatrical career was at an end, but he kept a detailed record of it in a scrapbook, including all the press cuttings relating to *The Choice*.

Stella was a great admirer of Kipling's verse and often quoted to me two lines from an early poem of his, 'The Mare's Nest':

She was so good she made him worse
(Some women are like this, I think);

I sometimes wonder whether she ruefully recognised in these lines a comment on her relationship with Allan, and whether this reali- sation helped her to forgive him.

CHAPTER 8

Gentle Powers

On 16 May 1950, Stella was made a Fellow of the Royal Society of Literature. She described the scene in a letter to her brother-in-law, John Oliver:

The ceremony took place in the Swedenborg Hall, which is devoted to the memory of Swedenborg who saw a lot of visions some time in the eighteenth century, and it has pictures of Victorian and eighteenth-century divines all round the walls. It is rather over-heated and during the lecture following the inauguration I jolly nearly fell asleep; truly, without exaggeration. Only the thought of how awful it would have been kept me awake.

When I got there, and announced myself to the secretary with the pretty, shy manner I assume on these occasions, I was introduced to a tall man named Kennedy Williamson who was also to be made a Fellow, and we sat down to wait the arrival of the Chairman (the President, Lord Wavell, is ill). Mr Kennedy [*sic*], on my saying how proud I was to have been chosen as a Fellow, said that *he* had taken good care that he could not be voted out, and had supplied himself with seven sponsors . . . all madly famous but I forget their names. Anyway, this announcement rather took the gilt off my Fellowship, as I did not know that one could force oneself into the Society like that. However, I consoled myself with the fact that at least I hadn't suggested I should be made a Fellow.

Kennedy Williamson, who had succeeded Algernon Blackwood as President of the Writers' Guild, was the author of a biography of W. E. Henley and some extremely undistinguished verse and criticism. The files of the Royal Society of Literature reveal him as a comic and slightly pathetic figure, a relentless self-promoter, forever bombarding the Secretary with information about his activities. On one occasion he wrote: 'Today, I have had one great happiness: I have seen myself in an anthology. And do you know that I am the only living poet who has had six broadcasts of one poem?' Stella with only a single proposer, the popular middlebrow novelist Angela Thirkell, had been voted in unanimously. Thirkell, who was on the committee of the RSL, was not a friend of Stella's and her competent, snobbish novels set mostly in a latter-day Barsetshire would not have appealed to her, but she did share with Stella a detestation of Charles Morgan. Stella went on:

> Then the Secretary arrived; very old and wheezy female, and full of grievances about the British Working Man, who was engaged on repairing a splendid new house in Hyde Park Gate which the society is to have as its new premises. Then the Vice President arrived, also extremely old and rather wheezy, male, and very learned in Shakespeare (and probably the musical glasses too). By a coincidence which was very interesting to me the lecturer was one Professor Doughty who first gave me lectures in English at University College thirty years ago, and he had hardly altered at all.
>
> Well, by this time the audience had assembled and without wishing to be uncharitable or choosy I am bound to say that a more rum collection of faces I never wish to see. Everybody except Ernest Raymond (who is a darling, about seven feet high and very easy, polite and obviously successful and happy) looked thwarted, and their *clothes* were most peculiar. One old man with a yellow face who looked like someone out of a story by R. L. Stevenson sat and blinked with his mouth open all the time, and there were many old ladies covered in lace and beads. Old Sir Edward Marsh was there; he looked fairly normal but very rakish, and as for James Bridie he looks exactly like a goblin. He has a little round stomach which makes his jacket stick out like a drum, huge eyes behind glasses, and a maddening pawky Scots manner. He kept making jokes in such a soft voice that I could hardly hear them and no doubt I laughed in all the

wrong places. Mrs Bridie is animated, elderly and pretty; *she* kept saying to everybody 'Come an' see us in Glasgow', with the happy knowledge that probably none of us could afford the fare. James Bridie was made a Fellow, and so was Hilary St George Saunders who wrote all those official accounts of the Battle of Britain etc. He writes wonderfully well, don't you think? He looked cheerful and intelligent and has something Churchillian about him; perhaps it is a curiously babyish look which seems sometimes to go with great ability of an unusual kind.

We all had to go up to the platform one by one, and have what the Secretary described as 'a little incantation' read over us, and then we signed our names in a huge parchment book, while the audience clapped us. It was an impressive moment to me while I was signing mine; never could I have imagined such a thing happening; and even now I think it's rather peculiar; I haven't dared to tell anybody except members of the family because I am pretty sure Eliz. Jenkins and Gwen [Clear] and others will think my work doesn't deserve it.

Then Professor Doughty gave his lecture, which was about the Poetic as conceived in Rossetti's poems and paintings. It was very learned, and not very interesting; too academic. Afterwards James Bridie had to propose a vote of thanks, and I had to second it; the first time I have ever done such a thing. We then had tea, which was very bad; and if ever I get into a position of power in the Society I shall concentrate on getting the teas better.

Stella never achieved any position of power in the Society because she never attempted to do so, but she attended many of its functions and once, in 1954, lectured to its members on *Cold Comfort Farm*. Though she disliked lionisation and literary coteries, she enjoyed the quiet distinction that the initials FRSL after her name conferred. In the same year that she became a Fellow, Allan, who had now left the stage for good, used some private money inherited from his mother to become a director of the Collectors' Book Club (Editions de Luxe Ltd). It was chiefly a bookbinding firm and produced some excellent work, but was never very profitable.

In 1950 Stella's *Collected Poems* were published. The volume contains her three previous collections and three new poems, two written in wartime. The longest of them, 'The Swallows of Ruheliegen', is a moving piece based on a story by Ernst Toller about swallows which returned each year to a concentration camp, despite the best efforts of the guards:

> Hope and courage were born on their wing-tips
> And burst in music on dying men
> Who know that the tide flows on in glory
> Because of the swallows of Ruheliegen.

She published verse more rarely from then onwards, and never produced another collection, but she kept a manuscript volume called *Verses for Friends* in which she made copies of poems that she would often send to friends and relations.

That year two young men came to tea with her to discuss a stage adaptation of *Cold Comfort Farm* which they had written, but she did not take to them. Their names were Peter Wildeblood and Kenneth Tynan. The introduction came through Renée, who had been directed by Tynan in *Man of the World* the previous December. Stella's prejudice may have been partly derived from Renée, who thought Tynan was the worst director she had ever worked for, but I doubt whether Stella would ever have taken to a man who, apart from having some claims to good looks (of a rather decadent kind), resembled nothing so much as a latter-day Mr Mybug. Besides, Tynan was a celebrity-chaser, a type Stella abhorred – especially when the celebrity was herself. Some years later Wildeblood, a distinguished journalist, was sent to prison as a result of a notorious homosexual scandal and wrote a remarkable book about his experiences. Tynan, to his great credit, had stood bail for him.

Though temperamentally antipathetic, Tynan and Stella did share a taste and a gift for parody. Stella quoted to me with pleasure from Tynan's brilliant guying of William Faulkner in his review of *Requiem for a Nun*: 'Down behind the morgue a few of the young people are roastin' a nigger over an open fire, but I guess every town has its night-owls. . . .' The parallels with *Cold Comfort Farm* are obvious.

She put her two visitors into a short story called 'The Time of Roses' which appeared in her 1954 collection *Beside the Pearly*

Water. Two exquisites are the guests of honour at a literary tea party. The narrator, a middle-aged woman who is obviously Stella herself, observes them as they speak with scorn of another guest, an elderly retired pedagogue. The old man, contrary to expectations, turns out to have had an extremely romantic past. The two young men, 'one elegant in Neo-Edwardian drainpipe trousers and short overcoat, the other too confident in his own brilliance to trouble about elegance', are clearly modelled on Wildeblood and Tynan. Nothing came of their projected version of *Cold Comfort Farm*.

In 1951 Stella's thirteenth novel, *The Swiss Summer*, was published. It has always been Renée's theory that Stella produced her worst work when she was least happy, and that the distressing incidents surrounding *The Choice* in 1949 account for the quality of *The Swiss Summer*. It is undoubtedly a very dull book, though by no means unpleasant to read. One might recommend it to a convalescent, much as doctors used to recommend milk puddings and other bland but nourishing forms of sustenance.

As soon as the war was over Stella had begun to travel again, and one of the first places she revisited was the country whose Alpine solitude had inspired some of her earliest published verse. The descriptions in *The Swiss Summer* of the heroine's rediscovery of a place where she had once known romance, and her revelling in the soothing 'smugness' of a people unscarred by the horrors of war, are entertaining enough – but they belong to a travel book rather than a work of fiction.

Mrs Lucy Cottrel is 'a peaceful romantic' and, like Stella, has a beloved husband who does not like holidaying abroad. She is invited to accompany Mrs Blandish to the Chalet Alpenrose in the Bernese Oberland. The chalet is owned by Lady Dagliesh, to whom Mrs Blandish is a paid companion. Mrs Blandish has hopes of inheriting the chalet, and, unknown to her employer, has decided to fill it with paying guests in order to augment her income. It is a reasonably amusing situation whose possibilities are exploited in a rather too leisurely fashion.

The central part of the book is concerned with the doings of four young people, Bertram, Astra, Peter and Kay, who are staying at the chalet. They are all credible, well-observed characters, but none of them is particularly interesting, and the anxious little love affairs that spring up between them are commonplace. Nothing much happens. Nice descriptions of walks up the Jungfrau and peasants making cheese are not enough. The reader feels a distinct sense of annoyance when halfway through the book Lucy comes down the mountain expecting to meet a friend of Mrs Blandish's called Stiggy, reputed to be a shady type, only to be told that she has just missed him. The reader, by this time desperate for something interesting and unusual to happen, misses him too. Relief, however, arrives in the shape of Miss Propter, a middle-aged Lancashire businesswoman whom Mrs Blandish, out of greed, takes on as yet another paying guest. She is a fine comic creation, at once individual and yet instantly recognisable as a type: one of those placid egoists who believes that everything they do or say is of interest, and that every person of the opposite sex is somehow in love with them. To make matters worse, she believes she has 'a sense of humour', which of course she does not. Miss Propter brings about the nemesis of Mrs Blandish, and this episode is skilfully and entertainingly handled. Indeed the book as a whole is clearly the work of an accomplished professional at the height of her technical powers. But it is still a dull novel.

Though Stella may have travelled a good deal without him in the following years, she now always had Allan at home to 'laugh with and lean on', as she used to say. At the end of 1951 Stella wrote to Beth McDonald (formerly Beth Daw, with whom she stayed at Elm Tree Farm in 1944): 'Allan hasn't been very well for the last year with a slight ulcer of the tummy, but his nerves are much better since he left the stage and he is still binding beautiful books with his new business.' That year Auntie Ru had had a stroke and Stella had to look after her; she died three years later, in November 1954.

The last book that Stella wrote for Longmans was *Fort of the Bear* (1953), a curious novel which she called 'a romance'. Its germ can be found in a wartime reverie which appeared in *St Martin's Review* in October 1940: 'One of the deepest reliefs for the mind in these days is to think of those lovely places in Canada, New Zealand, Tasmania, where people are safe and happy and our friends. I try to send myself off to sleep at night by imagining a lake in Canada; clear and blue and lonely, echoing only to the cry of water birds, reflecting the snows of mighty mountains, silent with the heavenly sounds of nature.' Stella had never been to Canada, but she decided to travel there in fiction by telling the story of an aristocrat, the Earl of Vernay, who in the 1920s travels to a remote part of Canada (the Fort of the Bear of the title) with his wife, daughter and assorted retainers.

Stella did not play to her strengths in this book. The characterisation is perfunctory for the most part, comedy of any kind is almost entirely absent, and the story moves slowly. But, though as a whole *Fort of the Bear* is perhaps even less satisfactory than *The Swiss Summer,* it is fascinating from a psychological point of view as the symbolic working out of some of Stella's deepest obsessions.

The creditable but over-copious descriptions of the landscape, flora and fauna are derived entirely from reading, in particular of Algernon Blackwood whose supernatural stories such as *The Camp of the Dog* and *The Wendigo*, set in the northern wastes of Canada, Stella admired. The Wendigo is the fiery wandering spirit of solitude that inhabits these desolate areas and can possess those who stay too long in them. Blackwood wrote: 'The spell of these terrible solitudes cannot leave any mind untouched, any mind, that is, possessed of the higher imaginative qualities.' The Earl of Vernay falls under this spell and, though there are no supernatural elements in *Fort of the Bear*, the legend of the Wendigo, symbol of his possession, is referred to more than once. Blackwood, with his unconventional religious beliefs, his solitariness and passion for raw nature, may well have been a model for Vernay. Stella met him once and remembered a striking personality with a penetrating, hypnotic stare.

Vernay is a man with a romantic longing for solitude who believes he can find personal peace in the harsh, unpeopled grandeur of Canada. He embodies that side of Stella which loved Alpine scenery and 'all the solitary things'. A genuine mystic, he is also an autocratic self-deceiver with a sublime disregard for the feelings of others. He says he only wishes to stay at the Fort for eighteen months, but his wife Cristina begins to suspect that he wants to remain there always, keeping her and the others with him. When one of Vernay's servants falls pregnant, the Earl causes her to miscarry so as to prevent her from leaving the Fort with Cristina. Cristina tries to escape with the help of an admirer, but is killed in the attempt. Vernay is finally brought to his senses through a meeting with a missionary – the best scene in the book.

The missionary himself is not an attractive figure; he is no match for Vernay either in spirit or in intellect, but the man's humility and the simplicity of his questions at last awaken the spark of humanity in Vernay that has become buried under a mountain of spiritual pride. Vernay is finally destroyed by the spirit of solitude and savagery which he sought. He meets a bear in a high mountain pass and dies as a result of wounds sustained in the encounter, but he dies in peace.

Stella identified strongly with Vernay's spiritual yearning, but in her own life had the sense and detachment to draw back from the path he took. Consciously or unconsciously, she had heeded Walter Beck's warning all those years back not to be 'too wildly amorous of the far'. She turned from pantheism to Christianity because she recognised the incompleteness of nature mysticism as a spiritual experience; not because she lacked the romantic imagination, but because she recognised its limitations. In Vernay too there is a vague sense of its inadequacy:

> Yet sometimes, while he was most deeply absorbed, a sensation of disgust with all this flying, creeping, preying life would overcome him, and with it another feeling, so tenuous and strange as to be only hinted at in words, that the visible world was a kind of model or sketch, mockingly assembled to imitate something else which he had never experienced; and then he would feel that he had lived for a very long time within the model, and that he thirsted for the Other which lay completely outside and beyond it.

Vernay's tragedy is that he recognises the demands of duty and human love too late. He is not, like Challis in *Westwood*, a hypocrite, but a fine spirit ruined by a lack of humility. It is a pity that in *Fort of the Bear* such an arresting and personal theme should have been buried under so much conventional romantic material.

In 1954 Malcolm Muggeridge, then editor of *Punch*, invited Stella to write for the magazine. In his diary for 8 January of that year he records that he gave her lunch, and found her 'highly intelligent and, what's more, sensible'. She wrote her first piece for the magazine in April, and, until the late sixties, she was a fairly regular contributor of articles and book reviews. The articles are light and amusing, but not especially distinguished. In one or two she shows off her gift for parody; and her science fiction story in the style of Jane Austen, *Jane in Space*, is evidence that she had not entirely lost her touch:

> Julia did not allow her knowledge of her father's disapproval of travel by rocket to restrain her for more than the few minutes that convention demanded. All was gratification and pleasure. Even the little, and that dusty, which could be seen while travelling at five thousand miles an hour pleased her, and she would not admit that the glimpses of the heavens through heavy clouds were too vast to be agreeable. . . .

Stella manages to convey perfectly not only Austen's stylistic quirks, but also her cast of mind, in particular that slightly suffocating exclusion of the wild and transcendent which made Jane Austen a true child of the Age of Reason.

But 1954 was in many ways a low point in Stella's writing career, and it is not hard to agree with the *Times Literary Supplement* that *Beside the Pearly Water*, the volume of short stories which she brought out that year, is 'a casual collection'. Perhaps it is unsurprising that it was published not by Longmans but by a lesser-known publishing firm called Peter Nevill.

'Beside the Pearly Water', the title story, is the longest in the book. Julia Lanier, a famous peace campaigner, falls in love with a man without knowing that he is a nuclear physicist engaged in atomic weapons research. On discovering this fact, and that he will not renounce his work, she shoots first him and then herself. Though well-paced and quite skilfully told, it is a preposterous tale. For the first time one is conscious of Stella striving for topicality rather than achieving it. The other stories, with one exception, are pleasing but slight. The exception is 'For Those in the Depths', a story about the unexpected power of prayer. It concerns a young boy with a simple faith who encounters the mystery of evil for the first time in a newspaper account of a concentration camp. As an acute study of a certain type of natural goodness it stands comparison with Flaubert's *Un Coeur Simple*, and the ending is almost as striking. With the possible exception of 'Sisters' and 'Roaring Tower' it is Stella's best short story.

Beside the Pearly Water and her last two novels had been either ignored or disparaged by the reviewers. She was having tea in Highgate village one day with her friend the writer Elizabeth Jenkins when she suddenly said that what she felt she needed just then was a really delicious piece of sugar cake. Elizabeth looked at her enquiringly and Stella explained. She had recently been in to see her agent at Pearn, Pollinger and Higham, and the girl on the reception desk had said: 'You're quite a stranger round here these days.' This Stella found discouraging; and she could be easily discouraged. Elizabeth suggested that she change agents and go with her own, Curtis Brown. The firm was then run by Spencer Curtis Brown, son of the firm's founder. Spencer, a writer himself and a man with a genuine love of literature, revived Stella's confidence and became a close personal friend. He also found her another publisher in Hodder and Stoughton, who published Stella's last ten novels.

In January 1955 Allan's wealthy Uncle Cyprian died. Both Stella and Renée remembered the funeral as a long drawn-out and supremely dismal occasion. Cyprian's life had been atrophied by snobbery and the pursuit of wealth, and his marriage to Rachel, who had died in 1953, had been loveless. She had married him for his money, while he had married her for her aristocratic lineage (she was an Erskine). Rachel had told her sister-in-law Jessie that the events of their wedding night had not encouraged either of them to attempt physical relations again, hence their childlessness. Cyprian left his considerable fortune to be divided equally between Allan and Renée, which gave Allan a financial independence that he had never known before. In July that year Stella wrote to her Gloucestershire friend Beth McDonald:

> Allan has bought himself the lease and good will of a nice old pleasant shabby second-hand bookshop in the Archway Road, near Highgate Woods [the Southwood Book Store]. He has always wanted one and now he has his heart's desire – at least, I hope that's me. But you know what I mean! He goes off there each morning about nine o'clock and has a twenty-minute walk to the shop. He runs it single-handed and it is doing well. He

brings home such amusing stories about the bores and the cranks and the queerities who drop in, as well as the ordinary nice customers.

In August 1953 Stella had travelled to Austria and Venice with Laura, now eighteen. In April 1955 Hodder and Stoughton published her novel *The Shadow of a Sorcerer*, which deals with a middle-aged widow, Mrs Lambert, travelling to Austria and Venice with her nineteen-year-old daughter Meg.

Relations between Stella and Laura were always loving but often difficult. Though it would be over-simple to see in Mrs Lambert and her daughter an exact reflection of Stella and Laura, the relationship which forms the core of the novel has an intensity and awkwardness founded on experience. The fact that Stella viewed the situation with a writer's objectivity from both the mother's and the daughter's point of view cannot have made the book any easier for Laura to take. There came a time, Laura told me, when she felt that Stella was making too much use of her life in the novels, and she had to ask her mother to refrain from this form of exploitation. Stella was a kind and loving person but she was not without that splinter of ice which, Graham Greene says, exists in the heart of every true writer.

The plot of *The Shadow of a Sorcerer* revolves around Mrs Lambert's worry that Meg will form an unsuitable liaison with a man. While they are both staying at a language-school-cum-pension in Austria Meg becomes entranced by a house overlooking the nearby lake and then by its owner, Esmé Scarron, the 'sorcerer' of the title. He is a rich man of indeterminate age and an expert on the Renaissance occultist Paracelsus, whose birthplace is the nearby town of Villach. Scarron takes up Meg and lavishes his learning and luxurious lifestyle on her. He is, like Challis and Vernay, another of Stella's misguided spiritual mountaineers, but unlike them he is finally revealed as genuinely malevolent. The gradual uncovering of Scarron's nature is skilfully and interestingly done. It is achieved not simply through the slow release of information, but through a change in the attitude of Meg and her mother towards him. He begins by being mysterious, glamorous and even charming; then he is shown to be sinister and powerful, and finally pitiable. When, in the latter part of the book, mother and daughter reach Venice, Meg half agrees to marry Scarron – not because she is the spellbound victim of his powers, but because she feels sorry for him. In the course of this movement from fascination to compassion – a more common progress for women than men would care to acknowledge – Meg matures. A last apocalyptic scene in Scarron's Venetian palazzo, when all these elements – mystery, horror, pity – are brought together, results in Meg's decisive rejection of him.

Scarron, like Paracelsus, is a healer and herbalist, but he only heals in order to attract followers and exercise power over them. His characterisation owes something to Browning's Paracelsus, who pursues power and wisdom but recognises in the end that he has failed because he lacks ordinary human sympathy and love. Scarron recognises, albeit less distinctly, a similar void in himself. Literary antecedents can also be looked for in those lonely sinners of legend, like the Flying Dutchman, who seek redemption through the unsullied love of a young girl. Perhaps there is also a touch of Prince Lucio Rimanez (actually Lucifer) in Marie Corelli's ridiculous but readable novel *The Sorrows of Satan*. As a study in the nature of evil, Scarron is an interesting modern variant of somewhat tired romantic stereotypes rather than a completely realised character in his own right.

The Shadow of a Sorcerer moves far too slowly to begin with, but, as so often with Stella's novels, it ends better than it begins. There is, however, an appallingly annoying character called Robin, a young man who speaks almost all the time in a jocose imitation of a black Southern mammy. Stella, of course, means him to be irritating, but he is not funny enough to be so amusingly, and one wishes him dead long before the end of the book.

Stella again drew on Laura for *Here Be Dragons* (1956), the most celebrated and successful of her post-war novels. Through the eyes of her nineteen-year-old heroine Nell Seely, Stella enters the world of fifties' beatnik bohemia, jazz clubs and coffee bars. Besides being a good novel in its own right, it is a remarkable feat of imaginative identification with the younger generation. Nancy Spain wrote in the *Daily Express* that it contained

> brilliant accurate reporting. I've been there too [to coffee bars, jazz clubs etc.] and I know. But I also know Stella Gibbons. So I rang her up and asked her, 'When were you last in a coffee bar?'

'Never,' she said, 'but my daughter Laura who is 21 this year used to tell me all about them when she was in with them. She's not any more, thank goodness. She's going to marry a very nice young man and we're very pleased.'

This was Joseph Richardson, a printer and aspiring writer, whom Laura married the following year.

It is hard to take Stella's words literally. Either she, or, more probably Nancy Spain, was exaggerating her use of Laura as a reporter. A description, for instance, of a visit to Humphrey Lyttelton's jazz club in Oxford Street has the authentic ring of something observed at first hand:

The party ... had seated itself at two tables near the band, which now, in jeans and shirtsleeves and with cigarettes hanging from lip, began to saunter onto the low platform at one end of the room; their instruments gleamed softly in the smoky dimness. They sat, blowing shortly and casually into their horns or tapping desultorily on their drums; pale, youngish men. They were a type, yet it was difficult to say in what their typicalness lay. Presently, when the room was almost full, one of them began to beat softly with a foot on the floor, and soon there was a deliberately hesitant yet decided theme wavering up into the air.

Elizabeth Bowen wrote in the *Tatler* that '*Here Be Dragons* has not only charm but something far better, perspicacity.' The charm is in the evocations of Hampstead life; the perspicacity in the anatomising of the tangled relationships of the young people who are its main characters. These young people are much more vivid than the credible but rather insipid figures of *Shadow of a Sorcerer* or *The Swiss Summer*. They belong to a new modern world of espresso bars and national service. They are the first of the television generation; but Stella presents them as they are without her customary moralising. To her they seemed both more self-confident than her own generation and ultimately more vulnerable.

Nell, a typical Gibbons heroine – ordinary, sensible, but with just a touch of the unusual – has come to London because her father, a vicar, has lost his faith and thus his means of livelihood. Nell's aunt, a television personality called Lady Fairfax, finds her a dull job, but through her cousin John, Lady Fairfax's son, she is introduced to the world of coffee bars and artistic types in bedsitters, the 'dragons' of the title. It is a world in which Nell's admission that she is a Conservative is greeted not so much with indignation as with amazement, almost admiration, that someone should have the naïveté to confess it. The novel charts Nell's progress through this world armed with her innocence and the common sense that often accompanies it.

Stella is not squeamish in her description of this world, and her detachment from it prevents her from becoming romantic, but, as Nancy Spain observed, she writes 'with affection'. In addition, her writing derived an extra confidence from the use of Hampstead as the main setting of the novel. No writer has ever evoked this part of London better or more comprehensively than Stella in some of her finest novels, ranging from *Enbury Heath* in 1935 to her last published novel, *The Woods in Winter*, of 1970. She covered its wide social spectrum, its grand houses and mean streets, and she captured the melancholy charm of the Heath where she loved to walk.

In 1957 Laura married Joseph Richardson. The marriage did not last, but Laura and Joe's two sons, Daniel and Benjamin, were to provide Stella with a deep source of happiness in her later years. 'They are my pride and delight,' she wrote in a letter to her friend Constance Rye.

The following year Allan was found to have cancer of the liver. His nervous temperament had always made him vulnerable to illness, and during the 1950s he had grown portly and aged rapidly. Photographs of him at Laura's wedding show a man who looks nearer seventy than fifty, his real age. But despite his physical deterioration his mind did not decay, and he was able to make sensible provisions in his will for his daughter and grandchildren by means of a trust fund. He faced the end courageously with Stella nursing him devotedly at home in Oakshott Avenue. His decline was rapid and he died on 22 July 1959. His death when it came was not unexpected, but no less hard to take for that; and the grief of parting remained with Stella for the last thirty years of her life.

Among her papers I discovered a folder containing photographs which Stella had taken of Allan on his deathbed.

During this period she also completed two novels, *White Sand and Grey Sand* in 1958 and *A Pink Front Door* in 1959. Even by her own prolific standards this was good going, but hard work was Stella's only distraction and relief during this exceptionally difficult period of her life.

White Sand and Grey Sand was perhaps inspired by Ouida's *Two Little Wooden Shoes* which, like Stella's novel, is about a female foundling brought up in a poor Belgian family. The novel is set in Bruges, and Stella gave herself the task of providing a detailed and convincing Flemish background for the book. She achieved this with a remarkable degree of success.

Like *Nightingale Wood* and *My American*, *White Sand and Grey Sand* is one of Stella's contemporary reworkings of fairy tales and legends; in this instance, *Beauty and the Beast*. It begins with the finding of a two-year-old girl abandoned on the dunes during the Nazi invasion of Belgium. She is named Ydette after the name tag found round her neck and is adopted by two sisters, a widow and a spinster who, with their mother, run a little grocer's shop in Bruges. Opposite the shop is the rich house of the aristocratic Madame van Roeslaere, whose son Adriaan is spoilt and selfish but pitiable because tormented by his own physical ugliness. He is the Beast.

Stella specialised in stupid heroines, and of these Ydette is perhaps the stupidest of them all. But Ydette manages to be interesting. Stella enters into the drowsy thoughts of a dreamy, beautiful young girl, and allows the reader to understand and enjoy the world of a guileless innocent from the inside. Ydette's romantic admiration for the rich house opposite is neither envious nor snobbish, and she bears no malice towards Adriaan in spite of his unkindness. Adriaan is, in turn, reluctantly fascinated by Ydette and expresses this fascination in small acts of cruelty towards her.

In the end Adriaan performs almost the first unselfish act of his life by rescuing her from England, where she has been lured by an ambitious young film executive who hopes to make her a star. Adriaan's nature has changed because he recognises, through her rather than in her, the absolute, pure beauty for which he had always secretly yearned. He brings Ydette back to Belgium, but they do not marry because he realises that he could not bear to live with such intellectual vacuity.

Up to the point of Adriaan's conversion, Stella has made him a very detailed and convincing study of a potential psychopath. Another writer with this build-up would have made Adriaan murder Ydette, thereby fashionably subverting the old myth. Had Stella done so, *White Sand and Grey Sand* might have received much more praise and attention than it did, but it would not necessarily have been a better novel. For the book is intended to be a fable about good and evil, and the strange power of innocence. Besides, Adriaan's conversion (by no means complete at the book's conclusion) is convincingly done and, as Stella might have said, 'it does sometimes happen'.

White Sand and Grey Sand has its *longueurs*. The *Times Literary Supplement*, with some justification, called it 'mellow, but rather monotonous'; but it also rightly praised the remarkably convincing Belgian background and the power of its mythical elements. *White Sand and Grey Sand* is also one of Stella's better titles. The white sand is the sand of the dunes on which Ydette was found. It is the sand which she associates with the sea and the romantic, dreamy side of her nature. The grey sand is the sand used by her guardians, the Maes sisters, to clean the floors so as to economise on soap. It stands for the uncompromising, unexciting, dutiful side of her life and character. Much of Stella's writing is about this opposition which existed in her own nature between the romantic and the practical, Elfine and Flora. Stella sometimes referred to these elements in herself as Stella and Dorothea (her second name), the latter being the stern, practical side.

She once started to write an autobiography (now lost) using these two characters, Stella and Dorothea, whom she envisaged as an elder and younger sister respectively. A late poem written in 1980 which she dedicated to her friend Suzanne Goodwin explores this idea. It is called 'Elder Sister's Song in Gratitude':

> When a pink convolvulus
> Me entrances
> And flocking fantasies begin
> Their useless dances

Around a score of household tasks
That cry for doing.
And letters left for several weeks,
Mean feelings brewing –
It's then my cry for help is heard
Loud and clear –
'Take over, younger sister,
Housework is a blister –
Please –
    Take over, Dorothea.'

She is the witty one, whose rational eye
Fills not, though Third World babes
By thousands die
She sends a cheque. And makes a list
And then
Works calmly through it
Ticking off items boring one to ten,
And likes to do it.
Buys foreign stamps and pays the bills
And 'keeps in touch'
With ancient aunts and agéd friends;
All suffering varied ills.
(Not caring much,
But, lying like an adept,
Sounds sincere)
She often has a plan.
Thank heaven you can
    Take over, Dorothea.

When Age's frosty claw shall lay me out
When thanks to strokes, or legs
I can't get out,
And lulled in dream, lie on the bed
Content to watch
The pictures in my head;
When Styx's sullen ripples chill and drear
Steadily draw near
And nearer to my feet . . .
Oh then may I

Call on the lifelong tie
That bound me to my second self here,
And on that journey grim
Across the river cold and dim
Into the quiet, laughless land
  Take over, Dorothea.

A Pink Front Door (1959) is another Hampstead book, and the first of Stella's frankly elderly novels, though none the worse for that. That is to say, it deals with elderly concerns such as growing old, the mystery of death, and misunderstanding between the generations.

The plot revolves around the doings of Daisy Muir, a young married woman whose main activity in life, apart from secretarial 'temping' and looking after a husband and baby, is helping out her friends, most of whom are 'lame ducks'. These generous efforts involve a large cast of shrewdly drawn characters and result in some notable comic incidents. Daisy finds accommodation for the Hultons, a destitute young couple with three children, at the house of Mrs Cavendish, an impoverished snob who clings on to a few fine old pieces of furniture as the last relics of a once elegant life. The scene in which Mrs Cavendish finds that a priceless table of hers has been defaced by the teethmarks of one of the Hulton children is a small masterpiece of painful comedy. Every detail of it is credible; and the author manages to extend sympathy to all the participants in the drama without detracting in any way from the humour of the situation.

Daisy is an up-to-date variant of that familiar figure in Stella's fiction, the woman who organises (or tries to organise) other people's lives. It of course represents a side of Stella herself, though Daisy in *A Pink Front Door* is in some ways modelled on Laura whose instinct for helping those less fortunate than herself was even stronger than her mother's. Stella contrasts Daisy's modern help-anybody approach, which ignores its effect on those closest to her, with the more reserved, punctilious values of an older generation represented by her father, aunt and elderly cousin. They may appear stuffy, even snobbish, but they have a point; for though their generosity is less spontaneous than Daisy's, it has more regard for the feelings of others.

One of Daisy's most absurd and manipulative protégés falls in love with her husband; this provokes a crisis which almost brings about the break-up of her marriage, but in fact saves it. An ending which is on the way to becoming a little too rosy is saved by the accidental death of Daisy's old spinster cousin Ella. The book closes in the sombre North London twilight which Stella evoked so well.

In the middle of the book there is a brief flashback to Ella's girlhood when, at the age of eighteen, on holiday in Switzerland, she fell briefly in love with a gentle young clergyman who became the victim of a homosexual scandal and had to be 'sent away'. Ella's recollection of the encounter is tinged with sadness, but its evanescent perfection has inspired her subsequent life. This episode, one of the best things that Stella wrote, is also the core of the book. It demonstrates the cruelty, as well as the innocence, of the old values, and it explains Ella's worldly fragility and spiritual strength.

A Pink Front Door is a funny, elegantly written, well-observed book. Dealing as it does mostly with spinsters and widowers, failed academics and genteel poverty, it has something of the quality of Barbara Pym, but without the damp odour of self-pity which so often hangs about her novels. The atmosphere of *A Pink Front Door* is a little melancholy – hardly surprising, considering the circumstances in which it was written – but it is a stoic melancholy, lightened by laughter.

Stella found life hard after Allan's death, and her grief was aggravated by the break-up of Laura's marriage not long afterwards. But she now had two grandchildren to whom she could devote herself; and she also had two young people living in her house, her nephew by marriage John Rose and Jane Rye, daughter of her old friend Anthony Rye. John, a former merchant seaman, was studying engineering and was the kind of lively, intelligent but not intellectual young man who often married the heroines of her novels. In fact, a reasonably exact likeness of him turns up in the shape of Lieutenant Barney Trewin RN in her next novel, *The Weather at Tregulla*. John would tax Stella's brains with the abstruse problems of physics and mathematics which he was endeavouring to master for his engineering exams; he would also argue with Jane about everything from animal rights to politics. For once Stella did not mind the arguments; they were a distraction of sorts, but Jane remembers Stella murmuring to her one morning at breakfast that she did not know how much longer she could go on.

She did go on, and every morning at ten she went up to her little writing room to work, though it was not until 1962 that another novel was published. The recovery from her grief was slow. A few years after Allan's death she told Suzanne Goodwin: 'It's better now. I don't lie on the ground sobbing any more.' Suzanne was surprised by this: it seemed melodramatic, and Stella was not a melodramatic person. But there was an extreme side to Stella which she usually did her best to disguise.

Stella never considered remarrying – she was as devoted to the memory of Allan as she had been to Allan himself – though she did receive one offer of marriage. It came from her agent, Spencer Curtis Brown. The offer was rejected but the friendship between them remained intact, and she often visited him at his house in Suffolk both before and after he married again.

She was grateful to Curtis Brown for reviving her literary career, and her loyalty towards him was fierce. But sometimes her deep loyalties clouded her judgement. When Angus Wilson, a writer who had been greatly helped by Curtis Brown in his early days, moved into the country not far from where he lived, he made no move to contact his old mentor. Wilson was then at the height of his reputation as a novelist and critic, and entertained lavishly. Curtis Brown thought, rightly or wrongly, that, having outlived his usefulness to Wilson, he had been discarded in favour of more fashionable company; and Stella felt the slight almost as strongly as Curtis Brown. 'Of course, he's very clever,' she used to say of Wilson, 'but his novels read as if he's taken bits and pieces out of all the most highly thought of modern literature, whisked it up into a sort of mousse and put it in his own books. There's no authentic personal voice, no originality.' It is perhaps not an entirely fair assessment. She told me that Wilson had once approached her at the Royal Society of Literature and told her that he had been influenced by her work: Stella was sceptical.

During this time Stella began to rent a house, The Bryn, for the summer near Trevone in Cornwall, which was the setting for *The Weather at Tregulla*. The heroine's home, The Lynn, is closely modelled on The Bryn; Trevone becomes Tregulla, Padstow becomes Selstow and so on. A local postman who tiresomely saw himself as 'a character' is entertainingly but acidly worked into the book.

The story concerns Una Beaumont, daughter of a newly widowed sea captain. She is an over-emotional Gibbons type with an unrequited passion for the stage who is bored with Cornwall and wishes she were in London. Then a brother and sister, Emmeline and Terence Willows, move into the locality. They are indolent, gifted and charming; and, with their subtly destructive amorality, they bear more than a passing resemblance to Henry and Mary Crawford, the brother and sister in *Mansfield Park*. Una becomes infatuated with Terence, and her childhood friend Barney Trewin with Emmeline. This situation slowly resolves itself, not entirely predictably, over 288 moderately diverting pages. A certain perfunctoriness about the narration of events towards the end of the book suggests that Stella herself became bored with the novel.

There are, as always, some amusing characters, like the Willows brother and sister, their appalling artist friends, the Pilchers, and the elderly Miss Keate who paints her toenails and 'who would have been married years ago had her desirable qualities matched in size her sexual self-confidence, that mysterious gift frequently bestowed on the vital and the ugly'. But, by and large, *The Weather at Tregulla* is a reiteration of themes – wayward daughters, the competing demands of love and art – more entertainingly treated in other books. Characters and situations are cleverly described but are not sufficiently arresting in themselves to hold the reader's attention.

In 1964 Stella wrote to Suzanne Goodwin: 'I feel guilty at the idea of letting the writing drop, because I know that if Allan is allowed to remember anything where he is, he would be so cross!' I doubt, however, if she could have let it drop, even if she had felt no guilt. Writing had become a refuge and a habit. The physical sensation of covering sheets of paper with her clear, well-formed handwriting was one she enjoyed. But her last books do give the impression that she was trying to interest herself as much as she was trying to entertain the reader. She set herself challenges.

The challenge of her next book, *The Wolves Were in the Sledge*

(1964), is that of first-person narration, which she had not previously attempted in a novel. She takes on the voice of Nancy Leland, a half-French, half-educated eighteen-year-old, and in so doing completely alters her style. She becomes light, and chatty – descriptive passages are kept to a minimum – and a kind of innocent shrewdness shines through. It is a very effective act of ventriloquism.

Nancy is married to Toby Leland, a young ex-public schoolboy who claims to be the son of an aristocrat. She and Toby are the wolves of the title – people without any permanent occupation who live a hand-to-mouth existence doing odd jobs for rich acquaintances. Toby's best friend Guy Murray, a racing driver, is obsessively in love with Nancy and a dangerous situation develops.

It is a tantalising book because parts of it are very well done. 'Miss Gibbons has narrowly missed bringing off a total if small-scale success,' wrote the *Times Literary Supplement*. The relationship between Toby and Nancy, and the subtle shift it undergoes when Nancy discovers that Toby's aristocratic pretensions are false, are very well realised. The raffish, dangerous world of the sixties in which they move, on the fringes of high society, is elegantly suggested; but the very considerable potentialities of the story are not exploited.

The Wolves Were in the Sledge was intended as a kind of fable about a young, irresponsible couple growing up. But the story is too inconsequential and insubstantial to deliver the moral punch. One is left with admiration at a bold stylistic experiment.

The book was dedicated to some cousins of Allan's, Edward and Noeni Young. Edward was a lieutenant colonel, not a great reader of fiction, and I recall the puzzled, almost pained tone of voice in which he mentioned that 'she once dedicated one of her books to us. I can't remember what it was called.' Edward may well not have read it – it would have baffled him if he had – but he was just the kind of brave, honourable, unintellectual man of whom Stella most approved.

The Charmers (1965) is, in many ways, the archetypal late Stella Gibbons novel. It is set in Hampstead in the mid-sixties and has a strong sense of period and location. The story concerns an elderly lower middle-class woman, Miss Christine Smith, thrown out of a long-standing and humdrum office job, who goes to keep house for a number of middle-aged artistic types. It is a novel about change: the change that is taking place in Hampstead with its rows of terraced houses being replaced by council blocks; of large houses being converted into flats, and the mingling of social classes (and races) that these upheavals bring about. Change is also expressed in the advent of a new Labour government in 1964.

More importantly, from the book's point of view, a change is taking place in Christine Smith. She is a person who is not quite ordinary. She once had a mystical experience, which she calls 'that day'; and the sensitive, spiritual side of her is developed by her proximity to the people for whom she keeps house. Ironically, though she changes through contact with them, they, the 'charmers', seem incapable of change. They are locked into a past when they were young and beautiful, and they are bound together by their common love for the brilliant Maurice Condron, a songwriter who died heroically in the war. When the charmers finally dismiss Christine she is ready for a new and adventurous phase in her life while they remain trapped in their amiable, irresponsible, bickering little world. There are obvious parallels with *Westwood* which is also a novel about someone growing as a result of contact with people of wider horizons who have, nevertheless, stopped growing themselves. Thematically *The Charmers* is one of Stella's most concentrated and coherent books, but, though it has many of her characteristic virtues of wit and observation, it is somewhat lacking in incident and cannot be considered one of her best novels.

Metaphysical preoccupations are also present in her next book, *Starlight* (1967), which is dedicated to Allan 'in perpetual love'. After Allan's death Stella became obsessively interested in the afterlife and the possibility of making contact with him, perhaps through a medium. Two things prevented her from doing so. In the first place, when, as Allan lay dying, Stella had brought up the subject of communicating with him posthumously, he had expressly forbidden her to do so. In the second place, the steely common-sense side of Stella – the younger sister, 'Dorothea' – realised that if she did enter the world of spiritualism and clairvoyants she would be chasing shadows and that nothing good would come of it. Nevertheless, the subject of the supernatural and the afterlife remained one of absorbing interest to her.

A number of the books that I inherited from Stella deal with out-of-the-body experiences, life after death and related topics. Some are of a quasi-scientific nature and purport to chart the stages by which the soul becomes separated from the body. Stella also became a member of the Society for Psychical Research. It would have been surprising, then, if this deep and agonised searching had not borne fruit in a novel.

In *Starlight* the eccentric, impoverished inhabitants of a pair of cottages in the back streets of Hampstead suddenly discover that the houses have been sold, apparently to a 'rackman' [*sic*. a generic name derived from the notorious sixties slum landlord, Peter Rachman]. The occupants are two sisters, Annie and Gladys Barnes, and Lancelot Fisher, an eccentric recluse who changes his name every month. These lovingly detailed figures belong to the underclass of elderly people living on the edge of society that Stella was writing about as early as 1936 in *Miss Linsey and Pa*. The 'rackman' is Mr Pearson, half Armenian, a man both sinister and vulnerable, who has a grown-up daughter and is still deeply in love with his wife. He installs her in part of the cottages hoping that in these quiet surroundings she will recover from the mental and physical debility from which she mysteriously suffers. Stella conjures up a sombre, suffocating world with more than a glimpse of violence on its fringes. It extends beyond the two cottages to the local vicarage and to the house of a rich, spoilt old lady by whom Mrs Pearson's daughter is employed as companion.

In the past Pearson had exploited his wife's mediumistic and clairvoyant gifts for profit, but she is now exhausted, and too weak to resist a discarnate entity which begins to possess her. The entity is possibly the familiar spirit which enabled Mrs Pearson to be clairvoyant in the first place. In her descriptions of this possession Stella makes use of her under-employed gift for the macabre:

It was in Mrs Pearson's eyes. Something glanced out of them; drew back and vanished, then returned, as if with a pounce of satisfaction, and glared out avidly into the room. The eyes had the expression of a creature that feeds. They settled on every visible object; the sleeping girl, the expanse of pink carpet, each little glass animal on the dressing table; sucking at them and caressing at them, and moving slowly over them, as if what was looking out had been starved for a very long time.

The sense of mounting evil leading up to the exorcism scene is powerfully evoked. It compares favourably with effects produced by acclaimed modern practitioners of the horror genre for a number of reasons. In the first place characters and locations are described with the depth and verisimilitude of a true novelist; secondly, descriptions of the psychic elements are based on a profound study of the subject; but, most importantly of all, the reader has the sense of a moral imagination at work, one that has original insights into the nature of both Evil and Good. Evil being a shadow, the intensity of its darkness is most apparent when contrasted with the light, something ignored by many modern specialists in the macabre. In addition, as with those two masters of supernatural terror Henry and M. R. James, the horror in *Starlight* is all the more intense for being hinted at rather than gruesomely detailed.

Starlight will not appeal to those for whom the world of the supernatural is one of pure illusion, partly because Stella managed to make the intrusion of that world into this so convincing and unfanciful. It is not Magical Realism, and its thinking, though original, is founded on the tenets of the Church of England. More open minds will be gripped by this most unusual novel, for Stella has allied her habitual gifts for characterisation and atmosphere to a compelling storyline not always present in her later novels. It has to be said, though, that, apart from intermittent flashes of characteristic humour, the book is about as far removed from *Cold Comfort Farm* as it could possibly be.

For the first time in her writing career, for *Starlight* Stella had the benefit of an editor. Her name was Elsie Herron, and her good influence can be seen in the unusually taut pacing and plotting of this novel. Stella at first resented Elsie's intrusion, but she came to appreciate her assistance.

Starlight was also the first of Stella's novels about which she consulted me. Not that I was especially privileged in this regard – Stella asked and occasionally took advice about her work from anyone who was prepared to give it. She said she was thinking of calling the novel either *Starlight* or *The Light of Stars*. Which did I prefer? I chose the latter and so did Stella; but apparently *The Light of Stars* had already been appropriated by another writer. So it was *Starlight*, which I now think is the better title.

By the late 1960s Stella's holidays were confined to staying with relations and friends, and visits either to Cornwall or to her favourite East Coast resorts such as Clacton or Frinton. She loved unfashionable English seaside towns with their mild, elderly atmosphere. The contrast between the restrained gentility of their architecture and the untempered wildness of the sea that fringed them pleased her.

Stella's last trip abroad was in 1966. She went to France with my parents, Renée and John, to visit her old friend the writer Elizabeth Coxhead, who had a house near Grenoble. Coxhead had worked with her on the *Lady* and given her the title of *Cold Comfort Farm*.

In Paris Stella and my parents had dinner with another friend, Monica Stirling, a novelist, and biographer of Ouida, and Monica's long-standing companion, Odette. Odette was a formidable lady, a literary agent who acted for, among others, Beckett and Ionesco, then at the height of their fame. My parents were intrigued. What was Ionesco like? 'Mad,' said Odette. And Beckett? 'Mad also.' In addition, Odette made it clear that she did not regard either of them as particularly talented; but they were fashionable and, as far as she was concerned, extremely lucrative. My parents were a little shocked, Stella merely bored. The conversation continued, Odette and Monica retailing bright Parisian literary gossip to their increasingly bemused audience. Eventually a slight lull occurred and Stella began to talk about her grandsons, Daniel and Benjamin, then eight and five respectively. She talked of their doings, their scholastic progress, their amusing sayings, their dietary preferences. My parents tried to stem the tide, but she was relentless. This time it was Odette's turn to look on stony-faced. The dinner was not a success.

On their way down from Paris, at Stella's insistence they made a special detour to Proust's home at Illiers. The little *concierge* was very morose and unobliging until Renée mentioned that Stella was a *Fémina-Vie Heureuse* winner, after which the man could not do enough for them and insisted on being photographed in the house's dank, Proustian garden.

This visit to France is used in her last but one published novel, *The Snow Woman* of 1968. Narrated by Maude Barrington, a very reserved English gentlewoman of seventy and the Snow Woman of the title, it begins promisingly with an uninvited guest suddenly giving birth on Maude's sofa during afternoon tea. Maude is outraged; in the highly comic depiction of this event, Stella is making fun of her own dislike of unpleasant emotional scenes both in fiction and in real life.

The whole novel, in fact, is an exercise in mild self-mockery. Stella gives Maude many of her own prejudices and foibles – her passion for order and obscure Victorian novels, her hatred of modernity, her occasional haughtiness and her capacity for harbouring long-standing grudges. More seriously, Stella is delicately probing her own emotional stasis after Allan's death. Maude's feelings have been locked up since the First World War when her three beloved brothers were killed.

The novel charts the process by which this Snow Woman gradu-ally melts. Unfortunately the circumstances which bring it about are, on the whole, uninteresting, inconsequential and improbable. As in the manner of a Victorian novel, the baby so unceremoniously born on her sofa turns out to be Maude's great-great-nephew. The ending is blissful and somewhat sentimental, but not without a certain charm.

Stella's twenty-third and last published novel is more successful. *The Woods in Winter* (1970) revisits the past, in both period and subject matter. It is set in the late twenties or early thirties and bears similarities to two of Stella's best early novels, *Bassett* and *Nightingale Wood*.

The book begins in Hampstead and travels to Buckinghamshire, where a middle-aged charwoman, Ivy Gover, has been left a cottage in the woods. The novel deals pleasantly with the effect that this gipsyish, solitary woman has on the local inhabitants from the squire, Lord Gowerville, whose dog she cures, to a young boy (modelled on Stella's grandson Daniel) who turns out to be a gifted artist. Its theme, a recurring one in Stella's novels and poetry, is the redemptive power of nature.

As in *Nightingale Wood*, a repressed upper-class spinster in her thirties scandalises the neighbourhood by running away with a local labourer; as in *Bassett* Stella's affair with Walter Beck is picked over, this time through the characters of Helen Green and Jocelyn Burke. Helen, a comparatively minor figure in the story, is perhaps Stella's fullest portrait of her younger self, complete with the raffish, artistic friends, a talent for poetry and a cottage in the Vale of Health.

The Woods in Winter is an agreeable novel, and the fairy tale element in its plot is much more satisfyingly rounded off than that of its predecessor *The Snow Woman*. A modern coda set in the seventies ruefully reflects on the mixed blessings of progress, and there are some good comic moments. The character of Win Smithers, the perpetually unwelcome guest, is very nearly Stella at her best.

*   *   *

Stella published no further books after 1970, though between 1972 and 1980 she wrote two more novels. She no longer felt able to deal with the anguish and anxiety of exposing her work to a publisher's editor, or to the critics. The two unpublished novels, *The Yellow Houses* and *An Alpha*, were to be left to her two grandchildren, Daniel and Benjamin, to do with as they wished after her death.

After the loss of Allan in 1959 Stella's horizons had, imperceptibly at first, begun to narrow. Her grandchildren became her most absorbing interest. Invitations to participate in some mildly adventurous project would often be declined on the grounds that she was 'old and frail', despite the fact that until two years before her death she looked neither. In fact, she tended to resent being told how young and fit she looked in case this was used in evidence against her lack of enterprise. She also detested being told about people even older than herself who had climbed a mountain, bicycled to Istanbul or performed some similar age-defying feat. Her contempt was especially reserved for those admittedly tiresome old men who used to be photographed by the newspapers plunging into an icy Serpentine or the North Sea on New Year's Day. 'Unseemly, ostentatious and aesthetically repulsive,' was her verdict on them. 'They ought to be thinking about their latter ends,' she added.

CHAPTER 9

Conversations with My Aunt

Throughout the seventies and eighties I would regularly walk from my home in St John's Wood to visit Aunt Stella in Highgate – over Primrose Hill, through Belsize Park, up Haverstock Hill and on to Hampstead Heath via Pond Street. In my memory those walks always seemed to take place in autumn when the leaves were deep in the ways through the woods, and the sounds, muted by mists, were of dogs and damp footballs kicked by distant children. In the earlier years, I would occasionally meet Stella at Kenwood House and we would walk together back to tea at her house in Oakshott Avenue.

Often our way back would take us down Millfield Lane. She would tell me that this was the place where Coleridge once met Keats, and how they had talked together about mermaids, and how Coleridge afterwards remembered that the young poet's handshake was that of a dying man. The fact that Keats had lived and walked there had always given Stella a particular feeling of closeness to the Heath and its environs. One of Stella's last poems was called 'Writ in Water', a reference to Keats' self-penned epitaph: 'Here lies One whose Name was writ in Water.'

> What stronger rune to be written in?
> Seething, or locked in arcane permafrost.
> Sans water, Man would shrunken be and lost.
> His very substance is of water made,
> Of water and of dust,
> Within its cloudy depth, secret and warm,
> A pulsing jelly burgeoned into form.
> Three days he can exist without the thin

Life-making flow. And music in full streams,
Pours down all hills, giving voice to dreams.

Sweet boy, bright star eclipsed at twenty-five,
Your genius erred in thinking water humble –
Water shall run while Earth herself's alive;
Iron rust, stone crumble.

Mostly our talk dealt with family gossip, books read and literature in general; sometimes the more general sphere of ideas was
ventured into. Stella was a good listener. Both her presence and
her house had a soothing influence. I was often reminded of the
opening lines of one of her poems:

Like a quiet room thy spirit is
Inviting men to rest
The young, the weak, the lonely find
A shelter in thy breast.

But the impression that many received of serenity and tranquil
fulfilment was not entirely accurate. There was a part of her which
was full of doubts and anxieties; there was also a part of her which,
despite the loving attentions of friends and relations, was intensely
lonely. To the very end she missed Allan. 'You don't get over it;
you learn to live with it,' she said to me. In 1975 she wrote to
Suzanne Goodwin:

It was Allan's 68th birthday yesterday, June 10. I think he would
have strongly disliked being 68, bless his darling, ordinarily
masculine-vain heart, and perhaps, perhaps it is best as it
is. I went up to the grave to put some roses on it; the Old
[Highgate] Cemetery is closed now, except for plot-owners, and
is unbelievably beautiful, like a silent fairy wood, with flitting
birds and their lovely ringing calls, waist-high meadowsweet
and hosts of buttercups.

Her melancholy, for the most part, was of a settled, accepting
kind. 'I suppose it's the result of being a minor poet,' she wrote.

'They always are sad – look at Betjeman, in spite of his delicious, rather catty humour. It's feeling the burden of mystery, as Keats said – or you might say instead with Mrs Gummidge [in *David Copperfield*] – "Everyone feels it, but I feels it more than most."'

The tranquil front she presented to the outside world was a product of discipline, and she offered it to those who visited her because she never liked to burden others with her problems. Besides, until very nearly the end her troubles were amply compensated for by the rewards of her life. The fulfilments she derived from nature, from reading and writing, from her grandsons and from religion were solid and deep.

I was standing with her one day on the slope looking down towards the lake below Kenwood House when Stella suddenly said to me: 'I wonder what C. S. Lewis is doing now.' He had in fact been dead for some ten years.

It was not an idle speculation. C. S. Lewis had influenced her religious thinking and, though she never met him, she heard about him through their mutual friend and literary agent, Spencer Curtis Brown. In 1965, through Curtis Brown's offices, she was asked to contribute to a volume of essays called *Light on C. S. Lewis*. Her piece on Lewis's fiction, with the exception of the essay by Owen Barfield, a lifelong friend of Lewis's, is the most interesting in the book.

Apart from the occasional review in *Punch* Stella had not practised criticism since she left the *Lady* thirty years before, but this essay is of the same high quality as her work on that magazine, jargon-free, succinct and perceptive. She noticed the streak of misogyny (often, like that of Charles Morgan, masquerading as Reverence for Woman) which runs through and often spoils Lewis's space fiction; and she summed up what prevents the Narnia books, excellent though they are, from being in the very front rank of children's stories when she said that all too often 'the tremendousness of the allegory mars the artistry of the tale'. However, she went on to write: 'Mr Leavis, the critic, has rebuked readers and other critics for crediting writers with possessing genius because they can "make a world", and none of us likes to be rebuked. Still, I feel that we shall continue to credit writers thus, and perhaps we may remind our mentor that it is not every writer who *can* create a world.' This is well said, in every sense of the phrase.

When Stella read that the theologian J. B. Phillips had experienced a post mortem visitation from C. S. Lewis, and that the Society for Psychical Research had a full record of this encounter, Stella joined the Society to obtain it. She also took a great interest in the Religious Experiences Research Unit which had been founded by the scientist Sir Alister Hardy. Once she sent them an account of one of her few brushes with the supernatural which she recounted to me. It was not very interesting and concerned a déjà vu experience with a defective courgette.

Towards the end of her life, Stella's thoughts began to turn increasingly towards religion: as a source of comfort perhaps, but much more as a source of understanding. It was an interest we shared and we talked about it on many occasions.

She once asked my advice when she was experiencing doubts. I came out with a few callow platitudes about certainty not being the same thing as faith, clouds of unknowing, dark nights of the soul, doubt being a necessary, even salutary companion on the spiritual journey and so on. She seemed satisfied. That she should ask me was testimony not to my understanding but to her own touching humility.

It was important to Stella that she should not be perceived to have mocked Christianity in the 'Quivering Brethren' of *Cold Comfort Farm*. When Elizabeth Proud was writing the radio adaptation of *Cold Comfort Farm* she wanted to add another verse to the Quiverers' hymn:

> Whatever shall we do, O Lord.
> When Gabriel blows o'er sea and river,
> Fen and desert, mount and ford?
> The earth may burn, but we will quiver.

Elizabeth began her second verse 'Whatever shall we do, O Christ . . .'. Stella objected strongly, and the words were altered. The Quiverers must be a theistic Old Testament sect, not a Christian one.

One book she studied in depth but did not altogether approve of was Aldous Huxley's *The Perennial Philosophy*. She resented its rather lofty approach, which embraced all religions, but part of her objection was *ad hominem*. She found it hard to take preaching from the man who was chiefly responsible, as she saw it, for making the drug cult of the sixties intellectually respectable. Nevertheless she found many of Huxley's judiciously culled quotations valuable. Against this passage by the seventeenth-century Catholic divine Fénélon, she has put a line and the single word 'Me':

> Many people are sincere who are not simple. They say nothing but what they believe to be true, and do not aim at appearing anything but what they are. But they are forever thinking about themselves, weighing their every word and thought, and dwelling upon themselves in apprehension of having done too much or too little. These people are sincere but they are not simple. They are not at their ease with others, nor others with them. There is nothing easy, frank, unrestrained or natural about them. One feels one would like less admirable people better, who were not so stiff.

My aunt said to me once, 'I'm not shy, I'm just unsociable.' It was a remark which made me feel a great kinship with her. It has to be said, however, that the stiffness in company to which Fénélon refers was only evident in her on certain occasions. If someone had said something with which she profoundly disagreed, or had made an unkind or coarse remark, her fine features would assume a certain rigidity and her voice would become fainter, sounding as if it were coming to you with great clarity over an enormous distance. Those who knew her well would detect the note of irony in her remarks. She would never argue, at least about the things that mattered to her. The experiences of childhood and youth had instilled in her a deep loathing of arguments. On the whole, she was right: few people can sustain an argument without at some point feeling that their moral integrity or intellectual capacity has been impugned; and then the argument degenerates into a reiteration of prejudices, or worse.

Despite this mild unsociability in her nature she did enjoy being taken about occasionally, and in her last years she made a number of new friends. She had a preference for the young, good-looking and intelligent. One was the photographer Tara Heinemann, another was a young man just down from Cambridge, Michael Pick, son of the Dr Fritz Pick who had translated *Nightingale*

Wood into German. 'I hope I can add him to my collection of Refreshing Men,' she wrote to Renée after first meeting him in the early 1970s.

Pick soon established himself as a distinguished writer on interior design, and was fascinated by the awareness of clothes and physical surroundings which is such a feature of Stella's books. A mutual interest in fashion cemented their friendship, and Stella told him that she had been one of the first women in England to wear the New Look. By the seventies Stella's clothes were not fashionable, but she had devised a style that exactly suited her: rich but not gaudy, discreetly idiosyncratic. Some idea of them can be gleaned from her letters to Pick:

> When I come to tea with you I will wear a sleeveless orange linen coat I have made, and a dark dress with orange and shadowy blue carnations printed on it, and a drawstring neckline – the drawstring is orange cord; I don't know where it came from, or remember buying it. Good Spirits, I expect; it came in perfectly. But first I shall re-sew a dart in the coat, because I'm pretty sure you would notice it's three inches below the one on the other side!

Pick, Estonian on his mother's side, would occasionally take Stella to receptions at the Estonian Legation where she would sit on a sofa and watch people. Occasionally he would ask her if she would like to be introduced to anyone, but she replied no, she was quite happy to sit and look.

Stella particularly liked to be escorted about the place by young men, and I frequently accompanied her to lectures and events at the Royal Society of Literature in Hyde Park Gardens. She enjoyed the lectures and the discreet, formal socialising, though she said that she would not and could not be vivacious. There were also certain members to be studiously avoided. The Brontë expert Winifred Gérin was, for some reason, a particular *bête noire*, perhaps because, like Mr Mybug, she had written a biography of Bramwell.

The little ceremonies of the Society she found irritating because they seemed to her arch and pretentious. When new Fellows were inducted, there was always a great deal of fuss made about the ritual of signing their name. Lord Butler, vast and apoplectic in a dinner jacket, would smile roguishly at the new Fellow and say: 'Now you must sign your name with Byron's pen!' Then there was a good deal of sycophantic laughter as the new Fellow took the poet's pen with a flourish, pretending to be both honoured and greatly amused at the quaintness of it all. 'That ruddy Byron pen again!' my aunt would mutter under her breath.

Irritation was always tempered by a secret pleasure in the absurdity of it all. In my diary on 23 July 1978 I recorded her description to me of meeting the Duke of Kent at the Royal Society of Literature:

> Poor Mrs Winston Graham was very badly dressed and forgot to curtsey. And I must say, and I know you won't misinterpret what I say, I was looking very nice. And the Duke of Kent looked quite relieved to see me because all the other old literary ladies looked like sacks, I'm sorry to say. And I didn't forget to curtsey. And Lord Butler said that His Royal Highness had been at a royal garden party, so he was quite relieved to sit down and have a rest! Of course everybody thought this was most amusing, so there was a lot of discreet laughter. And the Duke said he was very pleased to meet me and I said that I wondered if we writers had a kind of universal face. But the Duke didn't seem to be very interested in this remark and he said he didn't get enough time to read. Poor man! It must be all those garden parties, I suppose. Then a drunken old Baronet came up to me and said, 'I thought you were dead.' And he had proposed to the Secretary of the Royal Soc. Lit. because his estate was entailed and he wanted an heir. But the Secretary had had a hysterectomy, so that was no good. . . .

My visits with Stella to the Royal Society of Literature were never dull, because even if the talks were tedious they were enlivened for me by her occasional waspish asides. I went with her to a poetry reading by Christopher Fry who, among other things, read an interminable and slackly written poem by Robert Gittings about finding his soul on a summer evening. 'As if anyone cared whether he found his wretched soul or not,' Stella muttered uncharitably. Then she pointed out an elderly lady sitting just in front of us. 'That's Joanna Richardson,' she said, 'and sometimes she talks to me and sometimes she cuts me dead. Perhaps it's because she's short-sighted and doesn't always wear glasses.' Stella's voice was not loud but she always enunciated with exquisite clarity, so her comment may have been heard. Certainly Joanna Richardson's companion turned round and smiled rather nervously at me, and later in the evening Joanna Richardson *did* cut Stella dead.

The Yellow Houses and *An Alpha*, the two novels which Stella wrote with no intention of publication, were produced slowly and with enjoyment, unburdened by the anxieties of publisher's deadlines or the threat of adverse criticism. The writing, though sometimes excellent, often exhibits the comfortable carelessness of someone writing entirely for their own pleasure.

The Yellow Houses is about the operation of spiritual grace in the world, and takes as its starting point an idea of Kipling in *Uncovenanted Mercies* that 'guardian Spirits are ex-human souls re-conditioned for re-issue by the Lower Hierarchy'. In the novel these guardian spirits seem like ordinary human beings and take up residence in houses which are painted a peculiarly brilliant shade of yellow. This is the story of one particular yellow house in the Essex seaside town of Torford, and its beneficent effect on some of the inhabitants. The way in which the reader is slowly made to realise that the occupants of the house are more than mortal is nicely done.

As a whole, *The Yellow Houses* is perhaps an attractive curiosity rather than an important novel. Stella, as she often did in her later books, had set herself a challenge. I can remember her telling me: 'I'm going to make my hero Japanese,' much as someone else might tell you that they were about to swim the channel or walk the Pennine Way. Stella had never been to Japan, and her main sources were the works of Lafcadio Hearn, an American who wrote rather rosy-hued books about the Far East at the turn of the century. She had also read Arthur Waley's translation of *The Tale of Genji* and had heard of Yukio Mishima, even if she had not studied his works. Her Japanese hero is called Yasushiro and is devoted to the works of Mishima who, in Stella's mind, represented the harsh, inhuman side of the Japanese character. This aspect of Yasushiro is gradually but not entirely softened by his love for a very ordinary English girl called Mary.

Yasushiro is a believable, if slightly stereotypical, Japanese. Stella was delighted when her friend Suzanne Goodwin wrote in November 1979 to congratulate Stella on her achievement. In reply Stella wrote: '*Very* cheered, too, that you like Yasu – oh, so difficult to do! and, I *fear*, pure fiction, tho' perhaps *fictionally* convincing.' *The Yellow Houses* is saved from whimsicality and sentimentality by Stella's cool observant eye for character, and by the fact that she is using the book to explore unresolved problems peculiar to herself.

Towards the end of the book, the plot takes an unexpected turn. The Yellow House which has been such a haven of peace gradually becomes full of unease. The disturbance is caused by Katherine, one of the guardian spirits who live in it. Katherine is a melodramatic Gibbons type, with a restless, passionate desire to help the afflicted. 'I want to reach out, and haul in, until my arms ache and my hands are bruised and I'm *used*,' Katherine says. '*I want to feel used. Can't you understand?*' She represents what was good about the Gibbons character – a reckless self-giving, an unreserved compassion – which Stella had rejected along with the bad.

It was this spirit which Stella admired in her daughter Laura and yet found difficult to come to terms with. Stella's own approach to Heaven was a stroll rather than an assault. In the Yellow Houses good is done, as Stella did it, in small ways, by stealth and influence. This does not suit the character of Katherine, and so in the end she is allowed to leave the Yellow House to pursue her own peculiar and extreme path. In writing about this Stella had perhaps found her own idiosyncratic way of letting go of Laura at last. Obliquely she was acknowledging that she had been over-protective towards her daughter, and had at times intruded too much into her life. In a letter to Suzanne, Stella once referred rather resentfully to Laura as going through 'one of her My Life Is My Own phases'. Stella herself had a passion for 'the solitary things' which Laura evidently shared. *The Yellow Houses* is the only book of Stella's, besides *The Untidy Gnome*, to be dedicated to her daughter.

Stella's last novel, *An Alpha*, is about the development of a female mathematical genius. It has similarities to *My American* in that the heroine is immature, preoccupied and remote, and the novel charts both her rise to success and her gradual humanisation. But Juliet Slater, by contrast with Amy Lee in *My American*, is an intellectual rather than an imaginative genius, and the melting of the splinter of ice in her heart at the end of the book is only partial. It is a less successful novel than *The Yellow Houses* because the blend of realism and fairy tale fantasy is not so well achieved.

Stella said that after *An Alpha* she would stop writing except for poems. She told me that her aim on the whole was to be 'like the Persian poetess who said: "For forty years I have written poems about the moon, now I shall sit and look at it."'

One day in 1980 I found her pondering over a very flattering letter from the writer Richard Adams asking her to sign his treasured copy of *Cold Comfort Farm*. She was wondering how she could reply to him in a suitably appreciative way without betraying the fact that she had never read 'that rabbit book' (Richard Adams' *Watership Down*, a novel whose protagonists are rabbits). We discussed the problem for some moments and I suggested that she should read the book in question.

'Yes, yes,' my aunt said a touch irritably. 'I'm always being told that I should read it. And I'm sure it's very good indeed. But really, you know, one can't start reading novels about rabbits at my age.'

There was no answer to this, and besides, I never argued with Stella. As it happened, Stella and Richard Adams enjoyed a long and satisfactory correspondence and she signed his copy of *Cold Comfort Farm* 'for Richard Adams in admiration'.

She also contributed three poems to an anthology devised and edited by Adams called *Occasional Poets*, which was a collection of verse by distinguished writers more usually associated with prose, such as Iris Murdoch, William Golding and Doris Lessing. At first Stella was a little put out to be asked since she considered herself, with some justification, to be rather more than an 'occasional poet'. But, after all, it was over thirty years since her last volume of verse had been published. One of the poems which she contributed was 'Writ In Water', quoted at the beginning of this chapter. The anthology was published in 1986, the last time that new work by Stella appeared in print. Richard Adams told me that *Occasional Poets* went unnoticed by both press and public, which is a pity because it contains work of real poetic merit and is not merely a collection of curiosities.

Another admirer was the writer and entertainer Barry Humphries. Stella was delighted when he wrote to her saying how much he liked her poetry, and, as she put it to me, 'making no mention of You-Know-What' (i.e. *Cold Comfort Farm*). Humphries recognised that, though influenced by Keats and the Georgians, particularly de la Mare, her work had a flavour of its own. In the *Spectator* of 31 May 1997 he wrote that he thought her verse 'sometimes reads like the best Drinkwater which is very good indeed'. John Drinkwater was chiefly celebrated in his day for epic historical dramas, but he wrote some verse in the Georgian vein. 'Moonlit Apples' is probably the only poem of his that most people know. It was frequently anthologised, by J. C. Squire among others, and its haunted, dreamlike atmosphere does give it a certain family resemblance to Stella's poetry. But most of Drinkwater's verse reads more like a capable mixture of A. E. Housman and John Masefield.

Humphries invited Stella to lunch. 'I shall go,' she said to me, 'but I shan't enjoy it.' She did go, and did enjoy it. Humphries, however, did not consider the lunch to have been a success. 'I took her to a restaurant in Soho frequented by noisy yuppies and agents and their floozies, which served things like skate and parsnips in a kiwi fruit coulis.' It was perhaps an unfortunate choice of meeting-place, but Stella was impressed by Humphries, a courteous, knowledgeable and thoroughly civilised man. Not long afterwards she was invited by him, via her agent, to contribute an introduction to a book of household tips by Humphries' alter ego Dame Edna Everage. Sadly Stella declined – she brought out her familiar excuse of 'old and frail' – and the introduction was written instead by Margaret Drabble, a distinguished substitute.

Though Stella's feelings about 'that book' remained ambivalent almost to the end, she did enjoy it when *Cold Comfort Farm* became an A-level set text in 1978 and remained on the syllabus for some years. Many young people wrote to her and she replied to them. She loved receiving these letters, but did complain to me once: 'I do wish more of them would realise that the book is meant to be *funny*.' Many of the letters she kept. A Miss Nicola Colqhoun of Ormskirk in Lancashire wrote to point out severely a number of inconsistencies in the text about the relative ages of members of the Starkadder family. And what relation to Judith and Amos, she demanded, were Caraway, Harkaway, Ezra and Urk? (A good question: I have often wondered.) 'Would it be possible for you to send us a comprehensive family tree so that we can sort it out?'

Nevertheless many of these young people *did* find the book funny because they had grasped instinctively that *Cold Comfort Farm* is essentially a comedy about family life, and that the satire and the parody of the rural novel were brilliant embellishments. After all, many adolescents have felt, as Stella had at sixteen, that they were the one sane and rational being in a family of near lunatics.

It was mainly the large number of letters she received from eager and appreciative young students that finally reconciled Stella to 'that book'. One of the last things she said to me on the subject was: 'You know, after all, it is something to have made so many people laugh.'

In the early 1980s Stella wrote a number of short stories, one of them about the discovery of a prehistoric animal on a beach. She asked me to provide a suitable Greek name for it, which I did (*Pelagotherium*), and she gave me £5 for the information. She sent the story to the BBC, but they were not interested.

On Christmas Day 1983 I asked Stella if she were still writing: 'Oh, goodness, no,' she said. 'Besides, it doesn't do to have my stuff rejected. I sent a couple of stories to the BBC and the man said they weren't good enough. And it isn't good for one's magnificent self to have that happen too often, you know.'

Despite giving up writing, she maintained her deep interest in literature. As late as 1988 she was still adding to her commonplace book. One small notebook, begun in 1987, is entitled: 'Bad Examples or How Not to do It compiled by Stella Gibbons'. An anthology of bad writing, together with her own comments on the examples she gives, it testifies to the breadth of her reading and illuminates her very particular literary sensibility. The offenders range from Nabokov and Theroux to Mrs Humphry Ward and even her 'once revered and always loved' Walter de la Mare.

Musicality in verse she saw as a much neglected quality. Here she is on a line from Hardy's 'Wessex Heights' of 1896:

'But mind-chains do not clank where one's next neighbour is the sky.' (Thomas Hardy who may have been old enough to know better but didn't.)

Now I know that Hardy's use of 'roughness' in poems is accepted, even praised. I ignore this. No poet with any ear for music could have inserted that 'next'. Of course his poetry had other qualities; but I think he had a poet's *mind* but no technique – at least, no poetically-musical technique.

Without that 'next' we'd have a presentable alexandrine – oops! sorry – it *does* scan! But it's a fourteen-syllable – and I'll stand by my disapproval of 'clank'.

In a lighter, more waspish vein she wrote:

March 23 [1987]: 'A characteristic Muldoon lyric is as cryptic as it is intimate. It invites the reader's complicity *like a wishbone* [Stella's emphasis throughout], provoking a *nimbus* of shared apprehension and desires but making an *enigma* of its own desires as if it were bad luck to give them away.'

By John Mole in *Recent Poetry*, in *Encounter*, a literary magazine. I *suppose* you could say that a wishbone is in complicity with the person who eyes it with wishing to have it – but words fail me. What kind of a mind has John Mole? Wishbones – nimbuses – enigmas – it certainly is very bad luck on the average Poor Bloody Infantry reader.

March 25: '. . . hold *the whole egg* of an idea and follow it right to *the end of the line*.' Jeanette Halen, interviewed in *The Guardian*. She has, heaven help us, written a novel about Irish peasants, with a heroine named Enda. As usual, the bad writing is due to a commonplace fault – a mixed metaphor. (In her photograph, J.H. looks self-conscious, 'roguish', and vivacious – again, heaven help us. She has fat, ugly hands.) That wouldn't matter in the least if she weren't trying to look 'amusing' and 'full of mischief' – oh how I DISLIKE WOMEN – or men, who show off like small children without the innocence.

The *Guardian* was a regular source of irritation and amusement. When I was first having plays of mine produced Aunt Stella sent me a postcard: 'From *The Guardian* "I want audiences through heightened realism to look at what they've seen in a manner which they might not have expected to heighten their sense of what they might already have known about." Never forget the above, dear boy, and it will serve you well throughout your life. (Or will it?) Love A.S.'

Her reading did take in new writing because she cared about her craft, but it rarely met with her approval. She admired John Fowles's *The French Lieutenant's Woman*, and both admired and liked *The History Man* by Malcolm Bradbury, who subsequently wrote the filmscript of *Cold Comfort Farm*. Of the modern novelists she did read she claimed to prefer male ones, on the perhaps surprising grounds that they were less preoccupied with sex. I think she meant that men were less inclined to write the sort of books she categorised as 'sensitive studies of adultery in N.W.1'.

Modern poetry, unless you count W. H. Auden, had even less appeal to her than modern fiction, but she liked Philip Larkin and was a great admirer of Charles Causley, whose ballad style is in part derived from Auden. On the whole she preferred to return to her old favourites in verse and prose – the Romantic poets, Dickens, Brontë and those late nineteenth-century women writers who were her peculiar addiction. In a letter to Suzanne Goodwin in 1980 she wrote:

So I'm back to *Moby Dick*, darling Keats's *Endymion*, and *April's Lady* by Mrs Hungerford (bet you've never heard of *her* – Anglo-Irish, some 30 novels, circa 1880–1895) in which people go deadly pale in moonlit gardens and the distant fountain sobs. They also give each other veiled looks – not surprising in 1895, as the two of them are married to other people, the ladies have snowy arms and are always 'getting overdone' at dances, which accounts for the interesting air of weariness. Joycelyne Kavanagh, April's Lady, has just got stuck all night in a thunderstorm with Norman Beauclerk, who is carrying on with her while planning to marry rich Miss Maliphant – an enormous girl with Brummagen gold.

J and N put up at an inn run by an old family servant (All 'Miss Joyce darlints' and aware of the proprieties) and all would have been well if Norman had unselfishly driven the dogcart 15 miles in a thunderstorm to inform the house-party of what had unfortunately occurred.

Not unnaturally, he prefers brandy and soda and a cigar in the bar (we never learn where he sleeps – under the bar, possibly) while Mrs Connolly [the old family servant], taking absolutely no chances, beds down in a room *opening off* the one allotted to Joycelyne.

The latter is quite green with fear of what The County Will Say – (why need it know? but don't ask silly questions) but I am longing to hear the verdict of old Lady Clontarf on the goings on.

So far as I recall, having read it several times before, on hearing the Malicious gossip: 'I would gladly have passed the night with One of My Hinds in such circumstances.' – and though unfortunately phrased, this saves Joycelyne's good name.

Male writers of the same period fare less well. In another letter, she wrote: 'Slept all afternoon over *What Maisie Knew* (*What* Henry didn't!)'

It is true that a few of her closest friends, like Suzanne Goodwin and Elizabeth Jenkins, were writers, but by and large Stella steered clear of literary and artistic society. However, through the writer Monica Stirling she and Noël Coward – a great admirer of *Cold Comfort Farm* – exchanged greetings and expressions of mutual admiration. She was even invited out to his home in Switzerland, Les Avants, but declined. I think it was for the best. By all accounts Coward was at times a difficult host, and Stella might have proved a sad disappointment as she did not always sparkle in the company of strangers. She would almost certainly have talked far too much about her grandchildren, which might have irked the Master.

After his death she wrote to Cole Lesley, Coward's companion and biographer: 'He seems to me to incarnate the *myth* of the 'twenties (gaiety, courage, pain concealed, amusing malice) and that photograph . . . with prised fingertips held to hide the mouth, with the eyes delightfully smiling, is an incarnation in another form, even to the extreme elegance of the clothes.'

The qualities which she mentioned were ones she shared with Coward. She was always impatient with solemnity, particularly that of a more recent generation of writers. In 1980, after reading Coward's *Pomp and Circumstance*, she wrote appreciatively of the book to Suzanne Goodwin, ending with the comment: 'And absolutely NO ONE has an Identity Crisis!! Think of that.'

From the mid-1970s until 1987, on the first Saturday of every month, from four until about seven, Stella would hold open house at 19 Oakshott Avenue. 'But it is *good* for me to give these parties; it takes me out of myself,' she wrote in a letter to Renée. These occasions acquired a certain reputation and were mentioned in at least one newspaper profile of Stella in her later years. Guests would begin with tea and cake in the front room and then go on to wine in the back drawing room at about six. The company was varied and occasionally distinguished, with a bias towards literary interests. I remember in particular John Braine, who usually arrived with one or two female acolytes. He was large, shaggy, genial and physically repulsive. A distinctive presence, enhanced by an unusually loud and grating voice, allowed him to dominate the conversation. I got the impression that he was one of those writers – by no means uncommon – whose interest in literature is confined to that produced by themselves. Certainly I never heard him discuss any books but his own, and even those rarely. But he had pronounced views on almost everything else; and I can remember one enjoyable afternoon when he laid down strict guidelines for us all – rather in the manner of George Orwell – on the correct method of making a good pot of tea.

Michael Pick remembers him arriving one very hot day in a raincoat and complaining volubly about how much he had sweated on the way there, a fact already apparent to those in his vicinity. On another occasion he delivered a long tirade about dustbins and the inadequacy of refuse disposal in Hampstead. Stella, whenever possible, tried at these occasions to put a ban on what she called 'maintenance conversation' ('You have no *idea* how difficult it is to get a *washer* for a shower . . .' etc. etc.) but it was not always possible, especially with forceful characters like Braine. In spite of this Stella found him amusing and liked his complete absence of affection, though others may have felt that the acquisition of a few graceful affectations might have enhanced rather than diminished his charm. However, Stella once spoke to me less approvingly of a late work of Braine's in which he had expatiated on the charms of sex in late middle age. Stella's always vivid imagination was offended by the visions it conjured up. Her grandson Daniel, who was living with Stella at the time, found him 'obnoxious and intimidating'.

Among her less eminent guests, she had a strong bias in favour of the young and good-looking of both sexes. Most of those invited were pleasant and intelligent, but some of the people who made their way to these occasions were distinctly odd, and I was never quite sure how Stella had acquired them. Most probably they invited themselves, and Stella, unless severely provoked, had not the heart to turn them away. I remember meeting an American occultist who instructed me (alas, unsuccessfully) in the techniques of Astral Projection. ('When I was young, I talked to trees,' he told me.) Then there was an elderly writer who told me that he had just completed a long poem about T. S. Eliot with the uniquely unappealing title of 'Mystices Prufrockus'. I describe him in my diary as 'a heavy, bald, ragged bearded gentleman with a dark green shirt and stringy tie' who kept getting out a notebook and showing me mathematical formulae. He had a theory about a number called 'aleph null' and another theory about the Trinity which I found mildly interesting. In addition to being a poet, philosopher and mathematician he was also a kleptomaniac (or so he claimed), and once presented Stella with a poem entitled 'Humble Hands' which purported to justify his stealing from bookshops and other temples of capitalism. Stella's comment, as so often when confronted with life's absurdities, was: 'Well, really!'

In one of Stella's letters to Renée he appears simply as 'The Bore':

. . . this time his conversation was *utterly incomprehensible* even to Dorothy Sharpe [a frequent attender at these first Saturdays], and his huge Panama hat fell on the floor and *lay* there, because I was so cross with him I wouldn't pick it up. . . . The Bore said that the only people who could count up to 2 were the Americans who had landed on the moon, adding that personally he didn't believe they *had* landed there, and Dorothy Sharpe's husband said 'Oh – then I suppose to count up to 3 you have to land on Venus?' and The Bore looked daggers at him.

One is reminded of Mr Mybug's: '. . . there isn't an intelligent person in Europe to-day who really believes Emily wrote the *Heights*.')

The Bore had been introduced to the monthly Saturdays by Laura and, on the strength of this, sent Stella some poems of his, asking for an opinion. One 'first Saturday', 7 July 1979, my diary records that I found my aunt dreading the Bore's imminent arrival because she did not know what to say about his poems. She said: 'I could say: "Well, they have great insight and sensitivity, but I personally prefer poems with more of the senses in them." Of course, I don't know what the insights and sensitivities are all about, but I won't tell him that.' A chance conversation with a book dealer in 1996 put into my hands the two letters she sent him on the subject of his poetry. Their subtle blend of tact and irony – the latter surely wasted on the recipient – are characteristic.

The first letter is dated 8 July 1979:

It was kind of you to send me 'The Heaven Hungry' which I have read with close attention.

I will tell you what I think about the poems, having first warned you that my own taste is for poetry that is 'simple, sensuous and passionate' (with the exception of W. H. Auden who certainly isn't.) I am not an intellectual and I'm sure many of the more cerebral points of your poems elude me.

Well, I think '. . . skies were as black as pear seeds' is first rate; a completely original composition true to Nature as Tennyson's always are – (with the exception of 'dropping wells of fire' for laburnum – a superb phrase, but NOT suggesting laburnum, cool and pale!) I like all of 'Vin et Vinaigre', in fact I feel the poem is completely felt and vividly expressed without a single cliché.

I do not like 'The In'ard's Ethic' which I can't understand, i.e. which I find – perhaps deliberately? – unmusical to the point of harshness.

I must repeat that I am not really fit to criticise – in the sense of 'weigh' – the poems. I am old, and naturally influenced in my tastes by the poems I loved when I was young. I *can* say that I feel a distinct and strong personality shining through the book, and add that I hope it will get good notices from critics able to criticise and appreciate modern poetry.

With every good wish
Yours sincerely,
Stella Gibbons Webb
p.s. May I say that the writing of one successful best-seller 40 odd years ago *doesn't* mean that one has any brains or critical faculty.

The second and quite obviously final letter, dated 3 October that year, shows greater signs of impatience with her correspondent.

I am very sorry, but I am quite unable to 'appraise' the poems in 'The Running Birds'.

I am surprised to hear that they have never been reviewed, because they seem, to me, to possess the qualities of all contemporary poetry – obscurity, personal pre-occupation, the occasional very striking phrase, and no conventional rhythms.

You must remember that, although I was lucky enough to write a best-seller nearly 43 [*sic*, actually forty-seven] years ago, that does not make me into a critic, and I hope you will be good enough to accept my (very qualified) verdict as that of a very ordinary woman with some ordinary journalistic gifts.

I should have liked to analyse the poems in detail, but they are (or I find them) too cerebral to understand, and therefore to me they are antipathetic – you *cannot* expect a woman of 77 to either understand or appreciate them. Do you think that Pope would have liked the poems of Dylan Thomas? I grew up on the Georgian Group and Tennyson and, above all, John Keats. I still live by such poets.

I am not at all clever, and modern poetry wearies and irritates me. For all I know you may be a second Blake or Rimbaud – I simply can't tell.

At any rate I do truly wish that the load of grief you seem to carry may be lifted, either by literary recognition or some strong personal happiness.

Your book is returned herewith

Yours sincerely

Stella D Webb.

As if to emphasise her ordinariness, she has signed the letter with her married rather than her literary name. It was a final indication that their literary correspondence, as far as she was concerned, was at an end.

The Bore was eventually banished by Stella from her Saturday afternoons. The writer Jill Neville had encountered him once in a Paris bar, wearing 'an enormous clanking crucifix' and boasting about his attendance at these occasions.

Well-known people have an attraction for human oddities, but Stella accumulated more than her fair share. This was not because she felt particularly drawn to them. On the contrary, she loved restful normality, and *Cold Comfort Farm* is in some senses a hymn to it, but she had a kind heart and was not worldly enough to have developed a strategy for turning people away before they became a nuisance. She was particularly prone to odd cleaners. For some time she had a male cleaner, a very thin Buddhist who lived almost entirely on pulses and was forever trying to decide whether to become a monk or a writer. One morning, Stella told me, he was looking particularly distracted, and when she asked him what was the matter he replied: 'I am thinking of getting in touch with some people on Mars.' Another was an anarchist who chained himself to the altar railings of St Paul's Cathedral to advertise something called International Fraternity. 'And instead of having the moral courage to say "how silly", I said "how interesting", so we talked about it,' said Stella. 'Then he cleaned the bathroom and didn't do the corners properly. I do wish for once I could have someone normal, someone who'd come in and smile and say: "Turned out nice again, hasn't it?"' Soon after this the anarchist cleaner arrived on her doorstep and announced that he was the Resurrection, so she had to dismiss him.

As far back as the 1950s she had had a charwoman who was obsessed by the Christie murders. As each body was discovered in Rillington Place, she would arrive on my aunt's doorstep and announce the fact. When Christie was finally caught, she bounced in with the words: 'They've got him, the brute!' During the period when the police were making their grisly discoveries behind papered-over cupboards she once said to Stella: 'And to think he never took them out to see how they were getting on.' It was a thought, Stella observed, as bizarre as any that might have occurred to Christie himself.

By this time some of Stella's older friends had become a trial to her and her visits to them were often motivated purely by a sense of duty. In a letter to Renée she records how her cousin by marriage, Blanche Cardale, took her to see her old friend the poet and novelist Gwen Clear:

> ... she drove me over to visit poor Gwen who really begins to look painfully frail (small wonder – her living room was hot as the reptile house, she lives on biscuits, and hasn't been out for a *walk* since Christmas).
>
> Gwen insisted, to my inward horror, on demonstrating to Blanche the Little Device she has had fixed up in front of her front door; a board 3ft high, over which you have to step to get into the house, to keep out the *floodwater* when it rains. She explained its many uses, the disadvantages of being flooded etc. etc., in an almost inaudible croak. ... Blanche rose to the occasion as only she could and said stoutly that no-one liked having their sitting room flooded, and the Little Device was a very good idea.

Gwen died in September 1978 a week after Stella had visited her in hospital. Stella always felt slightly guilty about her, because she had had so much more success than Gwen both personally and professionally. Nevertheless she attributed the rather pathetic state into which Gwen had got herself very largely to the fact that she had never subjected herself to the bracing, self-denying discipline of a husband and children. Stella held religiously to the creed enunciated by the Balkan peasant, Vartouhi, at the end of *The Bachelor* that: 'Young or old, fair or ugly, man or woman (unless of course they be vowed to God ...) it is well to be married.'

Stella found it hard to accept that the gifted, lively companions of her youth had become disgruntled old parties whose charm had flown but whose wilfulness remained. This applied especially to Ina Dornan, who had been the model for the glamorous Mrs Smiling in *Cold Comfort Farm* with her hordes of admirers and her perpetual quest for the perfect brassiere. Ina must have had something: she once danced three times running with the Duke of Windsor when he was Prince of Wales.

By the time I knew Ina she was a cantankerous old lady with a husband, Gus, who looked, in Stella's graphic phrase, 'like a crushed raspberry'. She was restlessly argumentative and often created scenes which Stella hated, but the gusto with which she wrote them up to Renée suggests that my aunt did derive some entertainment from them:

> I had a dinner party, with a magnum of champagne, to celebrate dear Lewis's retirement from his firm after 37 years; and invited Ina and Gus. They kindly brought a bottle of champagne, and all was going rather merrier than a marriage bell, when Ina suddenly launched into a fearful scene, saying justice meant everything to her, and she had never been so insulted. She rushed into the drawing-room, and Gus followed and went down on his knees and said he would never leave her. We finally decided to leave her alone, and Gus rushed off for a walk (in the middle of my dinner party). I went to find Ina and found *she* had disappeared too. Gus reappeared and went off home over the Heath. No sign of Ina . . . and they left the dog, stone deaf, with me all night! She was the one who behaved properly [the dog, presumably]. However, dear Enid and Lewis and I finished the champagne. Ina said she 'didn't know what had got into her.' A lot of champagne, I imagine.

Only two years after Lewis's retirement he died. Stella's other brother, Gerald had died back in the 1950s. She felt Lewis's loss keenly, because he had been her favourite brother and they had been through much together. On the few occasions I met him I was struck by his wild, extravagant sense of humour – not unlike Stella's in certain moods. It had been forged in the same furnace.

Stella's natural tolerance was strained to the limit when, at Lewis's funeral in 1976, Ina approached the newly bereaved widow 'and', Stella wrote to Renée, 'said that *she* "had been dead for three minutes" (her cuss of a doctor told her this when she had a heart attack) "and it's really quite pleasant." Can *you* imagine? (Yes, I bet you can.)' Ina died (permanently) in 1978, and overlooking Kenwood House there is a teak bench commemorating her love of Hampstead Heath.

Though I could never understand her allure – I arrived too late on the scene – Ina never lost her grip on former admirers, and Stella had to write long letters to them after her death. '*Why* this task should fall on me, only inscrutable Heaven knows,' she remarked crossly in a letter to Suzanne Goodwin.

Up until the mid-1980s Stella was comparatively well and active and looked much younger than her age. She cherished her independent, solitary life. But when I visited her in March 1986, while she was suffering from an attack of bronchitis, it seemed to me that she had decided she could no longer live alone, that she needed looking after and was going to make the best of it. I noted in my diary 'the beginnings of a wish, always in some ways present since I have consciously known her, to release her grip on life and sink slowly beneath the advancing tide of death'.

In 1988 recurrent heart trouble began seriously to affect Stella's mobility. By this time, however, her grandson Daniel was living with her at Oakshott Avenue together with his girlfriend Karen O'Brien. The two of them looked after Stella devotedly.

It was not an easy task, Karen recalled; but Stella was deeply attached to Daniel and came to be very fond of Karen. ('Stella could be quite tough, but as soon as she found out I was not bullyable, I was all right,' Karen told me.) Though Stella recognised the necessity for it, she still resented the fact that her solitude had been invaded. At the same time, she grew afraid of being left alone and would often try to stop Karen and Daniel from going out. She refused to go into hospital and began to eat less and less. Towards the end, Karen told me, Stella was subsisting chiefly on brandy and Gauloises cigarettes. Smoking was a comparatively recent habit which she had taken up again in the mid-1980s after a long period of abstinence.

Karen believes that Stella had made a half-conscious decision not to go on living, but that this was a decision which, because of her conventional Christian beliefs, she was not prepared to admit to herself, let alone to anyone else. She had written all she wanted to write, and her two beloved grandsons were in stable relationships and gainful, satisfying employment. Laura's life, too, was now settled and content. As with Flora at the end of *Cold Comfort Farm*, Stella's work was done and it was time to fly off into the midsummer night sky with the loved one for whom she had never stopped grieving.

The natural grace of her bearing had not deserted Stella, even in extreme infirmity. She would be found sitting in the ground-floor front room by the bow window, swathed in shawls, with a book on her lap. She had a habit of talking to you with her head turned slightly away, perhaps because she knew that her profile was her best feature. Almost invariably there would be a lighted Gauloise poised between her long, vertically held fingers. One felt the cigarette ought to be in an ebony holder; the gesture was so reminiscent of the twenties. The hair, still not entirely white, was piled up as it ever had been with a sort of wild elegance which always reminded me of a steel engraving of a storm at sea. (I was once rude enough to tell her this, and she used to quote it back at me occasionally with a look of mild reproach.) In those final days she at last looked what for a long time she had insisted she was, 'old and frail'.

For my visits to Stella I saved up the kind of stories which I knew appealed to her sense of the absurd. I still occasionally find myself hoarding some anecdote or observation which might entertain her, only to remember that she is no longer there to share it. She particularly enjoyed stories about my brother Charles, with whom I was then sharing a cottage in Gloucestershire. On the last occasion I saw her – a week before she died – I had saved up two stories about him for her. One of them concerned an acquaintance of ours in the country who had just published a critically acclaimed first novel, the hero – or heroine? – and, if I remember rightly, the narrator of which was a greenhouse. My brother had become extremely indignant about this book. He is not a great reader of novels, but the idea of a narrative greenhouse had somehow struck a raw nerve; it outraged his sense of propriety.

I knew Stella would be amused. She was and said she sympathised with my brother's reaction, remarking that though an outbuilding had featured quite prominently in her first novel, she would never have seen fit to make it the protagonist.

I also told her that Charles had said to me: 'We ought to have more ancestors in the cottage.' My brother is obsessed by lineage and needs wherever possible to be surrounded by pictures of his forebears, steel engravings of ancestral seats, family trees and the like. My aunt appreciated this and at once pointed to a small watercolour on the wall, a portrait of our great-grandmother as a girl. She insisted that I take it and put it in our cottage to satisfy my brother's craving for more ancestry. It was a characteristically open-handed act of generosity. 'He's worth a guinea a box,' she would say of my brother. She was very fond of him, and his harmless eccentricity always pleased her.

On the evening of 18 January 1989, Karen found Stella collapsed outside her bedroom. After the doctor had been, Laura was summoned and remained with her mother through the night until Stella died the following morning. The cause of death was heart failure and the end had been peaceful.

Among Stella's books which I inherited are an edition of Chateaubriand in which I found some sheets of paper with the beginnings of a translation of *The Spirit of Christianity* and many works with marginal comments in her handwriting, most of them characteristic and interesting. Works on philosophy and religion are the most heavily annotated in her hand and bear witness to a profound and searching intellect, not always discernible in her published works. But it is the random thoughts among her marginalia that I particularly enjoy coming across. Next to these lines in Byron's 'Cain':

> Can it be?
> You small blue circle in far ether . . .

she wrote, 'When Man first saw the Earth from the Moon in the late 20th century – behold! it was blue. Did Byron have a poetic intuition?'

With some writers she seems to establish a kind of relationship.

It is evidence of the dogged, questing side to her character that despite finding Rousseau (of the *Confessions*) a uniquely irritating figure she clearly read his famous autobiography to the end. On one of the fly leaves she wrote in pencil: 'Is anything known of the FIVE children whom this creature, acting in a midge-cloud of self-deception, sent to an orphanage? FIVE.'

With Henri-Frédéric Amiel (of the *Journal Intime* translated by Mrs Humphry Ward in 1885) she is a little more lenient, but when he becomes maudlin and self-indulgent – a fairly regular occurrence – she is brisk with him. 'Oh dear – and it's only page 46!' she writes against one such passage. On 11 December 1872 Amiel wrote: 'A deep and dreamless sleep; and now I wake up to the grey, lowering, rainy sky, which has kept us company for so long. The air is mild, the general outlook depressing. I think it is partly the fault of my windows, which are not very clean, and contribute by their dimness to this gloomy aspect of the outer world.' Next to this my aunt has pencilled: 'Then why, in heaven's name, not CLEAN them? or get a servant to do it. *Really* –!' I can hear the tone of her voice again in these comments: irritable, but with the generous irritability of those who want others to make the best of themselves, and at the same time amused by her own irritation.

On one of the endpapers of the *Journal Intime* Stella has written her 'Verdict' (dated 29 January 1985): 'My notes are shallow, even cheap, on poor Amiel, but he brought out in me all the "nanny" common sense which has been *so* useful in my own life. . . . I never understand why, IF people are intelligent enough to see what's the matter, they can't DO SOMETHING about it. I know some things must be accepted, but even acceptance is a kind of DOING.'

As I read the books that once belonged to her, I still come across marginalia that I have not seen before. It is like catching a glimpse of an old friend.

Stella was buried in Highgate Cemetery in a grave next to Allan's on a gusty, rainy December day in 1989. The funeral service at St Anne's, Highgate was a modest affair attended by family and a few close friends. There was no eulogy, but I chose and read two poems of hers. The first of these was 'The Bell', quoted at the end

of Chapter 5; the second 'Fairford Church', the last in her volume
of *Collected Poems*. The final verse reads:

> Look, how it fights with its tower!
> This shield of worn stones
> With pallid blue glass and tall saints
> On the field rich with bones.
> Saying: 'Little is sure. Life is hard.
> We love, suffer, and die.
> But the beauty of the earth is real
> And the Spirit is nigh.'

Bibliography

Select Bibliography

BARALE, Michèle Aina, *Daughters and Lovers, The Life and Writing of Mary Webb*, Wesleyan University Press, Middletown, Connecticut, 1986

BEAUMAN, Nicola, *A Very Great Profession (The Woman's Novel 1914–1939)*, Virago, 1983

HART-DAVIS, Rupert, *Hugh Walpole, A Biography*, Macmillan, 1952

HOWARTH, Patrick, *Squire: 'Most Generous of Men'*, Hutchinson, 1963

SPALDING, Frances, *Stevie Smith, A Critical Biography*, Faber, 1988

WRENN, Dorothy P. H., *Goodbye to Morning, A Biographical Study of Mary Webb*, Wilding, 1964

Articles on Stella Gibbons

North London Collegiate Magazine, November 1933

Writers' Directory, 1943 and 1947

Leader magazine, 28 April 1945 (article signed 'Aquila')

Books of To-day, May 1949 (article signed 'Brodie')

Illustrated London News, January 1980 (by Sasha Moorsom)

Independent Magazine, 26 August 1985 (by Jill Neville)

Bibliography

Major Articles by Stella Gibbons

'Do Women Write Novels?', *Lady*, January 1931
'When Men Write about Women', *Lady*, 25 January 1932
'A School Moves House', *Good Housekeeping*, February 1938
'The Whole Duty of a Novelist', *St Martin's Review*, October 1938
'A Woman's Diary of the War', *St Martin's Review*, November 1939–November 1943
'C of E', *St Martin's Review*, April 1957
'Genesis of a Novel', *Punch*, 20 April 1966

Other Sources

HEILPERN, T. R., 'The Sources of *Cold Comfort Farm*', unpublished MA dissertation, Manchester University
The Mugar Memorial Library Special Collection holds a number of manuscripts by Stella Gibbons, including a 'Holograph with some typescript pages with extensive holograph corrections, 385p.' of *The Charmers*. The library also possesses holographs of over forty unpublished poems, some in several drafts, and three letters written in 1943 to a Miss Fisher about a proposed talk on Mary Webb to the Bristol University Literary Society on 15 November 1943

Published Works of Stella Gibbons

1930
The Mountain Beast (poems), Longmans

1932
Cold Comfort Farm, Longmans

1934
Bassett, Longmans
The Priestess (poems), Longmans

1935
Enbury Heath, Longmans
The Untidy Gnome, Longmans

1936
Miss Linsey And Pa, Longmans

1937
Roaring Tower and Other Stories (short stories), Longmans

1938
Nightingale Wood, Longmans
The Lowland Venus (poems), Longmans

1939
My American, Longmans

1940
Christmas at Cold Comfort Farm (short stories), Longmans

1941
The Rich House, Longmans

1943
Ticky, Longmans

1944
The Bachelor, Longmans

1946
Westwood, or The Gentle Powers, Longmans

1949
The Matchmaker, Longmans
Conference at Cold Comfort Farm, Longmans

1950
Collected Poems, Longmans

1951
The Swiss Summer, Longmans

1953
Fort of the Bear, Longmans

1954
Beside the Pearly Water (short stories), Peter Nevill

1955
The Shadow of a Sorcerer, Hodder and Stoughton

1956
Here Be Dragons, Hodder and Stoughton

1958
White Sand and Grey Sand, Hodder and Stoughton

1959
A Pink Front Door, Hodder and Stoughton

1962
The Weather at Tregulla, Hodder and Stoughton

1964
The Wolves Were in the Sledge, Hodder and Stoughton

1965
The Charmers, Hodder and Stoughton
'Imaginative Writing', contribution to *Light on C. S. Lewis*,
Geoffrey Bles

1967
Starlight, Hodder and Stoughton

1968
The Snow Woman, Hodder and Stoughton

1970
The Woods in Winter, Hodder and Stoughton

Index

Index

Index

Index

Chart